Suicide and the Gothic

Manchester University Press

INTERNATIONAL GOTHiC

The Series' Board of General Editors

Elisabeth Bronfen, University of Zurich, Switzerland
Steven Bruhm, University of Western Ontario, Canada
Ken Gelder, University of Melbourne, Australia
Jerrold Hogle, University of Arizona, USA (Chair)
Avril Horner, Kingston University, UK
William Hughes, Bath Spa University, UK

The Editorial Advisory Board

Glennis Byron, University of Stirling, Scotland
Robert Miles, University of Victoria, Canada
David Punter, University of Bristol, England
Andrew Smith, University of Sheffield, England
Anne Williams, University of Georgia, USA

Previously published
Neoliberal Gothic: international Gothic in the neoliberal age
Edited by Linnie Blake and Agnieszka Soltysik Monnet
Monstrous media/spectral subjects: imaging Gothic from the nineteenth century to the present
Edited by Fred Botting and Catherine Spooner
Globalgothic Edited by Glennis Byron
The Gothic and death Edited by Carol Margaret Davison
EcoGothic Edited by Andrew Smith and William Hughes

Suicide and the Gothic

Edited by William Hughes and Andrew Smith

Manchester University Press

Copyright © Manchester University Press 2019

While copyright in the volume as a whole is vested in Manchester University Press, copyright in individual chapters belongs to their respective authors, and no chapter may be reproduced wholly or in part without the express permission in writing of both author and publisher.

Published by Manchester University Press
Oxford Road, Manchester M13 9PL
www.manchesteruniversitypress.co.uk

British Library Cataloguing-in-Publication Data is available

ISBN 978 1 5261 2008 3 hardback
ISBN 978 1 5261 7184 9 paperback

First published by Manchester University Press in hardback 2019

This edition first published 2023

The publisher has no responsibility for the persistence or accuracy of URLs for any external or third-party internet websites referred to in this book, and does not guarantee that any content on such websites is, or will remain, accurate or appropriate.

Typeset by Deanta Global Publishing Services

For Carol Margaret Davison

Contents

List of illustrations	page ix
Notes on contributors	xi
Series editor's preface	xiv
Acknowledgements	xvi

	Introduction: the most Gothic of acts – suicide in generic context *William Hughes and Andrew Smith*	1
1	Scottish revenants: Caledonian fatality in Thomas Percy's *Reliques* *Frank Ferguson and Danni Glover*	18
2	Male and female Werthers: Romanticism and Gothic suicide *Lisa Vargo*	36
3	'The supposed incipiency of mental disease': guilt, regret and suicide in three ghost stories by J. Sheridan Le Fanu *William Hughes*	52
4	'The body of a self-destroyer': suicide and the self in the fin-de-siècle Gothic *Andrew Smith*	66
5	'To be mistress of her own fate': suicide as control and contagion in the works of Richard Marsh *Graeme Pedlingham*	81

6 Suicide as justice? The self-destroying Gothic villain in Pauline Hopkins' *Of One Blood*   96
Bridget M. Marshall

7 Gothic influences: darkness and suicide in the work of Patricia Highsmith   110
Fiona Peters

8 Better not to have been: Thomas Ligotti and the 'suicide' of the human race   124
Xavier Aldana Reyes and Rachid M'Rabty

9 Vampire suicide   139
Jeffrey Andrew Weinstock

10 Under the dying sun: suicide and the Gothic in modern Japanese literature and culture   160
Katarzyna Ancuta

11 'I will abandon this body and take to the air': the suicide at the heart of *Dear Esther*   176
Dawn Stobbart

Index   189

Illustrations

1.1	The frontispiece of the *Reliques*	page 23
1.2	The title page of the *Reliques*	24
9.1	The Combustible Vampire 1: Virginia from *Let the Right One In*, dir. Thomas Alfredson, prod. by EFTI, Filmpool Nord and Sveriges Television, 2008	143
9.2	The Combustible Vampire 2: Alison from *Daybreakers*, dir. the Spierig Brothers, prod. by Lionsgate, 2010. Perf. Isabel Lucas	144
9.3	The sole remains at the end of *Thirst*, dir. Park Chan-wook, prod. by Moho Film, Focus Feature Internationals, 2009	146
9.4	*Thirst* and the importance of sunscreen, dir. Park Chan-wook, prod. by Moho Film, Focus Feature Internationals, 2009. Perf. Song Kang-ho and Kim Ok-bin	148
9.5	Godric meets the sun, *True Blood*, Season 2, episode 9, 'I Will Rise Up', dir. Scott Winant, HBO, 2009	151
9.6	A morose Adam holds a pistol to his heart, *Only Lovers Left Alive*, dir. Jim Jarmusch, prod. by Recorded Picture Company and Pandora Film, 2013. Perf. Tom Hiddleston	153

9.7 Eben bakes and flakes at the end of *30 Days of Night*, dir. David Slade, prod. by Dark Horse Entertainment, Ghost House Pictures, 2007. Perf. Josh Hartnett and Melissa George — 156

9.8 & 9.9 Blacula throws in the towel, *Blacula*, dir. William Crain, dist. by American International Pictures, 1972. Perf. William Marshall — 157

Notes on contributors

Xavier Aldana Reyes is Senior Lecturer in English Literature and Film at Manchester Metropolitan University and a founder member of the Manchester Centre for Gothic Studies. He specialises in Gothic and horror film and fiction. He is the author of *Spanish Gothic* (2017), *Horror Film and Affect* (2016) and *Body Gothic* (2014), and the editor of *Horror: A Literary History* (2016).

Katarzyna Ancuta is a Lecturer at Chulalongkorn University in Bangkok, Thailand. Her research interests revolve around the interdisciplinary contexts of contemporary Gothic/horror, currently with a strong Asian focus. Her recent publications include contributions to *Neoliberal Gothic* (2017) and *The Routledge Handbook to the Ghost Story* (2017), as well as two journal issues on Thai (2014) and Southeast Asian (2015) horror film.

Frank Ferguson is Research Director for English Language and Literature at the Coleraine Campus of Ulster University, Northern Ireland. He is the editor of *Ulster-Scots Writing: An Anthology* (2008) and has published widely on Ulster-Scots literary and cultural subjects.

Danni Glover recently completed her PhD thesis, 'Thomas Percy: Literary Anthology and National Identity'. She has published on the musicality of Percy's *Reliques* and the poetry of Mary, Queen of Scots.

Danni is an independent researcher and is researching theology and terrorism in literature.

William Hughes is Professor of Medical Humanities and Gothic Literature at Bath Spa University. His twenty published books include *Beyond Dracula: Bram Stoker's Fiction and its Cultural Context* (2000), *Dracula: A Reader's Guide to Essential Criticism* (2009), *The Historical Dictionary of Gothic Literature* (2013), *That Devil's Trick: Hypnotism and the Victorian Popular Imagination* (2015) and *Key Concepts in the Gothic* (2018). A past president of the International Gothic Association, he was editor of the journal *Gothic Studies* from its launch in 1999 to 2018.

Bridget M. Marshall is an Associate Professor of English at the University of Massachusetts, Lowell. She is the author of *The Transatlantic Gothic Novel and the Law, 1790–1860* (2011) and co-editor of *Transnational Gothic: Literary and Social Exchanges in the Long Nineteenth Century* (2013). Currently, she is developing a project on Gothic literature and the Industrial Revolution.

Rachid M'Rabty is an Associate Lecturer and PhD candidate at Manchester Metropolitan University. He has published articles on the violence in *American Psycho*, Thomas Ligotti's corporate horror and the philosophy of Sade. Rachid's research explores contemporary 'transgressive' fiction, pessimism and, particularly, the extent to which acts/fantasies of self-destruction become a means to articulate a subversive response to, or escape from, existential discontent.

Graeme Pedlingham is Senior Lecturer in English at the University of Sussex, where he leads the university-wide interdisciplinary Foundation Years programme. He has published on Richard Marsh and curated the first Arts and Humanities Research Council-sponsored exhibition on Marsh. He has also published on anxiety in Gothic videogames. Currently, he is exploring approaches to teaching students in transition and the role of anxiety in education.

Fiona Peters is Professor of Crime Fiction at Bath Spa University. She is the course leader for MA in Crime and Gothic Fictions, director of the International Crime Fiction Association and founder and director of the annual international conference, Captivating Criminality, now in its fifth year. She is a Patricia Highsmith scholar, and her monograph *Anxiety and Evil in the Writings of Patricia Highsmith* was published by Routledge in 2011. She has published extensively on crime fiction, literature and evil, and psychoanalysis.

Andrew Smith is Professor of Nineteenth-Century English Literature at the University of Sheffield, where he co-directs, with Professor Angela Wright, the Centre for the History of the Gothic. He is the author or editor of more than twenty published books including *Gothic Death 1740–1914: A Literary History* (2016), *The Ghost Story 1840–1920: A Cultural History* (2010), *Gothic Literature* (2007, revised 2013), *Victorian Demons* (2004) and *Gothic Radicalism* (2000). He is a past president of the International Gothic Association.

Dawn Stobbart works in Lancaster University's English Department as an Associate Lecturer, specialising in contemporary literature and the way this translates to the videogame, with a forthcoming monograph titled *From Amnesia to Zombies, Run! Videogames and Horror*. She is a co-editor of the journal of Stephen King studies, *Pennywise Dreadful*, and is currently working on the links between H. P. Lovecraft and the videogame *Bloodborne*.

Lisa Vargo, Professor of English, University of Saskatchewan, has produced editions of Thomas Love Peacock's *Nightmare Abbey*, Mary Shelley's *Lodore* and *Spanish and Portuguese Lives, Mary Shelley's Literary Lives and Other Writings* (Vol. 2, ed. Nora Crook). Recent essays include as their subjects Mary Shelley's sources for *Frankenstein*, Anna Barbauld's 'Inscription for an Ice-House', representations of the moose in late eighteenth-century literature and Mary Shelley's 'The Swiss Peasant'.

Jeffrey Andrew Weinstock is Professor of English at Central Michigan University, USA, and author or editor of twenty one books – most recently, *The Cambridge Companion to the American Gothic* (2018), *The Age of Lovecraft* (edited with Carl Sederholm, 2016), *Goth Music: From Sound to Subculture* (co-authored with Isabella van Elferen, 2016) and *Return to Twin Peaks: New Approaches to Materiality, Theory & Genre on Television* (edited with Catherine Spooner, 2016). Visit him at JeffreyAndrewWeinstock.com.

Series editor's preface

Each volume in this series contains new essays on the many forms assumed by – as well as the most important themes and topics in – the ever-expanding range of international 'Gothic' fictions from the eighteenth to the twenty-first century. Launched by leading members of the International Gothic Association (IGA) and some editors and advisory board members of its journal, *Gothic Studies*, this series thus offers cutting-edge analyses of the great many variations in the Gothic mode over time and all over the world, whether these have occurred in literature, film, theatre, art, several forms of cybernetic media or other manifestations ranging from 'Goth' group identities to *avant-garde* displays of aesthetic and even political critique.

The 'Gothic Story' began in earnest in 1760s England, both in fiction and drama, with Horace Walpole's efforts to combine the 'ancient' or supernatural and the 'modern' or realistic romance. This blend of anomalous tendencies has proved itself remarkably flexible in playing out the cultural conflicts of the late Enlightenment and of more recent periods. Antiquated settings with haunting ghosts or monsters and deep, dark secrets that are the mysteries behind them, albeit in many different incarnations, continue to intimate what audiences most fear both in the personal subconscious and the most pervasive tensions underlying Western culture. But this always unsettling interplay of conflicting tendencies has expanded out of its original potentials as well, especially in the hands of its greatest innovators, to appear in an astounding variety of expressive, aesthetic and public manifestations over time. The results have transported this inherently boundary-breaking mode across geographical and cultural borders into 'Gothics' that now appear throughout the world: in the settler communities of Canada, New Zealand and Australia; in such post-colonial areas as India and Africa; in the Americas and the Caribbean; and in East Asia and several of the islands within the entire Pacific Rim.

These volumes consequently reveal and explain the 'globalisation' of the Gothic as it has proliferated across two and a half centuries. The general editors of this series and the editors of every volume, of course, bring special expertise to this expanding development, as well as to the underlying dynamics, of the Gothic. Each resulting collection, plus the occasional monograph, therefore draws together important new studies about particular examples of the international Gothic – past, present or emerging – and these contributions can come from both established scholars in the field and the newest 'rising stars' of Gothic studies. These scholars, moreover, are and must be just as international in their locations and orientations as this series is. Interested experts from around the globe, in fact, are invited to propose collections and topics for this series to the Manchester University Press. These will be evaluated, as appropriate, by the general editors, members of the editorial advisory board and/or other scholars with the requisite expertise so that every published volume is professionally put together and properly refereed within the highest academic standards. Only in this way can the International Gothic series be what its creators intend: a premier worldwide venue for examining and understanding the shape-shifting 'strangeness' of a Gothic mode that is now as multicultural and multifaceted as it has ever been in its long, continuing and profoundly haunted history.

Acknowledgements

The final editing of the manuscript took place while Andrew Smith was on research leave from the University of Sheffield. He would like to thank colleagues on the school and faculty research committees for supporting this leave period. He would also like to thank, as always, Joanne Benson for her love and tolerance throughout the editing of this project.

William Hughes would like to thank John Strachan, Fiona Peters and Kevin Yuill for their valuable contribution to an earlier phase of this project. He would also like to thank Gillian for her constant love and support through difficult, as well as good, times.

William Hughes and Andrew Smith

Introduction: the most Gothic of acts – suicide in generic context

The literary Gothic, if not actually initiated with a fictional instance of suicide, is certainly prefaced by the avowed intention by one character to exercise the ultimate preference of death over life. Manfred, the Gothic hero of Horace Walpole's frequently playful but still guilt-ridden *The Castle of Otranto* (1764), having enjoyed his baronial fiefdom in the capacity of a usurper, arbitrarily divorced a faithful wife and contemplated a technically illegal and incestuous union with his prospective daughter-in-law, finally commits the – admittedly accidental – crime of filicide and dispatches his own child, believing her to be the same reluctant maiden who has justly spurned his advances. On learning of the magnitude of his crimes, his reaction is the *lex talionis* of the ancients: 'Life *shall go* for life, eye for eye, tooth for tooth, hand for hand, foot for foot.'[1] The narrative recounts the fatal scene with breathless haste:

> Ah me, I am slain! Cried Matilda, sinking: Good heaven, receive my soul – Savage, inhuman monster! what has thou done? Cried Theodore, rushing on [Manfred], and wrenching the dagger from him. – Stop, stop thy impious hand cried Matilda; it is my father! Manfred, waking as if from a trance, beat his breast, twisted his hands in his locks, and endeavoured to recover his dagger from Theodore to dispatch himself. Theodore, scarce less distracted, and only mastering the transports of his grief to assist Matilda, had now by his cries drawn some of the monks to his aid. While part of them endeavoured in concert with the afflicted Theodore to stop the blood of the dying princess, the rest prevented Manfred from laying violent hands on himself.[2]

Manfred's vain attempt to turn the fatal dagger on the very self that has abnegated all hope of familial continuation is surely the only gesture that may adequately and appropriately compensate for the severity of the tyrant's own actions. The usurper-prince, as the attendant friar, Father Jerome, cuttingly notes, has indeed 'shed [his] own blood' through the stabbing of Matilda (159). With no other lineal descendant – his son having been killed by supernatural intervention at the novel's inception – Manfred has, through the killing of Matilda, effectively terminated the endurance of both his familial descent and its claim to lordship.[3] His subsequent fate – which, like his thwarted suicide, is an act undertaken explicitly by his own decision and hand – metaphorically ends his existence in the mortal world he has hitherto known and ruled. As the narrative laconically notes, on the morning following the death of Matilda, 'Manfred signed his abdication of the principality' and 'took the habit of religion' (165). His formal and irrevocable submission to monastic strictures ensures both his future celibacy and his withdrawal from society into an effective living death of rigorous silence, humble anonymity and regretful contemplation. His status, dynastically and communicatively, is that of one already dead. Even this living death may not constitute an adequate atonement for the crimes, which Manfred himself now freely confesses: 'what can atone for usurpation and a murdered child?' he queries, before concluding with the monitory statement 'may this bloody record be a warning to future tyrants!' (163). Though not visceral in its effect on his physical body, Manfred's withdrawal from the world has much the same effect as his suicide might have done. A self-consciously extreme action, it constitutes both a punishment for, and a release from, his crimes; it effectively removes him from social humanity but ensures his enduring presence there through the memory of his notoriety; uncanny in its implications, his social and dynastic self-annihilation imbricates both an apotheosis and a nemesis.

Suicide, as Manfred's analogous departure from the world may imply, is the most Gothic of acts. Its presence conditions death, profoundly reconfiguring the customary religious, moral and legal ramifications of the fleeting moment at which life is pronounced extinct, and thereby affecting the cultural value of both the individual who has taken their own life and the relationship of the deceased to their still-living associates. Suicide is, essentially, a momentary event with profound and lasting implications, a physical singularity that generates multiple social consequences, a point of crisis for the self and for those who perceive that self. As the fate of Walpole's Manfred demonstrates, the implications of suicide may function even where the act is deferred or never actually completed. Indeed, the interruption of the suicide of Walpole's Prince of Otranto anticipates a similar moment in the life of the protagonist of Byron's *Manfred* (1816–17), the eponymous hero of this verse drama being a character somewhat more tempered by the humanism and sensibility of a later era. It is surely not a coincidence that Byron came to select the specific name of Manfred for the emotionally tormented protagonist of his verse drama. It is likewise significant that the Byronic hero, in common with his Walpolean Gothic-hero forebear, should see self-extinction as an appropriate solution to the problems of his mortal existence. In Gothic, arguably, suicide is not merely a significant act but a crucial one, engaging as it does the central existential motivations which mobilise the genre from Walpole's eighteenth century to the twenty-first-century present.

Suicide is an act which simultaneously encodes anticipation, realisation and rationalisation – and the Gothic provides a central corpus of enduring and provocative images by which the act and its implications of self-murder might be both communicated and interrogated within a nominally Christian culture that has, historically, condemned those who commit suicide to, at best, immediate or temporary ignominy within mortal culture and, at worst, the unending tortures of Hell. As a provocative and culturally rich event, suicide may function – in a manner somewhat similar to other Gothic preoccupations such as incest, usurpation, violence, apostasy and death – in imbricating genre with non-fictional discourse, blurring the ostensible demarcation between the languages and conceptualities of figurative and literal existence. Suicide, in other words, is an act that – with its implications – may perhaps be most appropriately expressed in generically Gothic terms even outside the boundaries of imaginative or fictional writing.

The historical relationship between literary Gothic and the act of self-murder is graphically expressed in the manner in which Lord Byron appropriated generic imagery to provide a trenchant commentary on one of the most-celebrated suicides of his own era. Byron – a consumer as well as producer of Gothic textuality – responded to the death by suicide of the politician Robert Stewart, Viscount Castlereagh, on 12 August 1822 in his 'Preface to Cantos VI, VII and VIII' of *Don Juan*, published almost a year later in July 1823. As a suicide under British law, Castlereagh's property would have been forfeited to the Crown and his body denied a burial in consecrated ground.[4] The post-mortem imperilment of the statesman's body and chattels, however, was averted by way of a medico-legal inquest which, following statements from witnesses and a letter from the Duke of Wellington, ultimately concluded that Castlereagh's suicide was not the result of deliberate and conscious choice but a consequence of a temporary period of insanity.[5]

In the 'Preface to Cantos VI, VII and VIII' of *Don Juan*, Byron notes with particular distaste how Castlereagh's elevated station in life – he was the second Marquess of Londonderry as well as an elected English parliamentarian – and his political orthodoxy impacted on not merely the momentary reception of his private act of self-destruction but also the subsequent – and public – fate of both his body and his reputation. After suggesting that the politician was not only a divisive but also a *divided* figure – Castlereagh's 'amiable' private life being rhetorically contrasted with images of despotism, tyranny and weak intellect – Byron observed,

> Of the manner of his death little need be said, except that if a poor radical, such as Waddington or Watson, had cut his throat, he would have been buried in a cross-road, with the usual appurtenances of the stake and mallet. But the minister was an elegant lunatic – a sentimental suicide – he merely cut the 'carotid artery' (blessings on their learning) and lo! the pageant, and the Abbey! and 'the syllables of dolour yelled forth' by the newspapers – and the harangue of the Coroner in a eulogy over the bleeding body of the deceased – (an Anthony worthy of such a Caesar) – and the nauseous and atrocious cant of a degraded crew of conspirators against all that is sincere and honourable.[6]

This is a rich passage, and one with implications that extend far beyond its allusions to the reputation of, and conspiracy against, another celebrated politician as depicted in Shakespeare's *Julius Caesar*.[7] 'Poor', in context, refers to the politically unfortunate as well as comparatively penurious position of the two emblematical radicals – these latter being figures for whom the suicidal statesman would doubtless have found little sympathy.[8] Their projected fate – had the two indeed committed an act of self-destruction analogous to that of Castlereagh – would have utterly separated them from the sympathies as well as the presence of their fellow citizens.[9] Byron's allusion to the prophylactic qualities of the stake and the mallet – a favoured means by which the unquiet souls of suicides might be deterred from nocturnal perambulation – not only draws on historical British jurisprudence but also invokes the more recent Continental spectre of the vampire, popularised by lurid accounts translated for British journals from the mid-eighteenth century.[10] That the word 'vampire' had gained a conventional and an accessible metaphorical function by 1765 indicates the potential for the un-dead to function as an image in political and social critique with equal felicity to its literary deployment as a locus of supernatural horror.[11]

As a suicide – or, indeed, as a vampire, for the predatory un-dead are on occasions associated with the unquiet spirituality of those who have taken their own lives[12] – Castlereagh had forfeited the right to a Christian burial: the Anglican burial service is unequivocal that such spiritual comforts are denied to 'any that die unbaptised, or excommunicate, or have laid violent hands upon themselves'.[13] As Byron testily notes, however, the hypocritical eulogies accorded to Castlereagh were to be succeeded by no less an event than his ceremonial interment in Westminster Abbey, the revered burial place of English kings, poets and statesmen. Clearly, there is something that Byron perceives as conditioning – and disarming – Castlereagh's act of self-murder, entitling him to both enduring honour and sacerdotal repose.

Despite the poet's opening remarks on the mode of Castlereagh's demise, it is neither wealth nor political orthodoxy that has ensured the politician's honourable interment. Instead, Byron implies, Castlereagh has been exonerated of deliberate complicity in his own death by way of the exercise of the professional disciplines of medicine and law. The poet's pointed emphasis on the 'learned' detail of the 'carotid artery' – this physiological point being a direct quotation from the coroner's formal report – rhetorically draws the politician's death away from religious or moral jurisdiction and relocates it within the curtilage of medico-jurism. The coroner, whose professional training positions him between medicine and law, has, nonetheless, an implicit function in the ecclesiastical governance. It is his professional and legally binding conclusion that Castlereagh took his own life while 'delirious and not of sound mind' that exonerates the politician from conscious agency in his own death and thereby facilitates his burial according to the rites of his professed faith.[14]

Byron is somewhat less indulgent than the coroner, however. He states, testily, of Castlereagh: 'In his death he [was] necessarily one of two things by the *law* – a felon or a madman – and in either case no great subject for panegyric.'[15] This may be, strictly, true, but the poet's rhetoric continues in a vein such as might cast doubt on Castlereagh's implied lack of conscious complicity in his own death. Byron returns to two of his more mystifying asides – that Castlereagh was both 'an elegant lunatic' and 'a sentimental suicide' – in his Preface, when he turns to how the panegyric of the day comprehended the politician as a specifically *Irish* figure.[16] The poet suggests, later in his Preface, that a hypothetical Irish conscience might reasonably object to the statesman's interment in Westminster Abbey for reasons other than mere sectarian prejudice. Byron intones,

> Let us hear no more of this man; and let Ireland remove the ashes of her Grattan from the sanctuary of Westminster. Shall the patriot of humanity repose by the Werther of politics!!![17]

Though this polemic initially juxtaposes one distinguished Irish statesman who opposed the 1800 Act of Union with another, equally distinguished, who supported it, Byron's concluding sentence should be taken as being more than a sarcastic attempt to belittle Castlereagh through literary vogueishness. Castlereagh, as the critic Ellen Crowell suggests, was apparently perceived as being something of a dandified figure in early nineteenth-century London.[18] Leaving aside Byron's own involvement in a self-conscious fashionability of dress and manners, the poet's invocation of Goethe's 1774 novel *Die Leiden des jungen Werthers* here serves rhetorically to undermine the establishment consensus that Castlereagh should be absolved from complicity in his own death. Byron is not suggesting that Castlereagh is actually a *reader* of Goethe's fiction. Rather, he is associating the politician's dandyism with the fashionable Wertherism that effectively projected an awareness of Goethe's eponymous hero beyond his novel's pages and into contemporary cultural currency.[19] Thus, the poet's polemic implies that Castlereagh, like the fictional Werther, is morbidly sentimental, self-indulgently gloomy and – in consequence – liable to the type of studied *Weltschmerz* that led Goethe's hero to take his own life. In this reading of Castlereagh, Byron reconjures the suicidal politician as a figure culpable in his own death, his behaviour being a reflection of a lucid – rather than an insane – mental state.

Byron's parting suggestion that Castlereagh's death – like Manfred's abdication in *The Castle of Otranto* – might prove 'a "moral lesson"' to those in high office appears at first a somewhat conventional closure to the Preface's polemic.[20] Its more profound implication, though, is to affirm that *any* active engagement in suicide must be considered as being more meaningful than a passive submission to inevitable or unprovoked death. To commit suicide, in other words, is to make a statement, whether it be one of genuine and darkly profound despair or else a more theatrical seeking of attention which, nonetheless, still results in self-annihilation. Suicidal acts are thus a form of display and of performance. This much is implied by their initial appearance among the stock scenarios of Gothic fiction and Gothicised reportage. Walpole's Manfred attempts to lay 'violent hands on himself' in a tableau witnessed by, among others, the woman whose life he has just fatally compromised. Castlereagh took a penknife to his throat at the very moment at which his doctor entered the room, requesting that the witnessing physician catch him as he fell.[21] The latter event, indeed, was presented to the public as a graphic tableau by, among others, George Cruikshank.[22] In yet another tableau, this time in a context redolent of dramatic theatre, Byron's introspective Manfred is prevented from taking his own life by the timely intervention of a chamois hunter.[23] Suicide, arguably, must be *witnessed*, by a reader as much as by a fictional character or an inquest-summonsed witness. If there is no living mortal present to passively witness or to actively intervene, then the act of finding the suicide's body, the ritual of inscribing meaning to the act that has taken place, of imposing an explanation, must serve that same purpose of significance and containment. Such implications accompany, for example, the last testimonies of nineteenth-century fictional suicides such as Robert Wringhim and Henry Jekyll, just as much as they do the contemporary tabloid journalism which rationalises the suicide note, posed body and presumed mental condition of celebrity suicides such as Kurt Cobain.[24]

Byron's rendering of Castlereagh's death in Gothic terms serves to differentiate the poet's own dissident opinion from the conventional eulogies that lauded the dead man to his grave.[25] Byron's deployment of medical and legal casuistry, though, is indicative of a growing cultural awareness that suicide, as a significant and meaningful act, could not be understood by theological interpretation alone. Indeed, as Byron makes clear, suicide cannot be delimited, either, as a singular phenomenon confined to those afflicted by mental illness. Despair, in other words, may be a *facet* of mental illness, but it is not a mental illness in itself – and despair, caused by any number of personal, social or intellectual factors, might provoke any individual to take their own life, willingly, deliberately and knowingly. Byron's commentary upon Castlereagh is thus generated not merely by a literary consciousness which specifically draws on the poet's reading of Goethe, but likewise by a broader cultural understanding that suicide is a meaningful – rather than a mad – act, and an act further bound up with performance and self-fashioning. Castlereagh's death has often been cited as a factor in British culture's adjustment of legal, as well as moral, attitudes towards suicide – though, as Byron's own deployment of literary suicidal tropes arguably reveals, the parliamentarian's final act, be it despairingly mad or stylistically sane, is a relatively late component of a greater epistemological debate.[26]

Byron's choice of Gothic as a literary medium to interrogate the act of suicide is thus far from random. Indeed, the genre has been historically consistent in its deployment of self-murder as a distinguishing characteristic, and indeed ultimate fate, of many of its Gothic heroes. If Walpole's Manfred sets a precedent echoed by the despairing figure who shares his name in Byron's verse drama, then later characters – such as Radcliffe's Schedoni, who poisons both himself and his nemesis, Nicola di Zampari – develop further the possibilities of suicide as an evocative plot device. This is in addition to its status as a convenient, if not noble and poignant, way to dispatch thoughtful, though faulted, hero figures, implicitly associating their demise with the grandeur of self-sacrifice rather than the sordid matter of retributive execution.[27] Such figures effectively atone for their crimes, even when they die unrepentant, by their removal from human existence: that atonement, though, is compromised by the emphasis which their choice of self-murder places on their ultimate resistance to submission to the desires, justice or mercy of others.

For other Gothic heroes, suicide might be seen as somewhat less of a decision and more of an accident. When applied to the doppelgänger – a frequently encountered facet of the Gothic hero – the demise of one party necessarily involves the death of the other. The death of Henry Jekyll through the suicide of Edward Hyde – the servant Poole's account suggests that Hyde was incarnate for eight days before he administered the vial of cyanide to himself – appears to have been anticipated by both as a logical conclusion to their chemically conjoined lives.[28] For other doubled protagonists, the fatal consequences of aggression towards the doubled self are perhaps unforeseen. Poe's William Wilson stabs his more knowing second self, only contemplating his self-destruction when he comes to perceive a mirror rather than an antagonist.[29] Wilde's Dorian Gray, likewise, stabs his portrait to destroy its capacity, in his eyes, to serve as evidence of his crimes. Gray's instantaneous death (to say nothing of his consequent physiological transformation and the picture's restoration) appears not to have been contemplated in this destruction of 'this mirror of his soul'.[30] Accidental and unforeseen though they might be, these literary suicides are as pregnant with meaning as those deliberately engaged in by other desperate Gothic figures. They reflect, arguably, the inability of a self which self-consciously rejoices in transgression to perceive of its actions as transgressive: the simultaneous self, in other words, is never fully understood as a self – even as an abjected self – until it is far too late. Self-murder thus becomes an unforeseen act of atonement and disarmament for the suicide, one which perhaps brings a sense of closure and of restitution for the crimes committed in the eyes of the reader, but one whose bleakness leaves the moral status of the unrepentant protagonist still open and unresolved.[31] A suicide, whether undertaken volitionally or accidentally, is always significant, always capable of being related to the past actions of the protagonists by the reader, even where the character is less ready to participate in the text's moral script. The act of suicide is thus fundamental to the Gothic.

The chapters in *Suicide and the Gothic* reflect both the complexity and the diversity of this recurrent theme in the Gothic. They are all specially commissioned for this collection and, acknowledging the tenor of the International Gothic series, embrace an international as well as historical consideration of the place suicide occupies within Gothic stylistics. The works under consideration in *Suicide and the Gothic* range from the canonical to the scarcely read, and interrogate cultural traditions as diverse as those of Europe and Asia across a comprehensive range of media, from the eighteenth-century origins of the literary Gothic to the contemporaneity of the videogame.

In 'Scottish revenants: Caledonian fatality in Thomas Percy's *Reliques*', Frank Ferguson and Danni Glover discuss Thomas Percy's *The Reliques of Ancient English Poetry*, first published in 1765. A comprehensive three-volume set of British ballads, it was one of the most significant collections of the century, and its influence on British editors and writers was felt for generations afterwards. The backdrop for this literary endeavour was a culture war in English and Scottish literature which emanated from the Glorious Revolution in the late seventeenth century and found expression in a variety of texts. At the core of this battle was a struggle for cultural superiority between Scotland and England. Percy's approach was a Gothic riposte to this phenomenon in two senses. First, in a historiographical sense, he posited a conception of British literary history which maintained that the English were cultural inheritors of the Goths, a racial grouping which he believed was superior and different to Scotland's antecedents, the Celts. By advancing this idea, Percy was aiming to defend and consolidate a cultural position that favoured an interpretation of English predominance over other constituent members of the United Kingdom. Secondly, he anticipates Gothic literary approaches in his treatment of Scotland as practically a suicidal nation. If Ossianic poetry is a lament for the human subject caught in the predicament of age and death, the *Reliques* determines a judgement on Scotland that it is an unstable, barbarous place which precipitates self-slaughter. Though intended as a unifying text between the constituent nations of Great Britain, Percy's *Reliques* asserts Scotland as a dangerous, if minor, doppelgänger of England – a national space which exists in Britain's past and in the eternal moment of its own death.

Lisa Vargo, in 'Male and female Werthers: Romanticism and Gothic suicide', examines the influence of Goethe's *The Sorrows of Young Werther* (1774) on a generation of women writers including Charlotte Smith, Mary Wollstonecraft, Charlotte Dacre and Mary Shelley. Vargo argues that Goethe's text became influential on the Gothic when women writers reworked its theme of sensibility into a Gothic one. Sensibility, as a key register of women's writing during the period, is subject to a radical critical scrutiny in this transformation. The gendered aspects of 'Wertherism' as a cult of romantic suicide can, Vargo argues, be looked at anew in terms of how female-authored Gothic texts generated gendered readings of suicide and its motivation. Such a reading facilitates a new way of thinking about Wollstonecraft's *The Wrongs of Women* (1798), Dacre's *Zofloya* (1806) and Shelley's *Frankenstein* (1818), among other novels and poems from the period.

In '"The supposed incipiency of mental disease": guilt, regret and suicide in three ghost stories by J. Sheridan Le Fanu', William Hughes argues that, although in recent years J. Sheridan Le Fanu's ghost-story collection *In a Glass Darkly* (1871) has been interpreted through its Gothic, medical and theological contexts, its enactments of self-annihilation have never been properly explored. The first three narratives in *In a Glass Darkly*, 'Green Tea', 'The Familiar' and 'Mr Justice Harbottle', depict troubled, indeed persecuted, individuals – a diffident clergyman, a retired naval officer, a notorious and corrupt hanging judge – whose lives end prematurely following a personal contemplation of past actions known to themselves, but not to their contemporaries. This chapter considers the deteriorating mental states of the Reverend Jennings and Captain Barton, the respective protagonists of 'Green Tea' and 'The Familiar', and the retrospective account which charts the final days of the unfortunate Mr Justice Harbottle. The variant testimonies of Jennings and Barton, and of the witness who in each case reports and interprets the behaviour of these fatalistic individuals, are examined in the context of the ambiguous presences that both haunt them and hasten their end. In the case of Harbottle, the imposition of justice finally done through the act of self-destruction is emphatic. All three tales amply illustrate the complex relationship between introspection and self-destruction in the persecutory tradition of Gothic fiction.

Andrew Smith, in '"The body of a self-destroyer": suicide and the self in the fin-de-siècle Gothic', explores why so many fin-de-siècle Gothic novels conclude on equally complex, if different, forms of suicide, including Stevenson's *Strange Case of Dr Jekyll and Mr Hyde* (1886), Wilde's *The Picture of Dorian Gray* (1891) and Machen's *The Great God Pan* (1894). Smith argues that, in *Jekyll and Hyde*, images of the self-destructive self should be seen within the context of models of social self-destruction found in theories of degeneration. The writings of Edwin Lankester and Max Nordau, in particular, suggest that society is prone to self-destruction when it becomes overly refined and collapses back on to itself. Images of the individual body thus need to be related to wider issues of the body politic. However, Smith argues that the fin-de-siècle Gothic does not simply *replicate* the terms used in theories of degeneration but rather *scrutinises* how images of wealth, cultural refinement and class-bound models of 'civilisation' lead to Gothic representations of self-destruction that strangely liberate the subject from the demands of the ostensibly degenerate body.

In '"To be mistress of her own fate": suicide as control and contagion in the works of Richard Marsh', Graeme Pedlingham argues that the late Victorian period saw a marked anxiety around the seemingly inexorable rise in instances of suicide. Commentators from across Victorian society increasingly sought to understand the reasons for what William Knighton, in 1881, termed 'Suicidal Mania', and to assess its significance. The subject held a particular fascination for Richard Marsh, one of the most prolific and popular fiction writers of the period, with representations of suicide and reflections on it featuring widely throughout his Gothic *oeuvre*. But this interest goes further than the astute incorporation of cultural anxieties, which Marsh often used as a key technique for heightening the disturbing effects of his work, to considerations of its social, philosophical and scientific import. This is evidenced not only through his fiction between 1891 and 1910 but also by an unpublished essay (in the University of Reading archives), simply entitled 'Suicide'. In both the essay 'Suicide' and much of his Gothic fiction, Marsh captures a sense of ambivalence regarding suicide that speaks to its often contradictory status at this time. In his work, suicide takes on an unsettling uncertainty. This chapter considers Marsh's multifaceted conception of suicide in relation to the contemporaneous medical discourses in Britain that informed and provoked wider debates on the subject, including suicide's seemingly contagious potential.

Bridget M. Marshall, in 'Suicide as justice? The self-destroying Gothic villain in Pauline Hopkins' *Of One Blood*', begins by exploring how Ann Radcliffe and Charles Brockden Brown represent suicide as a way of achieving justice. Suicides by villains prevent the justice system (its processes and its outcomes) from further harming victims; they enable the legal system to have executions without executioners. Radcliffe and Brown's suicide solution for their Gothic villains is taken one step further in Pauline Hopkins' *Of One Blood; or, The Hidden Self*, originally serialised in *Colored American Magazine* between 1902 and 1903. On the first page of the novel, the main character, Reuel Briggs, asks, 'Is suicide wrong?', setting up an ongoing obsession of both the character and the text. After many plot twists and revelations, the novel's Gothic villain, Aubrey Livingston, commits murder. Another character intones, 'Justice will be done', and shortly thereafter, Aubrey's body is found floating in the Charles River. The narrator later explains that Aubrey was persuaded to commit suicide by a voice that tells him to, a voice which he had seemingly encountered while under hypnotic influence. According to the laws of Telassar – the imagined ancient kingdom in Africa that is the setting of half of the novel – men are made to commit suicide when they become murderers so that they become their own executioners. This chapter thus explores the ways that Hopkins represents the relationship between suicide and justice and how the African context impacts on that.

In 'Gothic influences: darkness and suicide in the work of Patricia Highsmith', Fiona Peters examines Patricia Highsmith's beliefs on suicide. When, for example, Highsmith's friend Arthur Koestler committed suicide along with his wife due to his leukaemia and Parkinson's disease, she was both shocked and furious. Peters focuses specifically on the Ripley novels by Highsmith and examines the relationship between the Gothic and crime fiction and the complex indebtedness between the forms. In her second Tom Ripley novel, *Ripley Under Ground* (1970), Highsmith's favourite 'hero' hounds an artist to death. Bernard Tufts has been forging paintings for Tom and his criminal gang, in the name of Derwatt, another painter who committed suicide several years before the novel begins. Knowing Bernard to be suicidal, Tom terrifies him until he leaps to his death from a cliff top in Austria. Prior to this, Bernard has faked his own death by hanging in the cellar in Tom's home near Paris. This novel contains multiple Gothic themes throughout; both mountains and the domestic home space are utilised to evoke the terrors both of the chase and the homely, the sublime and the domestic. Peters' focus on suicide across the Ripley novels provides an important new way of thinking about how the Gothic and crime fiction can be linked.

Xavier Aldana Reyes and Rachid M'Rabty, in 'Better not to have been: Thomas Ligotti and the "suicide" of the human race', explore what could be termed Ligotti's materialistic pessimism, or the belief that conscious and rational life is inherently tragic, as it is largely dominated by the experience of pain and the realisation of the inevitability of death. More specifically, their chapter focuses on one of Ligotti's recurring solutions to the quandary of existence – suicide – in selected stories from *Songs of a Dead Dreamer* (1986), *Grimscribe* (1991) and *The Spectral Link* (2014), but also in his non-fiction treatise *The Conspiracy against the Human Race* (2010) and his interviews in *Born to Fear* (2014). For Ligotti, antinatalism, or mass suicide as a way of preventing future generations from suffering the same fate, becomes an appealing – perhaps even the only real – option for a human race which has, thus far, preferred to believe in the absurdity of futurity and the fallacy of persistence.

In 'Vampire suicide', Jeffrey Andrew Weinstock argues that among the more counterintuitive tropes of the vampire genre is the propensity of vampires to attempt suicide (often successfully), which they do with curious regularity and for three main reasons: first, because they cannot bear what they have become; second, because their martyrdom will save someone they love; or, third, because the ponderous weight of centuries crushes their zest for life. Weinstock focuses on these three motivations for vampire suicide – *vampire guilt, vampire martyrdom* and *vampire ennui*. Weinstock explores Anne Rice's sustained attention to suicide in her Vampire Chronicles novels. After noting the motivations for vampire suicide in the literary Gothic, Weinstock explores vampire suicidal tendencies in a number of recent films and TV programmes, including Park Chan-wook's 2009 film, *Thirst*, and the HBO series *True Blood*. He argues that such narratives constitute a half-hearted attempt at recuperating the vampire genre from charges of immorality through a strategy of inversion. In folklore and in some popular culture texts, the punishment for the mortal sin of suicide is precisely to become a vampire. The consequence of the sin of unmaking is to become the embodiment of sin. Vampire suicide, particularly in instances of guilt or martyrdom, becomes a type of cleansing, made clear through the preferred means of self-slaughter: suicide by sunlight.

Katarzyna Ancuta, in 'Under the dying sun: suicide and the Gothic in modern Japanese literature and culture', discusses the changing representation of suicide in selected Japanese literary and visual texts, focusing on four twentieth- and twenty-first-century novels – *Kokoro* by Natsume Soseki (1914), *The Silent Cry* by Kenzaburo Oe (1967), *Norwegian Wood* by Haruki Murakami (1987) and Tomotake Ishikawa's *Gray Men* (2012), with reference to selected films and manga. Ancuta argues that these narratives have departed from the historic and nationalistic notion of suicide as a noble death in favour of a more Gothic version of the theme. This Gothic dimension is realised through the construction of the characters and the bleak landscapes they inhabit. Alienated from society, often living in self-imposed exile, prone to depression or other forms of mental illness, trapped in toxic, dysfunctional relationships and elaborate masochistic rituals, these melancholy individuals accept suicide with fatalistic abandon as an inevitable conclusion to their insignificant lives, or embrace it as the ultimate act of non-conformism and defiance against authority.

In '"I will abandon this body and take to the air": the suicide at the heart of *Dear Esther*', Dawn Stobbart examines how Gothic tropes and narrative form converge in the 2012 videogame *Dear Esther*. Set in a perpetual twilight, on a deserted Hebridean island, this game is part of a growing sub-genre known as the 'first-person walker', which involves the player exploring a typically Gothic space – a setting as evocative as that of *Frankenstein* or *Wuthering Heights*. Through a subversion of gaming expectations and tropes, Stobbart argues that *Dear*

Esther's control system, and lack of interactivity with the game's landscape, allows the player to take the role of a ghost, haunting the island, as she uncovers a narrative of loss and suicide. Stobbart further argues that through the game's construction, the player forces the narrator, an unnamed male whom the player hears as she walks across and even inside the island delivering fragments of letters to the titular Esther, to endlessly repeat his suicide and the events that led up to it.

This is the first chapter collection to consider at length the place of suicide in the Gothic. Its intention is to extend the critical parameters of scholarship on the genre and to stimulate further debate regarding how the Gothic explores challenging themes.

Notes

1 Deuteronomy 19, v. 22, italics as rendered in the King James Version of the Old Testament.
2 Horace Walpole, *The Castle of Otranto*, in *The Castle of Otranto* and *The Mysterious Mother*, edited by Frederick S. Frank (Peterborough, Ont.: Broadview, 2003), pp. 57–165, at p. 159. Subsequent references are to this edition and are given in parentheses in the text.
3 See, for example, *ibid.*, p. 94, where, on the death of Manfred's son, the garrulous servant Bianca informs Matilda that 'As you are become his heiress, he is impatient to have you married: he has always been raving for more sons; I warrant he is now impatient for grandsons.'
4 The bodies and personal effects of suicides were finally relieved of the punitive consequences enshrined in British law through the passage of the right to burial act (1823) and the abolition of forfeiture act (1870): see Alan H. Marks, 'Historical Suicide', in Clifton D. Bryant (ed.), *Handbook of Death and Dying* (Thousand Oaks, CA: Sage, 2003), Vol. 1, pp. 309–18, at pp. 315–16. Suicide was decriminalised in England and Wales through the passage of the suicide act on 3 August 1961 and via related legislation in Northern Ireland: in Scotland, however, suicide had not been a crime since the eighteenth century. See: www.legislation.gov.uk/ukpga/Eliz2/9–10/60, accessed 7 March 2018; Jennifer Green and Michael Green, *Dealing With Death: A Handbook of Practices, Procedures and Law* (London: Jessica Kingsley, 2006), p. 176; J. Neeleman, 'Suicide as a Crime in the UK: Legal History, International Comparisons and Present Implications', *Acta Psychiatrica Scandinavica*, 94:4 (October 1996), 252–7.
5 Anon., 'The Late Marquis of Londonderry: Coroner's Report', *Morning Post*, 14 August 1822, p. 3, cols 2–3.
6 George Gordon, Lord Byron, *Don Juan*, in *The Works of Lord Byron, Complete in One Volume* (London: John Murray, 1842), pp. 578–760, at p. 667. Byron was not alone in noting a canting change in tone by those who had on occasions been detractors of the late viscount: see Anon., 'The Marquis of Londonderry', *Morning Post*, 17 August 1822, p. 3, cols 1–2.

7 William Shakespeare, *The Tragedy of Julius Caesar*, in Jonathan Bate and Eric Rasmussen (eds), *William Shakespeare: Complete Works* (Basingstoke: Macmillan/The Royal Shakespeare Company, 2008), pp. 1801–58, at p. 1837: Act 3, sc. ii, ll.70–135. The passage contains a further allusion to Shakespeare, the 'syllables of dolour' being an adaptation of a phrase to be found in *Macbeth* Act 4, sc. iii, l.9 (*ibid.*, p. 1900).
8 Radical sentiment with regard to Castlereagh is inevitably bound up with Percy Bysshe Shelley's 1819 portrayal of the politician as Murder personified: see *The Mask of Anarchy*, in Stephen Greenblatt (ed.), *The Norton Anthology of English Literature, Ninth Edition, Volume D: The Romantic Period* (New York: W. W. Norton, 2012), pp. 779–89, at p. 779: Stanza 2, l.5. Though the later years of the two radicals named by Byron are obscure, neither is recorded as having met his end by suicide.
9 See Donna T. Andrew, *Aristocratic Vice: The Attack on Duelling, Suicide, Adultery, and Gambling in Eighteenth-Century England* (New Haven, CT: Yale University Press, 2013), pp. 116–17.
10 See 'Suicide', in John M. Ross (ed.), *The Illustrated Globe Encyclopædia* (London: Thomas C. Jack, 1884), 12 vols, Vol. 11, p. 159. Such crossroad interments retained an evocative, though residual, power at the time of Castlereagh's death: see Anon., 'Mr Abel Griffiths', *Sunday Times*, 6 July 1823, p. 2, col. 5.
11 See a pseudonymous letter in *Lloyd's Evening Post*, dated 10 May 1765, in which a previous correspondent is described as 'vampire like' [*sic*] in his defamation of the dead: *Lloyd's Evening Post*, 3 June 1765, p. 532, col. 1. Byron used the term in supernatural context in *The Giaour* (1813). See Lord Byron, *The Giaour: A Fragment of a Turkish Tale, Eighth Edition, with Some Additions* (London: John Murray, 1813), p. 72, ns 37, 38.
12 Paul Barber, *Vampires, Burial, and Death: Folklore and Reality* (New Haven, CT: Yale University Press, 1988), p. 30.
13 'The Order for the Burial of the Dead', in *The Book of Common Prayer and the Administration of the Sacraments ... According to the Use of the Church of England* (London: SPCK, n.d.), pp. 346–50, at p. 346. Though formally baptised into the Irish Presbyterian tradition, Castlereagh was educated as a member of the Church of England to qualify him for government service. See John Bew, *Castlereagh: The Biography of a Statesman* (London: Quercus, 2011), Ch. 2.
14 Anon., 'The Late Marquis of Londonderry: Coroner's Report', p. 3, col. 3.
15 Byron, *Don Juan*, p. 667. Italics in original.
16 Though not emphasised in the reporting of the coroner's inquest, Castlereagh's political career in Ireland, including his suppression of the 1798 Rebellion, was frequently referenced in the obituaries that immediately followed his death. See, for example, Anon., 'The Late Marquess of Londonderry', *The Times*, 13 August 1822, p. 3, col. 1.
17 Byron, *Don Juan*, p. 667.
18 Ellen Crowell, *The Dandy in Irish and American Southern Fiction: Aristocratic Drag* (Edinburgh: Edinburgh University Press, 2007), p. 67.
19 Byron was himself instrumental in perpetuating a residual Wertherism in the nineteenth century: see Bernard Dieterle, 'Wertherism and the Romantic Weltanschauung', in Gerald Gillespie, Manfred Engel and Bernard Dieterle

(eds), *Romantic Prose Fiction* (Amsterdam: John Benjamins, 2008), pp. 22–40, at pp. 35–6.
20 Byron, *Don Juan*, p. 667. Byron enforces his point through an allusion to Ben Jonson's Roman play, *Sejanus His Fall* (1603).
21 Anon., 'The Late Marquis of Londonderry: Coroner's Report', col. 3.
22 See Ron Brown, *The Art of Suicide* (London: Reaktion, 2001), p. 143.
23 Lord Byron, *Manfred: A Dramatic Poem*, in *The Works of Lord Byron, Complete in One Volume* (London: John Murray, 1842), pp. 175–92, at p. 181: Act 1, sc. Ii, ll.114–20. Despite its dramatic ambience, *Manfred* is a work designed for dramatised reading rather than full-scale theatrical production.
24 James Hogg, *The Private Memoirs and Confessions of a Justified Sinner*, ed. Adrian Hunter (Peterborough, Ont: Broadview, 2001), pp. 221–2; Robert Louis Stevenson, *Strange Case of Dr Jekyll and Mr Hyde*, ed. M. R. Ridley (London: Dent, 1964), p. 62; Olivia Waring, 'With the Lights Out: How Did Kurt Cobain Die, What Did His Suicide Note Say and What Are the Theories about the Nirvana Rocker's Death?', *Sun*, 4 August 2017, available online at www.thesun.co.uk/tvandshowbiz/4161956/how-kurt-cobain-die-suicide-note/, accessed 7 March 2018.
25 Whatever the niceties observed by the middle and upper classes, the proletarian heirs of Peterloo were less forgiving, at times to the point of ribald celebration. See, for example, Anon., 'The Marquis of Londonderry', *Jackson's Oxford Journal*, 24 August 1822, p. 1, cols 1–2.
26 See, for example, Brown, *The Art of Suicide*, p. 144.
27 Ann Radcliffe, *The Italian, or the Confessional of the Black Penitents*, ed. Frederick Garber (Oxford: Oxford University Press, 2008), pp. 403–4.
28 Stevenson, *Strange Case*, pp. 34, 39, 62.
29 Edgar Allan Poe, 'William Wilson', in *The Complete Works of Edgar Allan Poe* (New York: Chatham River Press, 1981), pp. 212–25, at p. 225.
30 Oscar Wilde, *The Picture of Dorian Gray*, ed. Joseph Bristow (Oxford: Oxford University Press, 2006), p. 187.
31 Note here Wilde's emphasis on Gray merely shrugging his shoulders when he considers 'his own sin' immediately prior to stabbing the portrait: *ibid.*, p. 187.

1

Frank Ferguson and Danni Glover

Scottish revenants: Caledonian fatality in Thomas Percy's *Reliques*

Thomas Percy's *The Reliques of Ancient English Poetry*, first published in 1765, was a seminal text in English literature.[1] A comprehensive three-volume set of British ballads, it was one of the most significant collections of the century, and its influence was felt on British editors and writers for generations afterwards. The backdrop for this literary endeavour was a culture war in English and Scottish literature which was part of the long-standing antagonism between the two nations. This antipathy had escalated after the Glorious Revolution and subsequent Union and found expression in a variety of texts. At the core of this battle was a struggle for cultural superiority between Scotland and England.[2] The *Reliques* superficially championed all anglophone British balladry, but in reality it demarcated profound cultural differences between English and Scottish peoples, history and mentalities. While its mission ostensibly sought to celebrate the heroic balladry of the British Isles from Gothic antiquity onwards, it did so by implicitly and explicitly depicting the Scottish psyche, particularly that of its nobility, as so prone to bellicosity as to be tantamount to being suicidal.

The mission of the collection was born from profound cultural antagonism, which manifested itself in many disciplines and encompassed interpretations of national language, literature, history, philosophy and economics. One of the major concerns of the *Reliques* was to discover literary origins and early practitioners so as to assert the cultural, literary and political supremacy of England over Scotland.

By doing so, proponents could then lay claim to cultural and thereby moral precedence and superiority over their rivals. In the early 1760s, this hunger to defend and promote Englishness had been given impetus by the publication of the alleged works of Ossian. With the discovery of the alleged translations of Ossian by James Macpherson in 1759, it was felt by many that Scotland had scored a decisive victory over the English in reclaiming an ancient Homeric poetic figure. Not only did Scotland have an ancient oral tradition in the Highlands, but Macpherson had the ability to fashion Ossian in a manner very attractive to a contemporary audience, replete with all the trappings of mid-century sensibility framed in a Celtic twilight as lachrymose as any Wertherian landscape. Death-haunted and dying in the mists of the Caledonian dusk as Ossian and his fellow bards may have been, their elegiac paeans did much to resuscitate the standing of Scotland's ancient nobles whose reputation had perished in the ignominy of Culloden. This revenant of sentimental Jacobitism returned as a spectral poetic genius of the first order and posed many problems for his critics, who sought to discredit the success of Macpherson by claiming his work was plagiarised and not authentic.

Percy's response to Ossian and Scotland in general in his *Reliques* was to deploy a Gothic riposte in two approaches. First, in a historiographical sense, he posited a conception of British literary history which maintained that the English were cultural inheritors of the Goths, a racial grouping which he believed was superior and different to Scotland's antecedents, the Celts. He was not alone in this belief and drew on the ideas of Nathaniel Bacon and Jonathan Swift who had identified political, legal and cultural similarities between contemporary English society and the Goths several decades previously. By advancing this idea, Percy was aiming to defend and consolidate a cultural position that favoured an interpretation of English predominance over other constituent members of the United Kingdom. This was ultimately an antiquarian response, basing his argument on having literary artefacts in the shape of manuscripts and items which proved the facts of his claims against what he believed were the spurious assertions made by proponents of oral evidence. This evidence he termed 'reliques', borrowing the quasi-religious terminology to add an extra frisson of meaning to his canon-building mission.

Secondly, he adopted Gothic literary approaches in his treatment of Scotland as a nation which, rather than being labile and imbued with sensibility, is violent, fraught and haunted to the point of terrorising itself – practically a suicidal nation. If the Ossianic poetry is a lament for the human subject caught in the predicament of age and death, the *Reliques* determines a judgement on Scotland that it is an unstable, barbarous place which precipitates self-slaughter. Though aimed as a unifying text between the constituent nations of Great Britain, the *Reliques* insists on Scotland as a dangerous, if minor, doppelgänger of England – a nominal national space which exists in Britain's past and in the eternal moment of its own death. By comparison, England and Englishness is determined as the dominant cultural force in the Union, and even when English suicides are discussed they are seen as an act of romantic sentimentalism – a by-product of overweening love and sensibility rather than the effects of an alleged rapacious Caledonian national character. Ancient and contemporary ballads, in Percy's often unsteady editorial stewardship, were reimagined as components of a Gothic metanarrative of British literary history and canonicity. His collection comprehends English and Scottish histories as a contrast between sentimental tragi-comedy on the one hand and a pathology of the nation on the other. This anthologising process employs an implicit classification of the act of suicide in each nation to affirm the respective character of England and Scotland and to valorise Percy's pro-English Gothic interpretation.

Susan Stewart wrote, 'In order to awaken the dead, the antiquarian must first manage to kill them.'[3] In Percy's case, the insinuation is that the subjects in many of the songs and ballads he assembled had helped in this process by dispatching themselves in the first place. What are left behind are textual artefacts and objects on which, much like a coroner, the antiquarian editor must conduct a form of literary postmortem. Despite his calling as an Anglican clergyman, Percy did not necessarily follow a discussion of his protagonists with a moralising of the deceased. This has less to do with a relaxation of such practices in the eighteenth century as it has with the more pressing moral and cultural points to be made in his editing. Certain statements made in the text would corroborate that Percy was aligning himself with trends in the discourse of suicide in the eighteenth century as one that was moving away from perceiving suicide as a sin towards understanding it more as a process of mental illness.[4] Instead, the texts which he edited allowed him to inter their remains within an intricately constructed Gothic reliquary.

To comprehend why Percy's work is 'Gothic' in its intent, it is necessary to briefly introduce his text. Ostensibly, the collection sought to publish a series of English and Scottish ballads. Percy spent a considerable amount of time creating eclectic texts of the various poems he would print, often collaborating with other literary experts. Furthermore, these poems were placed within a very complex system of headnotes, footnotes, glosses, notes, essays and illustrations. If the poems were the relics, then the editorial scaffolding around the poems was the reliquary that housed them and was a vital factor in the success of the whole collection. Without Percy's specific editorial techniques, the collection would not have benefited from the popularity it enjoyed during the eighteenth and nineteenth centuries. He may not have been a great innovator in the field of editorial collection, but the extent of his interpolation sets him apart from previous and contemporary editors. The majority of editors before Percy were concerned, as in Edward Capell's *Prolusions* (1760), to include as few additional notes as possible so as to keep 'the beauty of the page'.[5] Or, as in the *Collection of Old Ballads* (1723–25), an attempt was made to propitiate the book's audience for offering them such a low-status genre as the ballad, when the anonymous editor apologises, 'I never pretended to give him anything more than an old song.'[6] Percy provided an enormous amount of information around the poems that drew considerable consternation from advisors such as William Shenstone, who believed the poems should stand without introduction. Thus the *Reliques* appeared to be as much an academic or, in eighteenth-century terms, a 'philosophical' treatment of English song and balladry, approaching the scholarship of Thomas Warton's *History of English Poetry* in its scope and erudition.[7]

The presentation of the collection is of paramount importance, and an inspection of this aspect of the *Reliques* demonstrates how Percy attempted to deal with his materials. In addition, the prominence of the word 'English' in the title demonstrated his willingness to turn his collection into a nationalistic endeavour and tap into contemporary appetites for and anxieties about the state of his national culture. This ran parallel to his desire to turn the ballads into art objects. The collection was presented to readers in such a way as to try and convince them they were viewing national literary heritage. If the *Reliques* functioned as a museum of English literature, then Percy was the curator, guiding, informing and instructing his audience through unknown aesthetic possibilities. In comparison to Macpherson's *Fragments*, the production values of the *Reliques* were much higher. Percy's agenda to transform the ballads into national literary heritage was underlined throughout the various material levels of the anthology. The sense of materiality, indeed the corporeality, of the *Reliques* was emphasised due to the supposedly core texts being derived from a rescued manuscript of some years previous:

> This very curious old Manuscript in its present mutilated state, but unbound and sadly torn &c., I rescued from destruction, and begged at the hands of my worthy friend Humphrey Pitt Esq., then living at Shriffnal in Shropshire, afterwards of Priorslee, near that town; who died very lately at Bath (viz. in summer 1769). I saw it lying dirty on the floor under a Bureau in ye parlour: being used by the maids to light the fires.[8]

The frontispiece and title page of the *Reliques* provide a very important visual key to the whole collection. Percy had declared that the frontispiece should be 'in the Gothic style, no classical Apollo, but an old English Minstrel with his harp'.[9] This image was used to portray many of the objectives of the *Reliques*. It provided a snapshot of the stylised medieval world of knights and ladies transfixed by the song of a minstrel. The print showed medieval 'English' costumes, not the classical paraphernalia of Southern Europe, in an effort to demonstrate that art and high culture could be found as readily in an English setting. The minstrel was prominent in the foreground of the print, just as Percy would argue his social status demanded as an inheritor of the mantle of ancient bards. Just like the bards before him, he was a poet historian, a man of feeling, insight and sensitivity during an otherwise barbaric age.

This image is juxtaposed with the title and a second illustration on the recto page. Under the full title, a scroll or manuscript is placed with a harp in a ruined Gothic arch surrounded by ancient trees. All is in ruins. The ruin motifs of sentimental medievalism appear to have replaced the once vibrant medieval world of the verso page. The only thing that is left intact is the manuscript, and with that goes the implication that only a learned editor like Percy can guide the uninitiated back to past glories, for only he has the skill, knowledge and insight to decipher the text. The mottoes on both pages link to suggest this: '*non omnis moriar*' (verso, 'not everything decays, perishes') because '*durat opus vatum*' (recto, 'the work of the poets/bards/prophets endures, lives'). In the combination of these two images, Percy celebrates and compartmentalises the past. He opens up the possibility of glimpsing English history in all its imagined ceremony, and lamenting its passing at the same time. His antiquarian's version is one not so much of

1.1 The frontispiece of the *Reliques*.

graveyard poetry, as the poetic object firmly within its mausoleum, evidenced by the right-hand picture, suggests that he acts as the conduit for this literature. Percy took manuscripts out of the ruined vaults where they lay and transformed them into a modern collection that can open up both the past and the antiquarian appreciation for ruins and fragments as easily as opening a book.

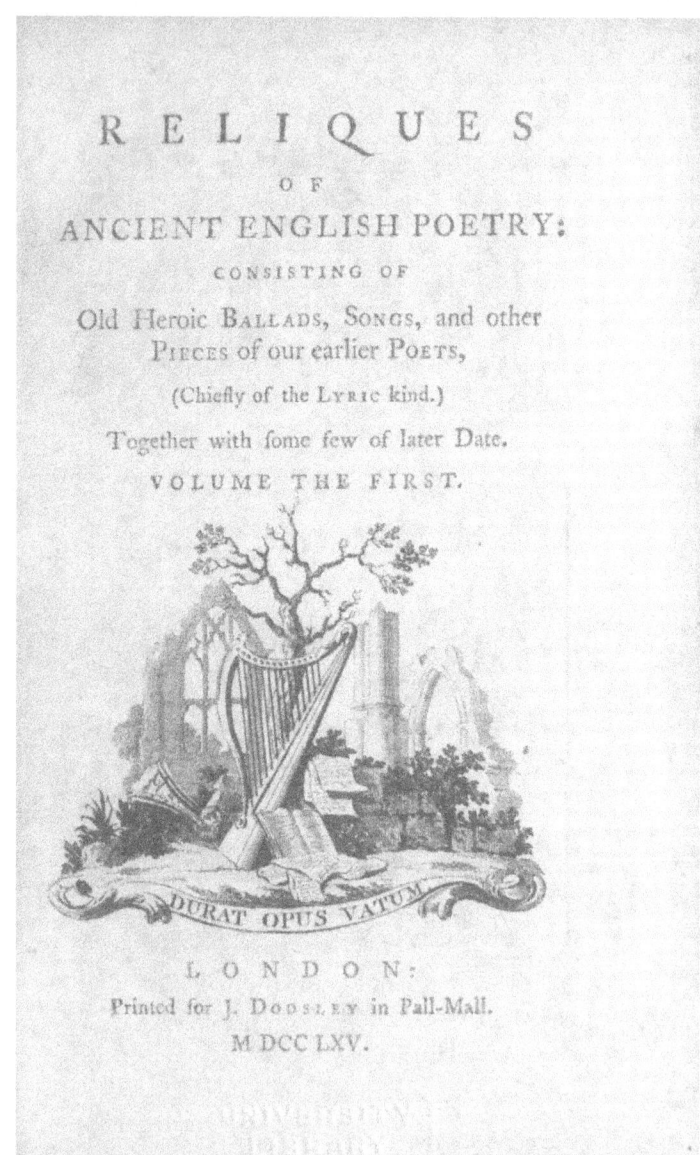

1.2 The title page of the *Reliques*.

The act of looking backwards was essential to the antiquarian editor and acted as a safeguard against the threat of time and decay. The past was valuable because of, not in spite of, the threat of decay; the antiquarian's job was to slow or stop entirely that decay by preserving the material objects of past lives as a placeholder for the lives which these symbols represent. Thus the antiquarian must ensure that the past is settled in its grave before he can assign significance to artefacts of its life. Percy's *Reliques* is predicated on this process as already having taken place. In the eighteenth century, this funeral-and-exhumation process takes on a specific national dimension, as the past which was being laid to rest post-1707 was a past in which England and Scotland were distinct geopolitical and cultural entities. By confirming Scotland and its ballad literature as a voice of the past, the antiquarian ballad collector gave credibility to a narrative of Great Britain as, in the words of Benedict Anderson, 'an unproblematic, primordial given'.[10] In fact, as the work of Steve Newman, Suzanne Gilbert and others has shown, the ballad tradition in Scotland was uninterrupted by the advent of Union; accusations of a 'revival' in the eighteenth century advanced by many modern critics would belie this.[11] While the antiquarian ballad collector claimed to be representing a fragile, fragmented thing, labouring-class balladeers in Scotland were producing poetry from the humorous to the politically subversive.[12] For Percy, who had interests both in ballad collection and in the maintenance of a stable, unified, Anglo-British identity, the death of Scotland and the limited, indeed controlled, 'resurrection' of the Scottish ballad tradition became part of the same wider project.

From a nationalist perspective,[13] the death of Scotland, and indeed the death of an old England which might have subversive capabilities, was presented as a foregone, desirable, even an aesthetically pleasing conclusion:

> The English ballads are generally of the North of England, the Scotch are of the South of Scotland and of consequence the country of Ballad-singers was subject to one crown, and sometimes to the other, and most frequently to neither. Most of the finest Old Scotch Songs have the scene laid within twenty miles of England; which is indeed all poetic ground, green hills, remains of woods, clear brooks. The pastoral scene remains: Of the rude chivalry of former ages happily nothing remains but the ruins of the castles, where the more daring and successful robbers resided.[14]

The choice of ballads also lent itself to the discovery of a heroic past from this space, but often one in which the heroism was English, not Scottish. The 'Ancient Ballad of Chevy Chase', chosen as the first ballad in the collection, might have presented problems because of the events it commemorated. It could be perceived as a medieval poem about a border skirmish between English and Scottish factions, which occurred because the then Lord Percy arbitrarily decided to make an illegal incursion into Scotland to hunt deer (1; 1, I, i). However, the ballad depicts this action as a holy and righteous exercise of Percy's power as an English nobleman:

> The Persé owt of Northombarlande,
> And a vow to God mayd he,
> That he wolde hunte in the mountayns
> Off Chyviat within dayes thre,
> In the mauger of [in spite of] doughtè Dogles,
> And all that ever with him be. (ll.1–6)

When the two nobles meet in battle, they are compared to epic heroes in combat, 'Lyk to captayns of myght and mayne' [like two captains of might and force] (1.26). When Lord Percy sees Douglas die, he takes no satisfaction but exclaims 'Wo ys me for the [woe is me for thee]' (1.58). Lord Percy's death, in turn, is depicted as the noble retaliation of the Scots, when Sir Hewe of Mongon-berry risks his life by riding through the ranks of the English archers to dispatch him with a spear (1.66). The slaughter of the English and Scottish soldiers that occurs in the Cheviot Hills is also dignified as worthy of epic grandeur, 'a marvel' that incites pity and compassion as well as martial pride that the blood spilt flowed 'lyk the reane doys in the stret [like the rain does in the street]' (ll.175–6). The Englishmen take 'no pryde' in the Scottish men they kill, and a long roll of the slain on both sides is commemorated in the closing stanzas of the poem (1.16).

Percy sought to represent post-Union Britain as a Whiggish, manifest destiny, with its constituent nations having undergone a symbolic self-slaughter for the growth of the new nation to take their place. This death was especially pertinent in light of the century of revolutions that would follow the act of union globally and within Britain, all of which threatened the notion of the state as an entity whose identity belonged to the social and political elite. The Jacobite rebellion of 1745 in particular advanced a political supremacy which was inherently Scottish in a time when the idea of inherent Scottishness threatened an emerging stability in British statehood. By 1814, Walter Scott had produced the first historical novel in English – *Waverley; or, 'Tis Sixty Years Since* – and in so doing had confirmed that the Jacobite threat was dead enough to become an appropriate vehicle for antiquarian fictions about Scotland. What happened in those sixty years to convert Jacobitism from a perpetual threat to British nationhood to a safe, nostalgic parable? The defeat at Culloden in 1746 and subsequent legal restrictions placed on Highland culture ended the Jacobite threat in a literal, real-world sense, but it might be argued that parallel to this military, political, juridical and economic quelling of Jacobitism, a cultural enterprise also developed to eradicate the threat to the British state. Percy's ballad efforts – which had a direct influence on Scott's own *Minstrelsy of the Scottish Border* (1802–03) – demonstrate an antiquarian literary determination not only to put Scotland in its grave but also to show that its defeat was a foregone conclusion, and that the cultural artefacts of pro-Scottish sentiment were suicide notes.

The formation of a canon is integral to the literary formation of the state; this becomes more complicated when the state is composed of a 'united kingdom' of different nations. Given that the title of Percy's collection is focused on English poetry, it might be deemed peculiar that Scottish balladry is included at all. Percy includes Scottish ballads in the *Reliques* partly because he had access to some unique examples of the genre which gave him a publishing advantage, but also because it enabled him to allow Scottish balladry into the British canon on his own terms. In the *Reliques*, the very fact of being Scottish is deemed to exist in the past. The post-Union Scottish identity as represented in the *Reliques* is either an ancient, forfeited identity or a volatile, subversive one. To Percy, the identity of progress and of the future was Britishness (informed by Englishness, rather than a conglomeration of the constituent nations in Britain which were assumed to adapt to English language, laws and cultural norms), which meant by extension that Scottishness was a stunted, primitive identity of the past. Furthermore, because Percy's nationalism was centred on Britain having developed out of Gothic rather than Celtic ancestry,[15] we can see something of the Gothic in the political subsuming of Scotland as the possession of a dead thing; the *Reliques* project consumes the decaying relics of what had once been Scotland. Not only has Scotland killed itself by becoming part of the Union, but it has been eaten by a stronger, more powerful entity.

Of course, the analysis of Scotland as a dead nation in the mid-eighteenth century (and even today) is absurd, but Percy's treatment of Scotland fits perfectly with his treatment of balladry. Because (to him) the nation was textual and literate, and antiquarian editing by its very definition referred to the holding of the object as the basis for its evidence, Percy only ever consulted textual sources for his ballad project.[16] This meant that he failed to recognise the living, thriving, changeable contemporary oral tradition in Scotland (and elsewhere) in favour of an antique, completed, fixed printed tradition.[17] Just as he undermines the vitality of the oral ballad tradition in Scotland, so too does he undermine the vitality of Scotland as a community-identifier itself. Percy's Gothic is identified explicitly in his introductory essays and footnotes, but also implicitly in the framing of Britain as powerful, primordial and printed; built on the foundation of an ancient textual tradition in the vein of Homer. His framing was predicated on the belief in the original Goths as being a textual culture distinct from the Celts, who were viewed as an oral culture. It was in many ways a response to the Homeric legacy proposed by James Macpherson in his *Fragments of Ancient Poetry* (1760), in which the legacy was characterised as Celtic and oral.[18] Macpherson's *Fragments*, like many of Percy's *Reliques*, are fatalistic and sentimental, and have a sense of the inevitability of death, but also offer a sense of the communality of death. Macpherson, who witnessed the defeat of his clan at Culloden, depicts a Highland landscape which is fatalistic not because of the suicidal action of its inhabitants, but because it is too inaccessible in terms of its sublime linguistic culture to outsiders to be preserved externally. Ossian was at the centre of the debate about how to characterise the national literary identity and became a kind of shorthand for Celtic poetry, because few antiquarian literary critics had the knowledge (or the inclination) to properly evaluate oral poetry. John Pinkerton, an admirer of Percy, wrote of the Celtic/Gothic dichotomy that:

> The Celtic poetry, as that of a weak and dispirited people might be expected to be, is almost wholly melancholic in a supreme degree. All the mock Ossian is full of death, misery, and madness. The Gothic poetry is the exact reverse of this, being replete with that warm alacrity of mind, cheerful courage, and quick wisdom, which attend a superior talent. Death, which is such a whining and dreadful affair in Celtic poetry, is in the Gothic a matter of laughter.[19]

Though this does not exactly describe many of Percy's ballads – Gothic as they are, there is plenty of weeping and mourning when their heroes die – it does speak accurately to Percy's characterisation of the Goths as being a race of doughty survivors and evolvers leading directly to the eighteenth-century Briton, and the Celts as being the ghosts of what was once Scotland. Perhaps most forcefully, English suicide ballads are signified in heroic, romantic or comedic terms.

Having advocated for a Gothic nationalism in his introduction to the book, Percy establishes a dichotomy between the English poetry that leaves behind relics for later literary historians to uncover (which is to say, printed and manuscript evidence) and the absence of Celticism in the form of Gaelic oral ballads whose exclusion suggests not even a spectral afterlife, as they are never deemed to have existed in the first place. The *Reliques* contains numerous Scottish ballads, and English ballads on Scottish subjects, and Percy uses his position as gatekeeper to the canon of folk literature to cement Scotland's position as a dead nation by pathologising it.[20] The ballads he selects for inclusion paint a picture of a nation which is fatalistic, traitorous and drenched in its own blood.

Scotland in the *Reliques*

Of the Scottish ballads Percy includes, 'Edward, Edward' is the most gruesome. Percy identifies it as 'From a MS. copy transmitted from Scotland', given to him by David Dalrymple, Lord Hailes, who contributed many Scottish ballads to the *Reliques*, but he fails to recognise – at least in the text – that the ballad was very likely a recent composition rather than an ancient one. The evidence for this is twofold; first, the composition of the ballad is uncommonly sophisticated, and its orthography appears antique to the point of affectation. 'Quhatten', for example, is unheard of in Scots poetry since the twelfth century and appears to be a needlessly elaborate re-rendering of the Scots word 'quhat' (what).[21] Secondly, the name 'Edward' is an anatopism in Scottish balladry, and apart from this example appears only when denoting an English king and almost never when naming another character in the wider ballad canon.

'Edward, Edward' is the fifth ballad in the first book of the *Reliques*. It takes the form of a dialogue between a mother and her son, in which she questions him on various sins, including murdering his father and preparing to abandon his wife and children, before he curses her to hell and sails away. The eponymous Edward appears to be of the low nobility, from the fact that he has horses, hawks and property, but his actions are not those of the *Reliques*' dignified English nobles. Compared to the bloodshed at the hand of the Earl of Northumberland in 'The Ancient Ballad of Chevy Chase', in which the 'Yngglishe archery / Gave many a wounde full wyde; / ... Which ganyde them no pryde' (1.1.10.13–16), Edward relishes in his gore and deception. The ballad is replete with symbols of destruction and decay: swords dripping with blood, abandoned halls doomed to ruin, noble families reduced to nameless beggars. Edward's defiance when faced with his sins and cowardly plan to 'set [his] feit in yonder boat, / And Ile fare over the sea, O'[22] are the self-inflicted actions which secure the fatal end to his line. Scotland's suicide is in part predicated on the fact that its nobility lack the urge for self-preservation exemplified by, for example, the Northumberland Percys, who patronised Percy (no relation) to publish the *Reliques*.

The theme of a self-destructive nobility is echoed in another ballad from the same volume, 'Sir Patrick Spence'. In all likelihood this ballad has authentic ancient Scottish provenance and is based on events surrounding the ill-fated retrieval of Margaret, the Maid of Norway, in the thirteenth century, whose death set in motion the Scottish Wars of Independence. In this ballad, a callous and distant king 'drinking the blude-reid wine'[23] sends Patrick Spence on a naval mission during a dangerous storm, and Patrick acquiesces in spite of his better knowledge and warnings from his fellow sailors:

> O quha is this has don this deid,
> This ill deid don to me;
> To send me out this time o' the yeir,
> To sail upon the se? (ll.17–20)

Patrick and his men all die at sea, leaving their wives in the tragically futile hope of seeing them again. 'Sir Patrick Spence' is more sympathetic to the Scots than 'Edward, Edward' – Patrick's determination to proceed towards certain death is borne out of loyalty to his King – but the result is the same. The Scottish nobility cannot survive as the English (specifically, the Northumberland Percys, to whom Percy was connected by patronage) do, because of the inherent suicidal nature of their actions. Keeping in mind the connection to the Scottish Wars of Independence, 'Sir Patrick Spence' had a further dimension of relevance to Percy's contemporary audience; how many Patrick Spences died protecting an ultimately futile line of succession during the Jacobite uprisings? Though his loyalty is to be admired, his misplacing of said loyalty is tragic. English nobility, by contrast, are presented as sturdier and more prudent, perhaps best exemplified in an English comic tradition presented by Percy as an example of national resilience. Book three of the *Reliques* begins with an Arthurian cycle, which balances the Arthur of 'The Boy and the Mantle', a cuckolded figure of fun, with the formidable military and political leader represented in 'The Legend of King Arthur'. Though the Arthur of the former has to contend with the accusation that his queen is '"a bitch and a witch, / And a whore bold: / King, in thine owne hall / Thou art a cuckold"' (3.1.9.147–50), 'The Legend of King Arthur' recounts that the fifteen-year-old Arthur was a king of such might that when 'All Britaine that was att an upròre / [He] did to quiett bringe' (3.1.38.27– 8). Though the English nobility (of whom Arthur is surely the paradigm) may have their personal foibles, they are ultimately powerfully, even mythically, suited to leadership; and besides, their failings serve more as instructional parables to the common folk than as evidence against their divine right. 'The Legend of King Arthur' excises and excuses the weaknesses presented in 'The Boy and the Mantle', and though satires of King Arthur are not uncommon in the English literary tradition, particularly after the seventeenth century, Percy's contribution to Arthurian balladry is overwhelmingly positive.[24] Scottish leadership, by contrast, is characterised by weakness and deficiency, a failure that ultimately concludes in national demise.

Unsurprisingly, the pathology of Scotland is further extrapolated in ballads about Scotland written by English balladeers. Scotland's supposed duplicitousness is laid bare in the opening line of 'The Murder of the King of Scots': 'Woe worth, woe worth thee, false Scotlànde!'[25] The notion of duplicity has run through evaluations of Scottish literature, culture and psyche since such evaluations have been made, reaching an apex with G. Gregory Smith's coining of 'Caledonian antisyzygy' in 1919.[26] In the eighteenth century it was a commonly expressed view that the Scots had an untrustworthy nature, as seen in the populist polemic of John Wilkes:

> The restless and turbulent disposition of the Scottish nation before the union, with their constant attachment to France and declared enmity to England, their repeated perfidies and rebellions since that period, with their service behaviour in times of need, and overbearing insolence in power, have justly rendered the very name of Scot hateful to every true Englishman.[27]

This national duplicity is explored in 'The Murder of the King of Scots', an English ballad which depicts the murder of Lord Darnley by Bothwell and his supporters. From the opening line of the ballad, it is clear that Scotland as nation is to assume the psychological responsibility of its own downfall. The murder of Darnley sets in motion Mary Queen of Scots' exile to England, trial and execution. This ballad suggests a duplicity in Bothwell's actions; his greed for wealth and social status is masked by his self-fashioning as the Queen's protector. A further dichotomy is explored in Mary's fate. The ballad seems to suggest that the strength and agency she demonstrated in choosing for her king 'The worthyest prince that ever was borne' (l.3) is undercut by her weakness in turning to the man who killed him for protection. Thus Mary has to go to England, where 'through the queene of Englands grace' (1.67) she lives out the rest of her days. The ballad-writer strips Scotland of its sovereignty by describing her as 'The queene of France' (1.5). The Scotland of this ballad is without a head of state of its own, making it all the more susceptible to the fatal manipulations of traitors such as Bothwell. Percy notes that the ballad appears to be contemporary to Mary's exile, but as an editor, his inclusion of it suggests a line being drawn from Darnley's murder to the present day. Scotland was no longer a separate sovereign entity, by act of Mary's own son and by the 1707 act of union. The evaluation of historical documents as evidence for the cultural and political situation in 1765 is an act of pathologising, like looking for anomalies in an autopsy.

'Jemmy Dawson' is perhaps the most explicitly suicidal of the ballads selected for the *Reliques*. This ballad, composed by Percy's collaborator and correspondent William Shenstone, tells the story of one of the Manchester rebels who participated in the 1745 rising, who was hanged, drawn and quartered for his crime, leaving behind his sweetheart who, broken-hearted, kills herself. Unlike other contemporary poetry about Jacobitism written in England, 'Jemmy Dawson' is fawningly sympathetic, painting Jemmy's participation as a tragic loss rather than an act of treachery. He is described as a 'gallant youth, / A brighter ever trod the plain',[28] until he was 'led astray' by the 'party's hateful strife' (ll.17/18). Like Patrick Spence, Jemmy's loyalty is not absent, but misplaced: when Kitty sees his heart after his body is mutilated, she notes that 'For tho' it could his king forget, / 'Twas true and loyal still to her' (ll.63–4). Kitty's suicide is played out explicitly at the end of the ballad:

> My death, my death alone can show
> The pure and lasting love I bore:
> Accept, O heaven, of woes like ours,
> And let us, let us weep no more. (ll.69–72)

Her death is directly contingent on the death of Jemmy, itself a form of suicide because it is framed not as justice but as tragedy. Shenstone does not identify any specific crime on Jemmy's behalf, except for wearing the 'fatal dress' of a Jacobite soldier. The very adoption of that identity is the fatal act. Jemmy's death is a direct result of the corrupting influence of Jacobitism; to advocate for Scottish sovereignty in the age after Scotland has been laid in its grave is to accept death. Like Patrick Spence, Jemmy has willingly boarded a sinking ship. How many of England's young lovers will die suicidally because of Scotland's treachery? By attempting to give life to something which is already dead, the Manchester rebels – and by extension, all naïve English youth – put themselves at risk of the same fate.

Conclusions

In *The Reliques of Ancient English Poetry*, we see several ideological influences converging. The book is nationalistic in its intent, as it establishes a literary history which prioritises English voices, stories and perspectives. This nationalism has a Gothic dimension, which Percy defines as a nationalism that can be traced to Northern Europe through print. This Gothicism is further emphasised through the bibliographical architecture of the collection; through its fascination with the inevitability of its subjects' deaths and in the obsession with these deaths as occasioned by English sentiment or Scottish disease. Finally, the book has an antiquarian interest which naturally favours cultures that leave behind printed and manuscript evidence which historians and antiquarians can use to prove a lineage. Percy takes the absence of this type of evidence by Celtic cultures as proof that these cultures neither survived nor evolved into the contemporary British landscape. To establish that these cultures were, in fact, 'dead', Percy chooses ballad examples from both England and Scotland that depict the Scottish nation and nature as inherently fatalistic and suicidal. Its aristocracy operates with duplicity and self-interest, while its most well-meaning citizens throw themselves into deadly situations through a sense of misplaced loyalty. English aristocrats, by contrast, act with benevolence and justice, while its citizens are suicidal only by virtue of their naivety to intoxicating false nationalisms.

Notes

1 Thomas Percy, *Reliques of Ancient English Poetry: Consisting of Old Heroic Ballads, Songs and Other Pieces of Our Earlier Poets (Chiefly of the Lyric Kind) Together with Some Few of Later Date* (London: R. and J. Dodsley, 1765); Nick Groom, *The Making of Percy's Reliques* (Oxford: Clarendon Press, 1999).
2 For the standard biography of Percy, see Bertram H. Davis, *Thomas Percy* (Boston, MA: Twayne, 1981) and *Thomas Percy: A Scholar-Cleric in the Age of Johnson* (Philadelphia, PA: Pennsylvania University Press, 1989). See Albert Friedman, *The Ballad Revival* (Chicago, IL: University of Chicago Press, 1961), p. 135; Murray Pittock, *Poetry and Jacobite Politics* (Cambridge: Cambridge University Press, 1994), p. 160.
3 Susan Stewart, *On Longing: Narratives of the Miniature, the Gigantic, the Souvenir, the Collection* (Durham, NC: Duke University Press, 1993), p. 143.
4 Kelly MaGuire, *Dying to be English: Suicide Narratives and National Identity, 1721–1814* (Abingdon and New York: Routledge, 2012), p. i.
5 Percy's copy, Bodleian Library Percy 91, iv.
6 *A Collection of Old Ballads* (London: J. Roberts, 1727), p. ii.
7 Thomas Warton, *The History of English Poetry, from the Close of the Eleventh to the Commencement of the Eighteenth Century* (London: J. Dodsley, 1774–81).
8 British Library Add. MS. 27879.
9 M. G. Robinson and Leah Dennis (eds), *The Correspondence of Thomas Percy and Thomas Warton* (Baton Rouge: Louisiana University Press, 1951), pp. 104–5. Ironically, for all of Percy's predilection for Gothic Black letter, no Gothic font appears in the title page; Christine Baatz, in Barbara Korte, Ralf Schneider and Stefanie Lethbridge (eds), *Anthologies of British Poetry: Critical Perspectives from Literary and Cultural Studies* (Baton Rouge: Louisiana State University Press, 1951), p. 115. See also, Joseph A. Dane and Svetlana Djananova, 'The Typographical Gothic: A Cautionary Note on the Title Page to Percy's *Reliques of Ancient English Poetry*', *Eighteenth-Century Life*, 29:3 (2005), 76–97.
10 Benedict Anderson, *Imagined Communities: Reflections on the Origin and Spread of Nationalism* (London and New York: Verso, 1991), p. 89.
11 See Steve Newman, *Ballad Collection, Lyric, and the Canon: The Call of the Popular from the Restoration to the New Criticism* (Philadelphia, PA: University of Pennsylvania Press, 2007); Sarah M. Dunnigan and Suzanne Gilbert (eds), *The Edinburgh Companion to Scottish Traditional Literatures* (Edinburgh: Edinburgh University Press, 2013).
12 Rather than exploring a living community that was continuing a tradition, Percy and other antiquarians were fixated on 'golden oldie' literary museum pieces. Diane Dugaw, *Warrior Women and Popular Balladry* (Chicago, IL: University of Chicago Press, 1989), p. 43.
13 The extent of Percy's nationalism warrants specific and detailed discussion, but briefly, he was a culturally Anglican Whig who believed that the native English were descendants of the Goths of Northern Europe and that by their racial virtues they were the most suitable dominant constituent of post-Union Great Britain.
14 *Reliques* I, 1, xi, 99.

15 See James Watt, 'Thomas Percy, China, and the Gothic', *The Eighteenth Century*, 48:7 (2007), 95–109.
16 See Groom, *The Making of Percy's Reliques*.
17 Nick Groom, 'Celts, Goths and the Literary Source', in Alvaro Ribeiro, SJ and James G. Basker (eds), *Tradition in Transition: Women Writers, Marginal Texts, and the Eighteenth-Century Canon* (Oxford: Oxford University Press, 1996), pp. 275–96.
18 Paula McDowell, '"The Manufacture and Lingua-Facture of Ballad-Making": Broadside Ballads in Long Eighteenth-Century Ballad Discourse', *The Eighteenth Century*, 47:2 (2006), 151–78, at 155.
19 John Pinkerton, *An Inquiry Into the History of Scotland Preceding the Reign of Malcolm III. Or the Year 1056* (London: John Nichols, 1794), p. 389.
20 Approximately 20 per cent of the 178 texts.
21 Linguistic data collected from 'Dictionary of the Scots Language', *Scottish Language Dictionaries*, www.dsl.ac.uk/, accessed 24 January 2017, a composite of *A Dictionary of the Older Scottish Tongue* and *The Scottish National Dictionary*.
22 'Edward, Edward', in Percy, *Reliques of Ancient English Poetry*, Vol. 1, I.31–2.
23 'Sir Patrick Spence', in Percy, *Reliques of Ancient English Poetry*, I.2.
24 Norris J. Lacy, 'The Arthur of the Twentieth and Twenty-first Centuries', in Elizabeth Archibald and Ad Putter (eds), *The Cambridge Companion to the Arthurian Legend* (Cambridge: Cambridge University Press, 2009), pp. 120–35, at p. 130.
25 'The Murder of the King of Scots', in Percy, *Reliques of Ancient English Poetry*, I.1.
26 G. Gregory Smith, *Scottish Literature: Character and Influence* (London: Macmillan, 1919), pp. 4–27.
27 John Wilkes, *The North Briton from No. I to No. XLVL Inclusive: With Several Useful and Explanatory Notes, Not Printed in Any Former Edition* (London: W. Bingley, 1969), p. 146.
28 'Jemmy Dawson', in Percy, *Reliques of Ancient English Poetry*, I.9–10.

2

Lisa Vargo

Male and female Werthers: Romanticism and Gothic suicide

If the Romantic Gothic hero is typically defined by his or her marginalisation from society and its norms and is characterised by excess, individualism and transgression, the ultimate act of defiance is self-annihilation. Romantic literature's dark side to a preoccupation with individuality and subjectivity is the extinction of the self. Given its associations with a longstanding interest in what has been characterised as 'the Romantic agony', it is perhaps surprising that suicide is not treated as a topic distinct from death in the critical literature on the Gothic – all the more so with respect to its connections with Johann Wolfgang von Goethe's *The Sorrows of Young Werther* (1774) and its notoriety as a work causing suicidal contagion, with sufferers donning his blue coat and yellow waistcoat as if exchanging their bodies for his own.[1] When it appeared, Goethe's novel generated anxiety about the 'Werther effect', so named by David Philips in 1974, drawing on the reputation the novel had for inspiring readers to follow the example of Werther and end their lives.[2] '*Wertherfieber*', or 'Werther-fever', transforms a work associated with sensibility to an extreme that gives way to the unknowable and inspires horror. If there is little evidence that *Werther* did indeed inspire suicide amongst its readers, what Tobin Siebers has called a 'compulsion of imitation' means that this notoriety might move the work away from those who view it in terms of the sentimentality of a man of intense feeling, towards a kind of infection that dismisses individual motivation in a manner that one might find horrifying.[3] Conversely, it might also point to a terrifying agency on the part of the individual, where suicide is a display of power. Allusions to *Werther* within British Gothic writing about suicide are found particularly in writings by women. Their retellings of Werther's story interrogate the relationship between infection and agency with respect to suicide.

Werther was written when Goethe was twenty-five and is commonly assumed to have been inspired by a friend, Carl Wilhelm Jerusalem, who committed suicide.[4] Its plot is simple, consisting of a series of letters written by Werther to his friend Wilhelm and a final section by an editor. Werther travels to the village of Wahlheim where he admires the peasants and meets Charlotte, who after the death of her mother takes care of her brothers and sisters. Werther falls in love with Charlotte even though he is aware that she is engaged to Albert, who is eleven years older. He befriends Charlotte and Albert, but his unrequited love makes him leave for Weimar, eventually returning to Wahlheim after Albert and Charlotte have married. His visits cause him great suffering, while events suggest that Albert, if admirable, is not as sensitive and cultivated as Werther and that Charlotte might reciprocate Werther's feelings even if she cannot act on them. After a final visit when he recites a passage he has translated from Ossian, he writes a farewell letter and borrows pistols from Albert, explaining that he is going on a journey. He shoots himself in the head and is found by a servant, mortally wounded. When Werther is buried in a corner of the churchyard under two linden (lime) trees he admired, Albert cannot bring himself to attend his funeral, and Charlotte's 'life is despaired of'. The work ends with the stark declaration that 'no priest attended' his funeral.[5]

Like many works that capture the popular imagination, the novel's reception is not necessarily dependent on Goethe's own words. Unless British readers could read German, they read mediated versions of the text. The edition of the novel that British readers would most likely encounter was a 1779 translation from the French, thought to be by Daniel Malthus, which omits certain incidents including the long passage Werther recites to Charlotte from Ossian.[6] A 1786 translation from the German also omits sections, as well as inserting moralising footnotes and pieces of poetry and prose that are not original to the work.[7] In his preface, Malthus anglicises Werther with his suggestion that the 'design' of the work is 'to exhibit a picture of that disordered state of mind, too common in our own country' (I.v). These mediations explain how, in Britain, the alleged suicide epidemic points to a powerful re-reading of the novel as a work of terror that both advocates and inspires self-destruction. There is some evidence for this perspective in the text. Near the end of the first volume, Werther contemplates how happiness moves to despair:

> That ardent sentiment which animated my heart with the love of nature, which poured upon me a torrent of delight, which brought all paradise before me, is now become an insupportable torment, a demon which pursues and harasses me incessantly. (I.139–40)

Whether the demon is an external force that takes away agency or is an internal one that directs action defines the ambiguities associated with the novel's reception.

These mediations of *Werther*, or *Werter* as it was known in the late eighteenth century, from a work of sensibility to one in the Gothic mode invite a revision of a well-known account of this process – A. Alvarez's study of suicide, *The Savage God*, in which he memorably observes that the 'Romantic Stance, then, was suicidal'. Alvarez wittily paraphrases Byron with the declaration that 'the Romantics thought of suicide when they went to bed at night, and thought of it again in the morning when they shaved'.[8] He calls suicide a kind of 'freedom from the rational' and a model of genius through which literature becomes 'a way of life in itself'.[9] Alvarez's broad strokes might be said to approach caricature; the reference to shaving suggests that his examples are male – Wordsworth, Coleridge, Shelley and Keats – for whom 'the example of Chatterton haunted the imagination of the poets in their moments of crisis; he was the standard by which they measured their despair'.[10] Alvarez suggests that it is Goethe's novel even more than Chatterton to which readers of the period responded: 'For the reading public Werther was no longer a character in a novel, he was a model for living who set a whole style of high feeling and despair.'[11] Subsequent scholarship offers a nuanced sense of engagement amongst what Syndy McMillen Conger has termed 'Werther's English Sisters'. Conger points out, 'Since by the time Werther became available in English translation (1779), sensibility and its literature had long since come under the guardianship of women, it is hardly surprising that women took note of the new German hero of sensibility.'[12] This offers a double significance. If sensibility might be seen to raise the reputation of women with respect to feeling's associations with morality and wisdom, it also belongs to a 'nightmare inversion' that endangers the individual.[13] The nightmare inversion posed by Werther accounts for why, for women writers, infection on the one hand takes away one's ability to act, and on the other advocates self-destructive agency.

In spite of Alvarez's suggestion that the Romantic stance is suicidal, it is a selective group of British writers who genuinely focus on what might truly be termed 'Gothic suicide'. Ann B. Tracy's summaries of 208 works published between 1790 and 1830 suggest that seventy of the novels contain suicides, with more referencing suicide contemplated or attempted and yet more that contain fake suicides.[14] These accounts of incest, rape and murder often seem little more than a means to offer retribution for transgression or simply add yet another taboo to their often intricate plots of intrigue, and the bemused tone of some of Tracy's summaries suggests their rather contrived character. A representative example is Elizabeth Helme's *The Farmer of Inglewood Forest* (1796), in which a chance encounter via a coaching accident leads a country family to libertinism, seduction, insanity, pregnancy outside marriage, duelling, attempted rape and threat of incest, and prostitution, ending with the suicide of the farmer's son Edwin and the characters of a subsequent generation who 'intermarry in suitable ways'.[15] If suicide plays a role in the plot, it seems more accessory than a central element to an exploration of the Gothic.

An exception to Tracy's comprehensive account of plots of largely forgotten works exists in the writings of Charlotte Dacre, whose best-known novel *Zofloya* (1806) questions the idea of a stable subject and unsettles assumptions about a woman's tradition of writing.[16] *The Sorrows of Werther* offers a vehicle through which Dacre interrogates whether the female subject is a victim of influence or if her fatal actions might reflect her agency. In her first novel, *Confessions of the Nun of St. Omer* (1805), the married heroine, Cazire, is seduced by a philosopher, Friebourg, who carries a copy of *Werther*. He eventually kills her husband in a duel and later commits suicide. E. J. Clery calls Werther Fribourg's 'secret weapon', which makes us realise that the heroine 'is doomed to transgress'.[17] In this respect, *Werther* is related to suicide as a form of infection whose effects are beyond the individual's control. Dacre registers her awareness that *Werther* was accused of promoting immorality; her transformation of Goethe's sentimental novel into a vehicle for seduction and the exploration of erotic desire on the part of women defines a transgressive agency that is alarming in its implications. This powerful re-reading of *Werther* is present in her most notorious novel. While *Zofloya* is more commonly viewed as a revision of Matthew Lewis's *The Monk* (1796), the work also can be seen as a reversal of the love triangle of Werther, Charlotte and Albert for Victoria, Lilla and Henriquez. Victoria is helped by a mysterious Moor, Zofloya (the servant of Henriquz), who assists her in poisoning her husband, murdering her rival Lilla and drugging and seducing Henriquez, who then commits suicide. Victoria meets her own end when Zofloya reveals himself to be Satan. The final sentence of the work, even as it draws back from the extremes it has raised, leaves matters unresolved: 'Either we must suppose that the love of evil is born with us (which would be an insult to the Deity), or we must attribute them (as appears more consonant with reason) to the suggestions of infernal influence.'[18] With *Zofloya*, Dacre takes a nightmare inversion of Werther's sentimentality to an extreme, which leaves open the possibility that women are not merely victims but can serve as agents of destructive desire.

Dacre's writings represent what is missing in Alvarez's male-centred perspective to suggest that primary examples of Wertherism in English literature are by women writing in the Gothic mode. The work of critics like Margaret R. Higonnet and Michelle Faubert is helpful towards defining why Gothic suicide has a prominence in women's writing. If there is a connection between women and death lying outside the frame of the known, as Higonnet has suggested, Gothic suicide likewise goes beyond sensibility and a social framework: 'this act so deeply resists our attempts at knowledge and explanation.'[19] Higonnet's discrimination between two modes of writing about suicide differentiates sensibility from the transgressive, thus locating its Gothic strain:

> Sympathetic narratives naturalise the puzzling act by attributing to it an inexorable logic of reaction to pain, political oppression, or emotional loss. Other narratives may build generically a pattern of deviance, of illogic: the suicide was irresponsible, dangerous to others, immoral, or transgressed the circuit of the socially acceptable.[20]

A sense of identification with transgression, deviance and the inexorable defines the nature of Gothic suicide. Like Charlotte Dacre, Charlotte Smith, Sarah Farrell, Mary Wollstonecraft and Mary Shelley adapt *Werther* to explore the terrors of the obliteration of the self, be it by external force or as an act of a person's own volition.

While Dacre's place within the Gothic is uncontested, Charlotte Smith remains closer to the border between sensibility and the transgressive in five sonnets in the voice in Werther included in her *Elegiac Sonnets*. In the first and second editions (both 1784), three sonnets attributed to Werther conclude the collection and follow three sonnets in the voice of Petrarch. A fourth Petrarch sonnet and two additional sonnets in the Werther series appear in the expanded third edition (1786). The original placement forges a link with the Petrarchan convention. While the sonnets in the voice of Petrarch affirm the power of unrequited love and its role in inspiration, the Werther sonnets trace their dangers. A progressive sense of how Petrarchan imagery entraps Werther begins with his encounter with a 'maniac' and his futile attempts to seek respite in solitude and direction through the North Star. The final two sonnets offer a description of his tomb and his state of mind just before his death. They represent a more complex reading of his suicide than the more sentimental readings in poems by Smith's contemporaries, Mary Robinson and Anna Seward.[21] Eric Parisot offers reassurance that Smith's sonnets negate the idea of suicide in her own poetic persona.[22] In this respect, Smith's position resembles Goethe, who suggested that after writing the novel he felt as 'after a general confession, joyous and free and entitled to a new life'.[23] And like Daniel Malthus, whose translation she likely read, Smith follows his connection between Werther's story and that 'disordered state of mind, too common in our own country'. Smith recognises how easily sensibility might, without proper limits, lead to self-negation and oblivion.

The movement from infection to death shapes their narrative. In Sonnet XXI, 'Supposed to be written by Werter', the familiar image of Cupid with his burning arrows is transformed to the ghastly and insignificant image of an insect immolated by the 'fatal fire' it 'courts' (1.14), as infection, represented by the wound from the arrow, turns to self-destruction of fatal attraction.[24] Images of love and madness allude to Werther's contemplation of a madman attempting to find flowers in the winter landscape, made clear through a quotation from Goethe added in a note to the third edition: 'Is this the destiny of man? Is he only happy before he possesses his reason, or after he has lost it? – Full of hope you go to gather flowers in Winter, and are grieved not to find any – and do not know why they cannot be found' (2.94). Allusion to Alexander Pope's *Eloisa*, who tells Abelard that she would 'drink delicious poison from thy eye' (note to 1.8), connects Pope's epistle with Werther's story.[25] In writing about the Werther sonnets, Elizabeth Dolan invokes 'the protective value of rational thought', which might anchor the Petrarchan lover with an understanding that metaphor is not reality.[26] This seems to be where the translations from Petrarch offer a counter to the Werther poems, which interrogate how poetic convention might infect one to commit or even authorise self-destruction. If reason is the thread that preserves life, once that thread is broken one falls into despair, madness and a terror of blankness offered by death.

A further step in Werther's decline is isolation. Sonnet XXII, 'By the same. To solitude', takes disconnection at its subject. The images of solitude, the vale in which one comes to hide sorrow and tears as a substitute for friendship, ruptures connection from the human realm. The winds that sound 'like soft Pity's sighs' employ simile to emphasise unlikeness and therefore pity's absence (l.8). The note quoting Werther's description of making his way 'among thorns and briars which tear me to pieces' to offer his pain relief (1.154) presents a disturbing image of self-violence (note to l.1). Sonnet XXIII, 'By the same. To the North Star', alludes to Werther's mention that the star shines opposite Lotte's window (note to l.1). Rather than a sense of sharing, as occurs in Ann Radcliffe's *The Mysteries of Udolpho* (1794) between Emily and St Aubert with the moon, or Coleridge blessing the rook that his friend Charles will see, the Pole Star signifies disconnection as Werther rejects its ability to offer pleasure. His soul maintains 'short rays of reason' which fade, and the failure of the North Star as a guide only leads him to his desire to 'despair and die' (ll.13, 14).

Movement from sensibility to the Gothic as the tropes of love fail to connect with reason is present in Sonnet XXIV, 'By the same', in which Werther imagines his grave, and Sonnet XXV, 'By the same. Just before his death'. The 'unhappy suicide' (Sonnet XXIV, l.8) imagines his unmarked grave in a secluded corner of a churchyard, where the luxuriance of grass and flowers contrast with his lack of memorial. As a suicide, the solitude he looked for in Sonnet XXII is now absolute; Charlotte must come in 'stealth' to weep with tears that will 'embalm the dead' over 'the mournful spot' (ll.7, 12, 13). Sonnet XXV focuses on how the 'worn heart' is in death obliterated, as 'worms shall feed on this devoted heart' which in its decay can no longer reflect the image of the beloved (ll.6, 11). Smith concludes the sonnet and the series with a sense that Werther's death might not achieve the peace he seeks, as he might haunt those he leaves behind: 'Yet may thy pity mingle not with pain, / For then thy hapless lover – dies in vain!'

(ll.13-14). Unlike the assurance that Petrarch and Laura will meet in death, the poem reinforces his separation and obliteration. Werther's description of his powerlessness before destiny and heart eaten by worms remind the reader of the horrors of self-destruction. Reference to the decaying corpse echoes the final line of Goethe's novel, 'No priest attended him'. He is isolated to the point of negation, and the poetic tropes he grasped for guidance have failed him.

Not all women writers focus on the demise of the hero. While Goethe's novel ends with uncertainty and fear for Charlotte's life after the shock of Werther's death, Sarah Farrell's poem in rhyming couplets, 'Charlotte, or a Sequel to the *Sorrows of Werter*' (1792), connects her fate with a retelling of Bürger's popular ballad 'Leonore', in which an absent lover's return at midnight to claim his bride transforms into a horse-ride to death.[27] Farrell re-situates Werther's burial place from two lime trees in a far corner of a churchyard to a crossroad, 'according to the English custom in cases of premeditated self-murder'. This alteration serves the premise of her retelling that '*No rest in sacred ground for passion's slave*' (6, italics in original). In Farrell's version, Albert's friendship for his wife cools, and she is haunted in her dreams by ghastly visions of Werther's body:

> See bleeding Werter's mangled form arise;
> Each wound expressive of the love he bore,
> Which gaping they confess, with reeking gore. (2)

Charlotte is lured from her bed and travels with loose attire and trembling limbs while listening to a widowed robin's mournful strain. On arriving at Werther's grave, she falls and is unable to rise. While she criticises Werther for his actions she confesses her love, explaining her own virtue which is met by Albert with distrust and neglect. She is imprisoned by her imagining of his death:

> My madd'ning brain will burst! – my head runs round,
> I see the flash! – I hear the dreadful sound!
> Yes! – there he falls! – it pierc'd his faithful heart,
> Ah! death stay – stop – nor strike the fatal dart.
> What bloody corse is that? – keep off – (she cried)
> O Werter! Werter! – 'twas for me you died. (16)

She calls for Albert, but the hapless Charlotte dies on Werther's grave (17). The poem does not end there but describes the father of

Charlotte, Sickbert, who goes to the grave where 'horrors chill you with an inward dread' as he sees his daughter's body and attempts to revive her with his tears. Charlotte's corpse is brought back to Albert's house, and the widowed red-breast often dresses her grave with flowers. The implication is that Albert could have saved her, but his coldness means that Werther is able to claim her in death if not in life.

While Orie William Long calls the work 'a specimen of pathos', the unexpected explanation for Charlotte's death suggests a deeper horror of infection.[28] Susanne Kord notes that the poem echoes Mary Wollstonecraft's argument that sentimental novels encouraged women readers to adopt and internalise gender roles that exacerbated their exclusion from public discourse.[29] English adaptations of the story stripped it of 'any kind of social or political content' and, in so doing, reframed it to highlight women's sentimentality in particular as a matter of 'individual failure', without consequence for the social world.[30] Kord adds the interesting suggestion that the work goes against the usual warning of 'the dangers of sentiment', noting that the 'problem here is not an excess of love but its absence, the horror is not that of ghosts arising from the grave, but that of loneliness and neglect'.[31] Farrell's story recognises a form of isolation for women via tropes of literature. Syndy Conger astutely reads Farrell's work as an 'entrapment in paradox' in which Charlotte's friendship for Werther and love for Albert are 'apparently beyond the ken of both her lovers', who misread feminine sympathy, 'seeing desire where there is disinterested love'.[32] Farrell's poem moves beyond the sense that women are victims who internalise sensibility to a more horrifying possibility of their isolation and lack of agency, and estrangement from the males who might protect them.

If Smith ventriloquises Werther, and Farrell contemplates Charlotte's fate, Mary Wollstonecraft's own notoriety as 'a female Werter' was bestowed on her posthumously by her husband. In his *Memoirs* (1798) of his wife, William Godwin accounts for her two suicide attempts over her rejection by Gilbert Imlay:

> We not unfrequently meet with persons, endowed with the most exquisite and delicious sensibility, whose minds seem almost of too fine a texture to encounter the vicissitudes of human affairs, to whom pleasure is transport, and disappointment is agony indescribable. This character is finely portrayed by the author of the *Sorrows of Werter*. Mary was in this respect a female Werter.[33]

He alludes to *Werter* on a further occasion, in a Preface to his wife's *Posthumous Works* (1798) introducing her letters to Imlay:

> The following Letters may possibly be found to contain the finest examples of the language of sentiment and passion ever presented to the world. They bear a striking resemblance to the celebrated romance of Werter, though the incidents to which they relate are of a very different cast. Probably the readers to whom Werter is incapable of affording pleasure, will receive no delight from the present publication. The editor apprehends that, in the judgment of those best qualified to decide upon the comparison, these Letters will be admitted to have the superiority over the fiction of Goethe. They are the offspring of a glowing imagination, and a heart penetrated with the passion it essays to describe.[34]

Michelle Faubert considers how in calling his wife a 'female Werter', Godwin casts her in terms of sensibility, thus rewriting Wollstonecraft's own letters and writings, which justify suicide as a rational act resembling an act of autonomy, to a state comparable to a slave suicide who 'represents far more than revolution and protest. He is also the ultimate figure of desperation who demands our pity'.[35] Godwin himself viewed suicide in terms of reason, but his effort to join his wife to sensibility locates an alternative vision within Wollstonecraft's view of suicide that emphasises horror.

As mindful as Godwin and Wollstonecraft were about suicide as an act of reason, Godwin's 'Wertherisation' of Wollstonecraft might lead to a recognition that she also views self-destruction as associated with horror. Roswitha Burwick points to the Gothic elements in the suicide letters and a more unsettling reading of a female Werther.[36] In a letter to Imlay, Wollstonecraft imagines that the guilty might be haunted by the innocent victims they tormented:

> May you never know by experience what you have made me endure. Should your sensibility ever awake, remorse will find its way to your heart; and, in the midst of business and sensual pleasure, I shall appear before you, the victim of your deviation from rectitude.[37]

Imlay is depicted by Wollstonecraft as a Gothic villain. The dead Wollstonecraft will haunt him, reminding him of her victimhood. It is this more Gothic version of the Werther story that also haunts the pages of her unfinished novel, *The Wrongs of Woman*.

With *The Wrongs of Woman*, Wollstonecraft's critique of marriage and women's association with sensibility is meant to argue for agency and rationality, but is unsettled by the Gothic imagery pervading a work in which suicide is offered as an escape from being 'buried alive'.[38] The first paragraph begins with the evocation of 'Abodes of horror' conjured by 'the magic spell of genius to harrow the soul' as being nothing in comparison to Maria's 'mansion of despair' (75). She is victim to a plot of 'civilized depravity' imprisoned in a 'dreary cell' with a 'small grated window', overlooking a 'desolate garden' (76). The souls of the inhabitants of the asylum in which Maria has been imprisoned by her husband, who wishes to control her fortune, are called 'the most terrific of ruins': 'What is the view of the fallen column, the mouldering arch, of the most exquisite workmanship, when compared with this living memento of the fragility, the instability, of reason, and the wild luxuriancy of noxious passions?' (83). Maria is described as fearing the other residents from whom she 'shrunk back with more horror and affright, than if she had stumbled over a mangled corpse' (84). Her dreams are haunted and she feels 'buried alive' (85). At night, she is 'waked by the dismal shrieks of demoniac rage, or of excruciating despair, uttered in such wild tones of indescribable anguish, as proved the total absence of reason, and roused phantoms of horror in her mind, far more terrific than all that dreaming superstition ever drew' (92). The weight of this language undoes the hope offered with the companionship of Jemima, the escape of reading books like Rousseau's *Heloïse* (1761) and the affections of Darnford, an inmate of the prison with whom she falls in love.

Wollstonecraft casts doubt on how she might have reconciled these Gothic elements with a positive outcome. The notes Wollstonecraft left as to how she might have concluded her work capture her own indecision as she wavers between Darnford's eventual unfaithfulness and Maria's suicide from a 'hell of disappointment' (202), or her heroine's restoration to life after a suicide attempt and decision to live for the sake of her daughter. Godwin's characterisation suggests that in wishing to 'drag into light' the 'details of oppression' that exist for women, the fate of Werther transformed into a tale of horror seems the more probable, if not the choice Wollstonecraft would have preferred to portray 'the wrongs of different classes of women, equally oppressive' (74). The logic of horror trumps her desire to suggest that rationality can triumph for women, though its fragmentary nature anticipates the tantalising irresolution of the final lines of Dacre's *Zofloya*.

The daughter of Godwin and Wollstonecraft read Goethe's novel in 1815, and her own writings further explore estrangement from the story of Werther as a source of horror. A number of critics have explored *Frankenstein*'s connections with *The Sorrows of Werther* – *Werther* is one of the books that the Creature employs to make sense of his life. While the mention of *Werther* is brief and restricted to a single passage, its influence is more pervasive with respect to *Frankenstein*'s epistolary form, love triangles, allusion to other literary works within its narratives and female characters, who are domestic icons like Lotte. Key to understanding the presence of *Werther* in the text with respect to the Gothic is a misreading of the work on the part of the Creature.

> I thought Werter himself a more divine being than I had ever beheld or imagined; his character contained no pretension, but it sunk deep. The disquisitions upon death and suicide were calculated to fill me with wonder. I did not pretend to enter into the merits of the case, yet I inclined towards the opinions of the hero, whose extinction I wept, without precisely understanding it.[39]

Roswitha Burwick connects the Creature with Mary Wollstonecraft, observing that the Creature is more of a 'female Werther' than a male one, as Goethe's hero had economic independence and choice.[40] Astrida Orle Tantillo argues that like Werther, who uses reading to influence his actions in a manner that is detrimental to his well-being, the Creature emulates this rather than understanding that Goethe believes that doing so is folly – something that both Goethe and Shelley arrive at via their reading of Rousseau.[41] Like Wollstonecraft, Shelley considers how the Gothic threatens the agency of reason.

What seems to be missing from these very helpful readings is that the Creature cannot be like any of those likely mythical readers of *Werther* who wore yellow waistcoats and ended their lives with pistols. If the extinction of Werter causes the Creature to weep and teaches him sensibility, a difficulty lies in his inability to connect his experience with that of the novel's hero. His punishment of Victor with the deaths of William, Clerval and Elizabeth bespeaks the absence of family, friendship and romantic love in his own life. The Creature can only misread Goethe's novel because of the horror of his isolation. He is not human; therefore, accounts of human existence have no relevance to him, and this absolute disconnection means his suicide. Walton suggests to his sister, on hearing Victor's story, 'do you not feel your blood congealed with horror, like that which even now curdles mine?' (209). The Creature's story is also one of horror which can only be both expiated and resolved by suicide:

> 'But soon,' he cried, with sad and solemn enthusiasm, 'I shall die, and what I now feel be no longer felt. Soon these burning miseries will be extinct. I shall ascend my funeral pile triumphantly, and exult in the agony of the torturing flames. The light of that conflagration will fade away; my ashes will be swept into the sea by the winds. My spirit will sleep in peace; or if it thinks, it will not surely think thus. Farewell.' (221)

An irony occurs in that while being unable to connect with Werther, he succumbs to 'Werthermania' with his anticipated suicide at the conclusion of the work. If Werther's unmarked grave is permitted a place in the churchyard in spite of his suicide, the Creature's traces are utterly obliterated.

The Creature's self-immolation is a response to the fact that he cannot enter into the discussion between Werther and Albert. Werther points out to Albert, who suggests they are 'paradoxical', 'I think it is as absurd to say that a man who destroys himself is a coward, as to call a man a coward who dies of a malignant fever' (1.219). Werther's debate with Albert suggests how the absolute of annihilation represented by Gothic suicide belongs to a wider discussion of suicide in the Romantic age. Certainly, it has its counters even by the very writers who explore its horrors. It is possible to see Mary Shelley, as Michelle Faubert argues in her edition of Mary Shelley's *Mathilda*, as engaging with the debate advanced by her parents, and, following David Hume, that suicide might be a logical and inevitable act to which one might have a right.[42]

That rights might be extended to self-destruction defines the limits of Werther's influence on Gothic writing. The parody offered by Thomas Love Peacock's *Nightmare Abbey*, published eleven months after *Frankenstein*, registers discomfort with such agency even as it creates laughter. His Shelleyan hero Scythrop Glowry, who does his best to immerse himself in a Gothic sensibility, has been doubly disappointed in love as a kind of reversal of Werther's love triangle when he is rejected by two women who marry other men. He is ready to emulate Werther and end it all, and asks his servant Raven for the necessary accoutrements:

> A pint of port and a pistol.
> A pistol!
> And a pint of port. I will make my exit like Werter.[43]

When Raven points out that the dinner is getting cold and 'There is a time for every thing under the sun. You may as well dine first, and be miserable afterwards' (130), Scythrop takes his advice. Not only do the pleasures of Madeira keep him anchored in this world, but in the 1818 version of the text so do the thought of taking an advanced degree in misanthropy and the desire to 'make a figure in the world' (134). Peacock laughs off the idea of Werther-fever and the thought that the infection of a Gothic sensibility is anything more than a fashion that Scythrop dons like Werther's blue coat. Peacock's insistence that Werther's effects were more literary than imitated by the reading public refutes Daniel Malthus's belief that Werther's story reflects the 'disordered state of mind, too common in our own country'. And if this is indeed true on a literal level, it overlooks the significance that women writers recognise in their own re-writings of *Werther*.

Notes

1 See Michelle Faubert, 'Werther Goes Viral: Suicidal Contagion, Anti-Vaccination, and Infectious Sympathy', *Literature and Medicine*, 34 (2016), 389–417; and Jan Thorson and Per-Arne Öberg, 'Was There a Suicide Epidemic After Goethe's Werther?', *Archives of Suicide Research*, 7 (2003), 69–72.
2 Tobin Siebers, 'The Werther Effect: The Esthetics of Suicide', *Mosaic: A Journal for the Interdisciplinary Study of Literature*, 26 (1993), 15–34, at 15.
3 *Ibid.*
4 Siebers questions this assumption (*Ibid.*, 15–19), suggesting that Goethe's reading of Rousseau on the subject of suffering is just as likely a source, as he 'did not need to live through the experience of suffering' (*Ibid.*, 19).
5 Johann Wolfgang von Goethe, *The Sorrows of Werter: A German Story* (London: J. Dodsley, M.DCC.LXXIX. 1779), 2 vols. Eighteenth Century Collections Online. Gale. University of Saskatchewan Library. 20 August 2018, Vol. 2, p. 172. Further references to the text are from this translation, which was contemporary to the writers here considered, and are given in parentheses.
6 Orie William Long, 'English Translations of Goethe's *Werther*', *The Journal of English and Germanic Philology*, 14:2 (April 1915), 169–203, at 177.
7 *Ibid.*, 179.
8 A. Alvarez, *The Savage God: A Study of Suicide* (London: Weidenfeld and Nicholson, 1972), p. 176.
9 *Ibid.*
10 *Ibid.*, p. 173.
11 *Ibid.*, p. 176.
12 Syndy McMillen Conger, 'The Sorrows of Young Charlotte: Werther's English Sisters 1785–1805', *Goethe Yearbook*, 3 (1986), 21–56, at 21.
13 *Ibid.*, 24.
14 Ann B. Tracy, *The Gothic Novel 1790–1830: Plot Summaries and Index to Motifs* (Lexington, KY: University Press of Kentucky, 1981).
15 *Ibid.*, p. 71.

16 See Adriana Craciun, *Fatal Women of Romanticism* (Cambridge: Cambridge University Press, 2003), pp. 153–5.
17 E. J. Clery, *Women's Gothic: From Clara Reeve to Mary Shelley* (Tavistock: Northcote House, 2000), p. 107. Robert Miles reads the novel through Wollstonecraft's critique of Rousseau, noting its dialogic qualities. See *Gothic Writing 1750–1820*, Second Edition (Manchester: Manchester University Press, 2002), pp. 91–6.
18 Charlotte Dacre, *Zofloya*, ed. Adriana Craciun (Peterborough, Ont.: Broadview Press, 1997), p. 255.
19 Margaret R. Higgonet, 'Frames of Female Suicide', *Studies in the Novel*, 32 (2000), 229–42, at 230.
20 *Ibid*.
21 For a list of poems, consult Conger, pp. 51–2 and Orie William Long, 'English and American Imitations of Goethe's *Werter*', *Modern Philology*, 14 (1916), 193–216.
22 Eric Parisot, 'Living to Labour, Labouring to Live: The Problem of Suicide in Charlotte Smith's *Elegiac Sonnets*', *Literature Compass*, 12 (2015), 662.
23 Belinda Jack, 'Goethe's *Werther* and Its Effects', *The Lancet Psychiatry*, 1 (2014), 19.
24 Charlotte Smith, *The Poems of Charlotte Smith*, ed. Stuart Curran (Oxford: Oxford University Press, 1994). All subsequent references are to this edition and are given in parentheses. Readings of the sonnets include Jacqueline M. Labbe, *Charlotte Smith: Romanticism, Poetry and the Culture of Gender* (Manchester: Manchester University Press, 2003), Elizabeth A. Dolan, 'British Romantic Melancholia: Charlotte Smith's *Elegiac Sonnets*, Medical Discourse and the Problem of Sensibility', *Journal of European Studies*, 33 (2003), 237–53. She expands her analysis of the sonnets in *Seeing Suffering in Women's Literature of the Romantic Era* (Farnham: Ashgate, 2008).
25 In his edition of the poem, Geoffrey Tillotson points out that the line echoes John Hughes' 1736 translation of the letters of Eloise and Abelard as well as Shakespeare's *Anthony and Cleopatra* (1.5.26ff). See *The Rape of the Lock and Other Poems*, ed. Geoffrey Tillotson, Vol. 2. *The Twickenham Edition of the Poems of Alexander Pope*, General ed. John Butt (London: Methuen, 1940), 309n.
26 Dolan, 'British Romantic Melancholia', 249.
27 Mrs Farrell (Sarah), *Charlotte, or, a Sequel to the Sorrows of Werter: A Struggle between Religion and Love, in An Epistle from Abelard to Eloisa: A Vision, or Evening Walk; and Other Poems* (Bath: Campbell and Gainsborough, M.DCC. XCII. 1792). Eighteenth Century Collections Online. Gale. University of Saskatchewan Library. 20 August 2018. All subsequent references are to this edition and are given in parentheses. In his, John G. Robertson suggests that 'not even Goethe's *Werther*, which appeared a few months later – was more stimulating in its effects on other literatures as Bürger's *Leonore*'. See *A History of German Literature* (Edinburgh: William Blackwood and Sons, 1902), p. 304.
28 Long, 'English and American Imitations of Goethe's *Werter*', 198.
29 Susanne Kord, 'From Sentiment to Sexuality: English Werther-Stories, the French Revolution, and German Vampires', in Maike Oergel (ed.), *(Re-)Writing the Radical: Enlightenment, Revolution and Cultural Transfer in 1790s Germany* (Berlin: de Gruyter, 2012), pp. 25–43, at p. 28.

30 *Ibid.*, pp. 33, 42.
31 *Ibid.*, pp. 37.
32 *Ibid.*, pp. 41–2.
33 William Godwin, *Memoirs of the Author of a Vindication of the Rights of Woman. The Second Edition. Corrected* (London: Joseph Johnson, 1798). Eighteenth Century Collections Online. Gale, pp. 114–15.
34 Quoted in Roswitha Burwick, 'Goethe's *Werther* and Mary Shelley's *Frankenstein*', *The Wordsworth Circle*, 24 (1993), 48.
35 Michelle Faubert, 'The Fictional Suicides of Mary Wollstonecraft', *Literature Compass*, 12 (2015), 652–9.
36 Burwick, 'Goethe's *Werther* and Mary Shelley's *Frankenstein*', 47–52.
37 *Posthumous Works*, IV, Letter LXIX. Quoted by Burwick, 'Goethe's *Werther* and Mary Shelley's *Frankenstein*', 48.
38 Mary Wollstonecraft, *Mary and The Wrongs of Women*, ed. Gary Kelly (Oxford: Oxford University Press, 1983), p. 185. All subsequent references are to this edition and are given in parentheses.
39 Mary Shelley, *Frankenstein*, Third Edition, eds D. L. Mac Donald and Kathleen Scherf (Peterborough, Ont.: Broadview, 2012), p. 142. All subsequent references are to this edition and are given in parentheses.
40 Burwick, 'Goethe's *Werther* and Mary Shelley's *Frankenstein*', 51.
41 The Creature as a reliable or an unreliable reader of Werther is discussed in Astrida Orle Tantillo, '*Werther, Frankenstein* and Girardian Mediated Desire', *Studia Neophilologica*, 80 (2008), 177–87.
42 Mary Shelley, 'Introduction', in *Mathilda*, ed. Michelle Faubert (Peterborough, Ont.: Broadview, 2017), pp. 26–7. See also S. E. Sprott, *The English Debate on Suicide: From Donne to Hume* (Peru, IL: Open Court, 1961). William Godwin represents an alternative view which justifies suicide, though he also cautioned that the motives for it might be wrong, and there are more significant examples in Godwin's *Fleetwood*, where a suicide occurs early in the novel.
43 Thomas Love Peacock, *Nightmare Abbey*, ed. Lisa Vargo (Peterborough, Ont.: Broadview Press, 2007), p. 129. All subsequent references are to this edition and are given in parentheses.

3

William Hughes

'The supposed incipiency of mental disease'[1]: guilt, regret and suicide in three ghost stories by J. Sheridan Le Fanu

Somewhat surprisingly, researchers working in the medical humanities have directed comparatively little attention to the works of J. Sheridan Le Fanu. This is curious, considering the Irish author's reputation not merely as a recluse but also as something of a hypochondriac following the death of his thirty-five-year-old wife, Susanna, in 1858. Indeed, poor health seems to have been almost a constant shadow across the life of the author: as Le Fanu's biographer, W. J. McCormack notes, 'Ill health dogged both Joseph and Susanna – scarletina, rheumatism, gout in his case, and a recurring ailment probably of psychosomatic origins in Susanna's.'[2] McCormack's surmise regarding Susanna Le Fanu's frequently fragile mental – as well as physical – state is not without foundation.[3] As he notes, even in an era of relatively high mortality, her family – the Bennetts – seem to have been plagued by the presence of premature death. This 'family burden', McCormack suggests, is one that 'Sheridan Le Fanu was ill fitted to acquire as a dowry'.[4] Given the fifteen lonely years for which the reclusive author mourned his dead wife, the consciousness of the looming presence of death should surely be considered as arguably less of a soon-spent dowry and more of an enduring legacy.

McCormack infers that the frequent periods of ill health experienced by the author, his wife and his relatives-in-law underlie the 'recurring images' of 'illness and convalescence' that punctuate the breadth of his fiction.[5] McCormack's view, indeed, is that Susanna's early death, which followed a crisis the biographer describes as 'an hysterical attack', was rationalised by the 'disorientated' author in rhetoric that resembled the fiction he had already published.[6] For McCormack, the theology of the troubled mind lies at the centre of the author's 'personal neurosis': death itself, or the impending visitation of mortality, have an immanent psychological value centred on an afterlife perceived through Protestant apologetics.[7]

Le Fanu's often conflicted relationship with the Protestantism associated with his cultural identity is well documented by McCormack, as is the author's apparent resignation of the ultimate fate of his wife's physical, as well as spiritual, self to the care of a beneficent – if somewhat distant and inexplicable – Deity.[8] McCormack, though, understates somewhat the way in which Le Fanu's theology perceptibly interacts with the more secular care exercised over her body in the period leading up to her demise. Le Fanu's acute consciousness of the physiological and the psychological, indeed, is indicated in a diary entry, readily quoted by the biographer as evidence of an enhanced religious fervour consequent on Susanna's death. Following what McCormack terms 'a long invocation of God the creator of life and controller of death', Le Fanu intimates, candidly,

> I will not trouble myself with the faithless thought that the errors of art or the misapprehensions of the beloved patient hastened her death. In these events there is no such thing as chance, and, over all seeming accidents preside [sic] the eternal dominion of our Heavenly father, a controul [sic] the most minute and power immeasurable.[9]

McCormack clarifies these remarks by noting how Susanna was quite possibly treated under a fashionable homeopathic medical regime immediately before her death, and further suggests that the couple may have been divided in their opinions regarding the treatment's efficacy.[10]

Le Fanu's words, brief though they are, deserve a greater consideration than the passing attention paid to them by McCormack. There is something in Le Fanu's rhetoric, admittedly, that suggests an abnegation of blame, a deflecting of ultimate responsibility for Susanna's death on to a presiding Deity and away from those who exercise, or submit to, the 'art' of the – in this case, homeopathic – physician. But there is, equally, an intimation of at least a suspicion on the part of the diarist that medical negligence, actual malpractice or mere ignorance may have possibly hastened the patient's end – or that she, herself, may ultimately have entertained little faith in the presiding practitioner and his chosen restorative regime. Whatever conclusion the author may have eventually reached regarding the Deity's role in Susanna's physiologically premature death, his momentary candour suggests that he has considered, at least in passing, the possibility that her decline might be a matter of medical rather than theological import.

Unlike the broader issue of prostrating illness, this complex interfacing of theology and medicine enjoys no significant presence in Le Fanu's fiction until almost the close of his literary career. In 1872, the Irish author published a collection of short stories under the biblically inflected title of *In a Glass Darkly*.[11] Four of the five narratives contained in the volume had been released previously in a variety of periodicals, including *All the Year Round, Belgravia, London Society* and *The Dark Blue*, between 1869 and 1872; the other – 'The Familiar' – was a retitled and reworked narrative from Le Fanu's 1851 volume *Ghost Stories and Tales of Mystery*. Significantly, though, *In a Glass Darkly* was synthesised into an ostensibly organic whole through the imposition of a presiding physician, Dr Martin Hesselius, from whose case files the narratives are supposedly derived. This framing, though, is a brittle conceit. Hesselius is physically in attendance on the patient in only the first of the narratives, 'Green Tea'. In this one exemplification of his practice, the physician's inability to project diagnosis satisfactorily into prognosis, and his lack of due care towards a vulnerable patient, leads to the death of the latter by suicide. The subsequent tales in the collection are historical accounts from various periods and countries, again selected by Hesselius's executor supposedly to illustrate a range of theoretical and clinical works by the physician – namely 'MS Essay A.17', 'The Interior Sense and the Conditions of the Opening Thereof', *Mortis Imago* and a further unnamed essay – none of which is made available to the reader.[12] Their putative presence adds nothing to the late physician's reputation and, indeed, only serves to foreground the demonstrable deficiency of his comprehension of deviant psychology.

Deviant psychology, indeed, is the true focus of *In a Glass Darkly*. These are not ghost stories in the strict sense of that genre's conventional definition. The supernatural, which manifests itself in all but one of the six tales, is emphasised far less than its physiological and mental impact on the subject to whom it is revealed.[13] In this sense, the spectre-smitten body is rendered simultaneously a conventionally diseased one, expressing symptoms, inspiring diagnosis and prognosis, travelling beneath the medical gaze towards recovery or death. The supernatural in itself, however, provides far too superficial an explanation for the mental issues exhibited by the five afflicted protagonists of *In a Glass Darkly*. The supernatural is, in many respects, a catalyst rather than a discrete cause, for all five characters are otherwise subject to the stresses associated with the repression of what they perceive as being unacceptable desires or else unatoned-for crimes. These are the occluded issues that escape those observers – medical as well as lay practitioners – charged in the novel with applying diagnoses and prognoses to the troubled minds of the protagonists. Their diagnoses are based primarily on a physiological approach to psychology, and the assumption that a change in bodily regime – most emphatically, diet – will neutralise or diminish the abnormal symptoms suffered by the patient. It is notable that in 'Green Tea', 'The Familiar' and 'Mr Justice Harbottle' – the first three stories within *In a Glass Darkly* – the afflicted and spectre-smitten characters are all men of sedentary habits. Issues of diet – and of diet-related disorders such as gout and dyspepsia – punctuate the commentaries on their gradual mental decline. Of the three, the first and last are unequivocal narratives of self-annihilation; 'The Familiar' is somewhat more ambiguous, though still couched in terms that recall the rhetoric associated with suicide in the two stories that bracket it. These three stories are narratives of persistent and apparently supernatural persecution which terminate in the apparent self-annihilation of the central protagonist. They are likewise fictions that revolve around the ostensibly indiscernible presence of secret lives, the stresses associated with past actions repressed in current mental consciousness, and the inability of the protagonist to successfully integrate these competing and alternative visions of the self.

Unlike in 'Mr Justice Harbottle', where the titular judge's vices and vindictiveness are something of an open secret, the central protagonists of 'Green Tea' and 'The Familiar' are reticent men whose outwardly respectable lives occlude an inner consciousness of recent activities known only to themselves.[14] In 'Green Tea', the Reverend Mr Jennings is a 'kind' and 'shy' Warwickshire cleric, 'a charitable man', described by one of his London associates as 'the most happy and blessed person on earth'.[15] 'Little knows she about him' (7), Hesselius pithily concludes. In 'The Familiar', Captain Sir James Barton is a retired – and relatively young, at forty-three or forty-four – naval officer, an 'intelligent and agreeable companion' whose manners were 'remarkably easy, quiet, and even polished' (43) despite an occasional moodiness. Both enjoy unblemished public lives, and their lapses into physical disability and mental distraction are sufficiently rare as to be promptly remarked on by their associates (58). Both place themselves under the searching gaze of professional physicians – Hesselius in the case of Jennings, the fashionable Dr R–––– of Dublin, in that of Barton – and for both, diet and lifestyle are assumed to be the first and immediate cause of their current indisposition.

This diagnosis is, of course, a convention of mid- to late Victorian writings in the supernatural tradition. Dickens' Ebenezer Scrooge, when visited by the ghost of his former business partner, summarily dismisses the spectre as nothing more than a dyspeptic hallucination: 'You may be an undigested bit of beef, a blot of mustard, a crumb of cheese, a fragment of an underdone potato. There's more of gravy than of grave about you.'[16] Bearing this convention in mind, it should come as no surprise that Jennings himself comes to a similar conclusion when he is faced for the first time by his own attendant demon, the spectre of a small black monkey, visible only to himself. On seeing his nemesis, Jennings attempts to placate and comfort himself:

> 'The thing is purely disease, a well-known physical affection, as distinctly [sic] as small-pox or neuralgia. Doctors are all agreed on that, philosophy demonstrates it. I must not be a fool. I've been sitting up too late, and I daresay my digestion is quite wrong, and with God's help I shall be all right, and this is but a symptom of nervous dyspepsia.' Did I believe all this? Not one word of it. (25–6)

Hesselius, significantly, considers more than once the likely effects of Jennings' dietary regime (34, 39). Barton's attendant physician, likewise, specifically prescribes for 'some slight derangement of the digestion' (53), a view similarly communicated to Barton by a clergyman in a lay diagnosis which recommends 'the aid of a few tonics' as a supplement to 'a little attention to diet, exercise, and the other essentials of health' (60, 61). The captain clearly does *not* share this diagnosis, as is demonstrated by the summary manner in which he subsequently and deliberately burns the doctor's prescription (54).

Dickens' moral tale is generically more humorous than it is Gothic. The misdiagnoses imposed on Jennings and Barton lead not to an amusing though sobering review of their pasts, but rather to a worsening of their respective physical and mental conditions. Both men, Hesselius suggests, have somehow abraded the physical yet psychic veil that protects gross human perception from a direct encounter with things fearfully spiritual. Jennings, in his protracted nocturnal theological and philosophical studies, has energised his senses with copious doses of green tea. Hence, for Hesselius, the cause of Jennings' hallucination is obvious: an 'inner eye' has been opened, 'a surface unduly exposed, on which disembodied spirits may operate' (39, cf. 32). Likewise, in the case of Barton – whom the German physician did not actually meet – Hesselius compares an individual susceptibility to apparently preternatural visions to 'the loss of the scarf-skin, and a consequent exposure of surfaces for whose excessive sensitiveness, nature has provided a muffling' (41). Harbottle, notably, suffers from gout (110), which is a conventional consequence of his lifestyle, though one which is associated in Le Fanu's narrative specifically with the tortures imposed on him by those he has sent prematurely – and, for the most part, without statutory legal justification – to the grave. Harbottle, like Jennings and Barton, consults a doctor, who diagnoses the judge's disease as hypochondria and gout, and orders him to convalesce at the spa town of Buxton (111).[17] His own lay diagnosis – "Tis nothing but vapours, nothing but a maggot' (111) – is, perhaps, more accurate: the preoccupied judge is sinking into a depression, and his gout is a symptom, rather than the cause, of his declining mental state.[18]

For Hesselius, the crux of the case in both instances is that the sufferer *sees* visions, and that these visions link straightforwardly towards a diagnosis which unites the spiritual and the material. A material action of some sort – eating, drinking, living, for want of a better word – opens the gaze of the self to things it should not see, and these things are instrumental in unsettling personal sanity with fatal consequences. Jennings' spectral black monkey is invisible to others, and first distracts him merely by its presence, disagreeable visage and rocking movements (30). It ultimately goads him with blasphemies (31) and then prompts him, at first unsuccessfully (32), to take his own life (32). Barton is stalked by a stunted and disagreeable-looking man, visible at times to others (67, 68), and capable of expressing himself in concrete communication by way of handwritten notes signed 'THE WATCHER' (47, 49). Both men dread their attendant nemesis, and accord that figure a central role in their declining physical as well as mental state. The nemesis figure, monkey or Watcher, is seemingly – in the eyes of Hesselius – the prime cause of the early demise of both characters. This is how the matter is most openly presented to the reader. A visual and auditory delusion destabilises the mind, and the mind's instability prompts the destruction of the body – by an actual physical action, in Jennings' case; by simply resigning oneself to inevitable dissolution, in that of Barton (cf. 29). It all seems so simple, so straightforward: the sight of the uncanny in itself is supposedly sufficient to destabilise the mind and to bring death.

Hesselius attempts to further enforce the inevitability of Jennings's death by suggesting that the clergyman's fatal paranoia was merely 'a complication' (39) of an undetected 'hereditary suicidal mania' (40). *In a Glass Darkly*, however, is consistent in associating self-destruction with internalisation and brooding – with actions undertaken in the distant or recent past, reflected on exhaustively and obsessively in the present, with self-judgement, with regret and with deathbed grief. It is a cumulative process, as Jennings notes when describing the accretion of his woes to the consulting Hesselius:

> But as food is taken in softly at the lips, and then brought under the teeth, as the tip of the little finger caught in a mill crank will draw in the hand, and the arm, and the whole body, so the miserable mortal who has been once caught firmly by the finest fibre of his nerve, is drawn in and in, by the enormous machinery of hell, until he is as I am. (31)

The rhetoric of divine punishment is common also to Barton's account of his perceived persecution, despite the captain's professed status as a free thinker (45).[19] His fear would seem to be that the Deity has either permitted his torture or else is incapable of preventing it (63). Barton's partial confession, though, is delivered not to a doctor but to a clergyman, and the latter, after suggesting a purely physiological source for the captain's indisposition (61), voices what really is the substantial psychological key to his decline – one which has almost equal relevance to the parallel case of Jennings: 'My dear sir, this is fancy ... you are your own tormentor' (63).

Barton's response to this remark is enigmatic yet also proclaims a personal belief that there is no delusion here, no mistake: 'fancy has no part in it' (63), he proclaims:

> 'There are circumstances connected with this – this *appearance*', said Barton, 'which it is needless to disclose, but which to *me* are proof of its horrible nature. I know that the being that follows me is not human – I say I *know* this; I could prove it to your own conviction.' (63, original italics)

Those convincing 'circumstances' are never vouchsafed to the clergyman, and are only given to the reader in a coda following Barton's sudden death. Yet his words at this first juncture elide easily from the language of theology to that of paranoia. Barton admits, with perceptible despair, how he is never free from 'the consciousness that a malignant spirit is following and watching me':

> I am pursued with blasphemies, cries of despair and appalling hatred. I hear those dreadful sounds called after me as I turn the corners of the streets; they come in the night-time, while I sit in my chamber alone; they haunt me everywhere, charging me with hideous crimes, and – great God! – threatening me with coming vengeance and eternal misery. (62)

It is the 'charging' and the 'threatening' that are surely significant here. These arguably motivate not merely Barton's physical and mental deterioration but also his passivity at the approach of death. Like Harbottle, who hangs himself (117), Barton – who succumbs to a fatal seizure – is rendered passive in the face of both the perceived persecutor (an individual who has died because of the actions of the spectre-smitten) *and* the certainty that death will come as predicted by that retributive presence. The spectre does not prompt the death: rather, it energises the reflections and remembrances which cause death to be enacted or contemplated by the sufferer.

Death is thus the outcome of no sudden decision for Barton or Harbottle. Throughout the duration of their persecution, both are made to continuously recall the past, with its sexual as well as sadistic components, and that process of internalisation is fatal to mental well-being: 'my life has become all but intolerable', Barton confides, 'I have grown to hate existence' (62). If he does not actually do fatal violence unto himself, the captain succumbs to a desire to end his mortal tenure. Harbottle, it might be noted, is observed to be progressively 'sinking into the state of nervous dejection in which men lose their faith in orthodox advice, and in despair consult quacks, astrologers and nursery storytellers' (111–12) – Harbottle, indeed, might well have consulted a homeopath for his gout, though no doubt such a figure would have been incongruous in Le Fanu's vision of fashionable eighteenth-century London. Notably, the collapse of the viable mental self for both men does not prompt a discharge of guilt or stress in privy or public confession. They take the *exact* details of their sordid secrets, the men they killed, the women they seduced, the principles of high office they violated, to the grave. To extinguish the consciousness is apparently to numb the power of perception, to strive towards a state of being when such burdensome memories may be known no more. It is an act of desperation, however, that might as easily be specious, given that both have contemplated the everlasting tortures of hell (60) and the indignation of an angry and retributive Deity (60).

Harbottle is a sexual predator who possesses himself of another man's wife and then judicially hangs the wronged husband to consolidate his position (95–6). Barton is a seducer who has, through misuse of naval discipline, fatally tortured the father of the girl he has disgraced (81–2). These things, 'grievous' and 'discreditable' (81) as they are described in 'The Watcher', provide both 'origin and motives' (82) for the externalised persecution that visits both men, and an ongoing prompt for their own contemplation of past misdeeds and coming retribution. Their respective watchers – the men they have killed – provide a reminder of tangible and terrible deeds, force the remembrance of things suppressed, prompt if not confessions then at least acknowledgement of occluded crimes which the subject might well have hoped would have remained buried up to and after their own sepulture.

If Harbottle and Barton unequivocally deserve moral condemnation on account of their fatal abuses of power, Jennings represents a more problematic reflex of the motif of spectral persecution as it is presented in the first three stories of *In a Glass Darkly*. The shy clergyman is neither a seducer nor a bully, and his actions appear never to have impacted on any living being other than himself. Yet it is Jennings who commits the most spectacular and despairing act of self-annihilation, incising his own throat with 'a frightful gash', and being found dead in an 'immense pool of blood' (35). If Jennings has committed some unatoned-for crime, it is one which seemingly only he perceives in its purported immensity, and one which he assumes is the subject of divine condemnation (15). This awful and unspeakable transgression is, however, a matter of knowing rather than of actually doing. Jennings has studied unorthodox theologies, giving credence to the elaborate demonology of Swedenborgian thought (14–15) and undertaking a prolonged study of paganism – a subject which, on reflection, he admits is 'a degrading fascination' (21) for a man of the cloth. If Jennings is strikingly reluctant to comment further on the pagan thought which, he confesses, has 'thoroughly infected me', he is more forthcoming when rationalising Swedenborg's magisterial prose. Works such as the *Arcana Caelestia* 'are rather likely to make a solitary man nervous' (16), Jennings confesses to Hesselius. Indeed, Jennings *is* a solitary man, for he eschews company throughout the sad narrative of his demise and faces his attendant demon alone in an omnibus (23), his carriage (29), his chambers (26) or his pulpit (29). Unlike the human spectres which pursue Barton (51) and Harbottle (113–14), the malignant monkey is not visible to any other mortal. In common, though, with those spectres, Jennings's insubstantial monkey is a watcher as well as a dogged companion. This aspect of Jennings's persecution is stressed consistently, from the first moment he observes its red eyes englobe him in a London omnibus (23), to its watching him from a wall near his home (24), until its entry to his house (26). It is fascinating to Jennings – 'An irrepressible uneasiness as to its movements kept my eyes always upon it' (26) – but the cleric is equally an object of compulsion for the monkey's scrutiny. As Jennings recalls, 'Its eyes were half closed, but I could see them glow. It was looking steadily at me. In all situations, at all hours, it is awake and looking at me. That never changes' (26). Again, 'Its eyes were never off me. I have never lost sight of it, except in my sleep, light or dark, day or night, since it came here, excepting when it withdraws for some weeks at a time, unaccountably' (27, cf. 28). Jennings's coda here is significant. It is the monkey that retains the power to withdraw its gaze, not the clergyman. Jennings is passive, gazed on, tacitly assuming that which gazes on him is engaged in solemn and portentous judgement.

Not surprisingly, as is the case with Barton and Harbottle, both of whom are subjected to a considerably shorter regime of scrutiny, Jennings begins to suffer a debilitating mental decline. Jennings admits of the monkey, 'it is prevailing, little by little, and drawing me more interiorly into hell' (28). This hell might well be that conventionally reserved for transgressors and sinners after death, though it may just as likely refer to the living state of torture suffered by all three men in Le Fanu's successive narratives of supernatural persecution. As with Barton, who plateaus to a state of resignation towards the end of his life, Jennings succumbs to a feeling of powerlessness suggestive of a despair numbed and accepted rather than one that pointedly pains the self. Hesselius notes towards the end of the consultation that Jennings

> was beginning to speak with a great deal more effort and reluctance, and sighed often, and seemed at times nearly overcome. But at this time his manner was not agitated. It was more like that of a sinking patient, who has given himself up. (29)

Indeed, that is what he has done. Though Hesselius ostensibly brings hope, the physician's removal of his own comforting and controlling gaze from the patient coincides with the return of the spectral monkey and its powerful, hostile vision. The last letter written by Jennings before he is prompted to suicide reveals just how searching that hostile gaze is. To Hesselius he writes, 'It is here. You had not been an hour gone when it returned. It is speaking. It knows all that has happened. It knows everything' (34). This sense of revelation, of evacuated privacy, of total powerlessness in the presence of a knowing and implacable counterpart, whatever its nature, is surely the central premise on which Le Fanu's vision of suicide operates throughout *In a Glass Darkly*.

In a Glass Darkly thus presents a vision of self-annihilation that is intimately linked not merely to supposed hallucination but also to a destructive and intense train of thought generated in association with the uncanny vision. The concrete existence of what the sufferer *sees* matters little in context: it is what the sufferer perceives he has *done*, embodied symbolically in the spectre, which forces him towards his untimely end. Dietary regimes and correctives may be prescribed, but these can have no effect on a troubled conscience. There is no medicine, no therapy, no skill that can thwart the interiority that preoccupies an obsessed and reflective selfhood. Such figures live public lives, but die alone – for the detested company of their personal nemesis, be it man or monkey, is but a conceit for the self-loathing that prompts their final and untimely end.

The patient, in Hesselius's diagnosis – whether the physician is present or absent – always seems to be somehow complicit in his or her decline. The attendant medical practitioner is, however, as intimate to the mortality of the sufferer as the patient himself. Acknowledging the medical events which brought Le Fanu's marriage to an untimely end, it is possible to project into these three fictions – and, to a certain extent, into the later *Carmilla* – a signal lack of trust in the judgement customarily exercised by the medical profession, and a suggestion that medical practitioners at all levels of clinical experience rely more on conventional text-book nosologies than they do on the evidence advanced by the sufferer him- or herself. Le Fanu's doctors, and those non-clinical individuals who likewise vouchsafe conventional lay diagnoses, fail for the most part to recognise, let alone cure, morbid mental illness. The diagnoses that are advanced by these medical and para-medical attendants – diagnoses which simply associate disturbing visions with the patient's 'habits, dietary' (34) or susceptibility to 'vapours' (111) – implicitly refer each unique case to a predetermined and rigid nosology that fails to comprehend the patient as a living individual rather than a projected casebook model. Likewise, the remedies, be these the clinical medicines of Hesselius (34) or the homeopathic herbalism of Barton's Clontarf hostess, 'a great pretender to medical science' (72), lack sufficient specificity as antidotes to individual varieties of depression.

The fatal balance in these three fictions is predicated between patients who are overwhelmed and attendant doctors who are purblind and unimaginative. One might recall here Le Fanu's 'faithless thought' regarding the 'misapprehensions of the patient' – his wife – in respect of her treatment at the close of her final illness.[20] In the first three narratives of *In a Glass Darkly*, the patient temporarily places his trust in a programme of medical supervision which demonstrably fails to contain, let alone cure, a progressive mental and physical decline. As the failure of the curative regime becomes evident, the patient becomes passive – Barton does not resist death, and the spectre-haunted Jennings, like the gout-ridden Harbottle, embraces its oblivion almost as a relief through the definitive act of self-murder.

Susanna Le Fanu, of course, did not take her own life. The entry in her husband's diary, which resists the notion that her death was 'hastened' by ineffective homeopathy, though, might appear somewhat ambivalent when taken in the context of the decline and death of Jennings, Barton and Harbottle. It is possible that the author was, in his diary, lamenting not the ministrations of the homeopathic physician, nor indeed his wife's initial enthusiasm for a medical regime in which he himself placed little trust. Rather, his woeful intimation may well have been directed at the patient herself, and the final collapse of *her* faith in the ability of her doctors and their nostrums to restore her to lasting health. Susanna Le Fanu, like Barton, may have simply sunk into a hopeless despair, and allowed the seemingly inevitable to finally and fatally overwhelm her. All this makes Hesselius' closing remarks on the mortality of Jennings – 'If the patient do not array himself on the side of the disease, his cure is certain' (40) – all the more pointed. Jennings – like Le Fanu himself – would seem to lack faith in the curative ability of a mental and physical science that fails to see what the patient sees, which mistakes a symptomatic vision for a hallucination, and which implicitly despises the opinions and observations of those it deems unqualified. The explicit invoking of the Deity – by Le Fanu in his diary, and indeed by Hesselius in his coda to Jennings' case, 'A Word for Those Who Suffer' (38) – as the final arbiter of mortality may be, quite simply, a convenient and conventional fiction.[21] The final resignation, arguably, is not to the will of God but rather to the inevitability of, and the peaceful oblivion to be found in, the state of lifeless non-being.

Notes

1. J. S. Le Fanu, 'The Familiar', in Robert Tracy (ed.), *In a Glass Darkly* (Oxford: Oxford University Press, 1993), pp. 41–82, at p. 65. All subsequent references are taken from this edition. Page numbers will appear in parentheses on the body of the text.
2. W. J. McCormack, *Sheridan Le Fanu*, Third Edition (Stroud: Sutton Publishing, 1997), p. 122.
3. Based on access to Bennett and Le Fanu family papers, McCormack notes several periods in which Susanna's health and associated irascibility gave cause for concern within the family. See *Sheridan Le Fanu*, pp. 126, 128.
4. *Ibid.*, p. 122.
5. *Ibid.*, p. 125.
6. *Ibid.*, p. 128.
7. *Ibid.*, pp. viii, 129–30.
8. *Ibid.*, pp. 129–32.
9. *Ibid.*, pp. 129–30.
10. *Ibid.*, p. 130, cf. pp. 132, 133.
11. The allusion is to 1 Cor. 13:12.
12. Le Fanu, *In a Glass Darkly*, pp. 42, 83, 119. 'Green Tea' is published with reference to a further work, *The Cardinal Functions of the Brain* (p. 38), which is, likewise, never presented to the reader.
13. The penultimate story 'The Room in the Dragon Volant', a tale of treachery and drug misuse in immediately post-Napoleonic France, is the exception. This latter narrative, though, is a metafictional romance replete with Gothic signifiers of mystery, sublimity and high adventure.
14. J. S. Le Fanu, 'Mr Justice Harbottle', in Tracy (ed.), *In a Glass Darkly*, pp. 83–118, at p. 88. All subsequent references are taken from this edition. Page numbers will appear in parentheses in the body of the text.
15. J. S. Le Fanu, 'Green Tea', in Tracy (ed.), *In a Glass Darkly*, pp. 5–40, at p. 7. All subsequent references are taken from this edition. Page numbers will appear in parentheses in the body of the text.
16. Charles Dickens, 'A Christmas Carol', in *The Christmas Books* (London: Cassell, 1910), pp. 11–86, at p. 23.
17. A 'hypochondriac', according to one widely available 1879 dictionary, is 'One who is morbidly disordered or melancholy in imagination': see P. Austin Nuttall (ed.), *Routledge's Pronouncing Dictionary of the English Language* (London: George Routledge and Sons, 1879), p. 320.

18 To suffer from 'vapours', according to *Routledge's Pronouncing Dictionary of the English Language*, is be subject to 'Nervous debility; hypochondria; melancholy; spleen' (717). The same work indicates that to be 'maggoty' is to be 'capricious; whimsical' (390). A somewhat later lexicon defines 'vapours' as 'an old name for a nervous hypochondriacal or hysterical affection; the blues': see Charles Annandale (ed.), *The Student's English Dictionary* (London: Blackie and Son, 1895), p. 777.

19 Though he apparently rejects the authority of Church and Bible, Barton is almost certainly not an atheist: his membership of a Masonic lodge specifically militates against such a philosophical positioning: see J. S. Le Fanu, 'The Watcher', in Tracy (ed.), *In a Glass Darkly*, p. 55.

20 McCormack, *Sheridan Le Fanu*, pp. 129–30.

21 *Ibid.*, p. 130.

4

Andrew Smith

'The body of a self-destroyer': suicide and the self in the fin-de-siècle Gothic

Utterson's comment, on discovering the twitching, dying body of Edward Hyde, that he 'knew that he was looking at the body of a self-destroyer', is both a tragic moment of discovery and a pun.[1] Jekyll may have committed suicide, but Hyde is a destroyer of selves, including that of Jekyll. This chapter begins by exploring how accounts of civilisation, constructed in theories of degeneration, articulated anxieties that civilisation could not be trusted because it incorporated within it the very forces which would overthrow it. Civilisation is, in other words, a destroyer of selves, and this self-destructive impulse would seem to explain why so many fin-de-siècle Gothic texts, including Stevenson's *Strange Case of Dr Jekyll and Mr Hyde* (1886), Machen's *The Great God Pan* (1894) and Wilde's *The Picture of Dorian Gray* (1891), culminate in suicide. However, these points of contact to theories of degeneration are largely superficial because, as we shall see, the fin-de-siècle Gothic repeatedly employs suicide as a trope through which to examine a new model of the teleological subject which was becoming formulated within the scientific (Darwinian) and philosophical (Nietzschean) contexts of the time. The fin-de-siècle Gothic inhabits a discourse of degeneration to redirect it for radical ends by championing a cultural impulse for self-destruction which permits this new model of the subject to be born. This chapter thus argues for a new way of thinking about the fin-de-siècle Gothic's relationship to theories of degeneration.

First, it is important to outline the type of oblique cultural work undertaken in theories of degeneration, as this indicates what is challenged by these Gothic texts. Edwin Ray Lankester, in *Degeneration: A Chapter in Darwinism* (1880), identifies the precise conditions under which degeneration appears:

> Any new set of conditions occurring to an animal which render its food and safety very easily attained, seem to lead as a rule to Degeneration: just as an active healthy man sometimes degenerates when he becomes suddenly possessed of a fortune; or as Rome degenerated when possessed of the riches of the ancient world.[2]

Although Lankester's position would be lampooned by H. G. Wells for its poor grasp of Darwin (whose theory of adaptation precludes the type of atavism that Lankester advances), it established an image of a supposedly problematic over-refinement that would be developed by Nordau in *Degeneration* (1892).[3] Nordau would condemn what he saw as an effeminate 'emotionalism' that characterised the 'mental stigma' of the degenerate for whom 'a commonplace line of poetry or prose sends a shudder down his back' and who 'falls into raptures before indifferent pictures and statues' and 'is quite proud of being so vibrant a musical instrument'.[4] Nordau gains some reassurance that the philistine middle classes would be immune to the art that inspires this devotion, but, overall, *Degeneration* represents a fragile attempt at cultural quarantine which cannot quite see off these troubling new emotional engagements. The effeminate man is the villain in Nordau (and implicitly in Lankester), because he is regarded as symptomatic of newly diseased cultural forms. At the fin de siècle, this cultural death gains a visibility that can also be found in accounts of suicide and in emerging models of epistemology which suggested that the world may have its own, scientifically reasoned, sense of an ending.

Frederick Marshall, in 'Suicide', published in *Blackwood's Edinburgh Magazine* in June 1880, claims that suicide 'is, in civilised countries, an inevitable malady'.[5] Indeed, he goes so far as to claim that a contemporary 'fever of self-murder' can in part be attributed to the growth of a better-educated population which has become dissatisfied with the modern world.[6] S. A. K. Strahan, in *Suicide and Insanity: A Physiological and Sociological Study* (1893), also argued that the numeric rise in suicides was paralleled by the spread of civilisation. He states that

> None of the earlier peoples ever experienced the feverish haste, the terrible wear and tear, and the prolonged mental strain suffered by most of the civilised peoples of this latter quarter of the nineteenth century. Tranquillity and repose have become almost unknown.[7]

The key problem for Strahan is the pace of knowledge in which 'The news of yesterday from the whole known world is presented to us each morning with our coffee', so that 'It is the pace that kills, and the pace is the same in all classes from the highest to the lowest.'[8] Strahan distinguished between 'false' suicides (provoked by an overreaction to circumstance) and 'true' suicides. The figure of the 'true' suicide possesses a latent biological tendency for self-destruction which Strahan likened to (and to some degree linked with) patterns of inherited epilepsy. Such attributes are brought out under these new social circumstances, in which too much knowledge, consumed too quickly, creates a mental derangement which stimulates these self-destructive degenerate tendencies.

Strahan may claim that 'earlier peoples' did not suffer these burdens, but he evokes Lankester's view of Roman decline when he argues that 'the Romans during the latter part of the Empire' practiced 'vicious indulgences of every kind', so that

> It was during this period that suicide was so rife among the Romans, and there cannot be a doubt that much of the self-destruction indulged in must have been true suicide, the direct outcome of degeneration induced by vicious excess.[9]

For Strahan, 'Where civilisation is highest there life is most artificial, and there we meet with the most rapid degeneration of the stock.'[10] The problem is not just the pace of life and the capacity to develop unwholesome indulgences that too much money can buy; it is also education, which Marshall too had identified as a key agent in suicide. Strahan claims that 'suicide increases everywhere with civilisation, for the main element in civilisation is the cultivation of the intellect, and that is done by education'.[11] For Strahan, this is not formal education *per se*, but rather modes of cultural understanding articulated within 'the acquisition of all knowledge which goes to make up the culture of a people'.[12] During the period, a certain type of science helps to form this model of cultural suicide.

Linda Ray Pratt, in a discussion of the representation of suicide in Matthew Arnold's *Empedocles* (1853), situates Arnold's poem within the type of epistemic shifts that Foucault in *The Order of Things* (1966) identified as being of paradigmatic importance to the nineteenth century.[13] Pratt notes that according to this genealogy,

> The deepest fear behind the new sciences of geology and evolution was not the question of our ancestry but of our end, the realization that humanity was only one of many species sharing the earth for a span of time, and that like other species, the human animal had its origins in evolutionary time and could reach its conclusion by the same process.[14]

This position constitutes a major theme in fin-de-siècle Gothic fiction which centred on suicide and forms of social self-destruction – especially in relation to the figure of the scientist. The fin-de-siècle Gothic also links these scientific deliberations to the cultural factors which give rise to them. Stevenson's *Jekyll and Hyde* illustrates how models of personal dissipation are implicated within wider socio-political dramas which suggest that self-destruction is rooted within class-bound cultural forms (and not just enabled by the science of chemistry).

Jekyll's account of why he sought for a chemical liberation of an inner self is situated within the context of his past. He acknowledges the presence of 'a certain gaiety of disposition, such as has made the happiness of many, but such as I found it hard to reconcile with my imperious desire to carry my head high' (81), in the pursuit of social advancement. Jekyll's commitment 'to a profound duplicity of life' (81) indicates that the condition of entry into the respectable middle classes depends on the renunciation of pleasure. Jekyll destroys a private self to manufacture a public one. This renunciation is not unique to Jekyll, as it is also reflected in the empty lives of the other representatives of the middle-class professions (namely, medicine and law) who populate the novella. The opening scenes of *Jekyll and Hyde*, for example, focus on Utterson and Enfield, who are indulging in their ritual Sunday afternoon walk despite the obvious boredom that it induces:

> It was reported by those who encountered them in their Sunday walks, that they said nothing, looked singularly dull, and would hail with obvious relief the appearance of a friend. For all that, the two men put the greatest store by these excursions, counted them the chief jewel of each week, and not only set aside occasions of pleasure, but even resisted the calls of business, that they might enjoy them uninterrupted. (30)

This grim, mindless adherence to ritual is what Stevenson critiques. Such figures have destroyed themselves and harbour within them the remnants of their earlier, lost, selves. At one level this implicates middle-class civilisation in the generation of degeneration, and what is truly horrifying in Enfield's description of his encounter with Hyde, who has crushed a child, is that Hyde asks the angry family to name their price because '"No gentleman but wishes to avoid a scene"' (32). Hyde, with his – or rather Jekyll's – Coutts chequebook, troublingly, for Enfield, claims both membership of the middle class and the status of a gentleman.

Hyde's concealment in Jekyll is referred to as a 'temporary suicide' (96), leading to a resentment which gained outlet through the 'apelike tricks' (96) that Hyde would play on Jekyll, such as 'scrawling in my own hand blasphemies on the pages of my books, burning the letters and destroying the portrait of my father' (96). Strahan argued that 'true' suicide was to be found within latent degenerative tendencies, and *Jekyll and Hyde* superficially appears to illustrate this in Hyde's apparent Darwinian associations. Strahan would even go so far as to assert that an evolutionary principle lay behind acts of suicide, so that

> the true suicide becomes an unnatural natural production, like the blind, the deaf, or the idiotic. He is rarely or never the product of a single generation, that is, he generally inherits a more or less degenerate constitution from his parents.[15]

In such instances, suicide is in accord with the principles of 'natural selection', meaning that 'In some cases [the] suicide does society little, if any, injury, and in others he actually confers a favour upon it by quitting it.'[16] However, *Jekyll and Hyde* moves beyond this context by emphasising the social – specifically middle-class – causes of suicide. In this argument, Hyde is conjured from *within* a cultural absence which is emphasised from the start and which pre-emptively challenges Nordau's assertion that the middle classes were immune to degeneration. A middle-class model of civilisation is thus represented as self-destructive by Stevenson as it becomes transformed into a model of alienation in which characters are unable to connect, or to establish, meaningful points of social contact beyond a superficial adherence to bourgeois ritual.

In one of the very few critical accounts on suicide in *Jekyll and Hyde*, Barbara T. Gates argued that at the end Jekyll kills Hyde because Jekyll 'must ultimately be his own murderer to avoid full disclosure of (his) duality' – a point somewhat belied by the presence of Jekyll's confessional narrative which explains the reasons for this duality.[17]

Also, the slippery pronouns in Jekyll's confession – which move from 'I' to 'he' and back again to 'I' – make it unclear whether, at the end, Jekyll or Hyde is narrating. Stevenson leaves the ending radically open, as we cannot be sure if Jekyll kills Hyde (in which scenario suicide becomes honourable self-sacrifice) or if Hyde kills Jekyll (which suggests that Hyde is, paradoxically, a murderer). The suggestion that Hyde is a killer, generated out of bourgeois respectability and created to undermine it, redirects ideas of degenerative self-destruction for radical ends by suggesting that civilisation is indeed responsible for its own surpassing, but in terms which challenge the reactionary notion that the ostensible 'degenerate' is a negatively destructive figure.

Jekyll and Hyde thus represents a fragile world of middle-class respectability. Suicide is associated with the self that is destroyed as a cultural requirement for entry into the middle class. This idea of social clubability and suicide was discussed by Strahan who, in a discussion of copycat suicides, argued that

> Closely related to suicide from imitation is the course followed by those abnormal specimens of humanity who establish what are called 'suicide clubs'. These persons agree to kill themselves upon certain fixed days, or when their names may be drawn by lot. This course is entered upon voluntarily, and for no conceivable reason.[18]

Stevenson considered this trend in his *The Suicide Club* (1878), the whimsical tone of which is at odds with the morally minded pursuit of those who run such a club. Membership requires that, after pulling cards, the participant with the Ace of Spades will be killed by whoever receives the Ace of Clubs, so that suicide becomes transformed into a willingness to be murdered and makes murderers of those who wish to die. Set in a socially elite world, it appears to gloss ideas about a degenerative over-refinement, but in actuality it is about holding those to account for their soul-destroying actions and so enforces a type of redemption. Self- and socially destructive urges are replaced by a cause which reawakens ideas of decency and chivalry within the seemingly dissipated world of Prince Florizel of Bohemia, who leads the pursuit of those who organise the club.[19]

For Strahan, such acts of socially managed suicide are atypical and difficult to ascribe to 'true' suicide as he conceives it, as they appear to be the result of whim rather than hereditary tendency. As he notes, 'Persons capable of such an idiotic performance as this cannot be taken as normal beings, nevertheless, without further evidence of intellectual disorder, they cannot be pronounced insane.'[20] *Jekyll and Hyde* lacks the redemption found in closing the Suicide Club because the emphasis is on the inescapability of what is found within the body, in a novella which indicates that corruption is found, likewise, within the cultural body of the body politic. The body politic can be cleansed in *The Suicide Club*, a work which is difficult to read as a Gothic text as its tone is closer to the comic, and which also has much in common with the form of the detective story. However, ideas of physical and social corruption reappear in Machen's *The Great God Pan* (1894).

There is a moment in *The Great God Pan* when Villiers, a high-society figure, ponders that '"London has been called the city of encounters; it is more than that, it is the city of Resurrections."'[21] This thought immediately prefaces his discovery of an old college friend, Charles Herbert, who has fallen on hard times and whose tale of decline focuses attention on Machen's femme fatale, Helen Vaughan, who is responsible for Herbert's desperate circumstances. After their marriage, she introduces him to certain undisclosed metaphysical truths, which means that within a year '"I was a ruined man, in body and soul"' (26). Helen has been created out of a scientific experiment conducted by Dr Raymond, who practices 'transcendental medicine' (4) – a phrase taken from *Jekyll and Hyde*. Helen is the hybrid offspring of the seventeen-year-old Mary, whom Raymond rescued as a child from the slums, and the deity, Pan. Helen works her way up through the elite social world of London, prompting those who encounter her to commit suicide. Her presence evokes the duality found in *Jekyll and Hyde*. An unnamed doctor states of her appearance, when attending a police court convened to ascertain the cause of death of an earlier victim, that

> Everyone who saw her at the police court said she was at once the most beautiful woman and the most repulsive they had ever set eyes on. I have spoken to a man who saw her, and I assure you he positively shuddered as he tried to describe the woman, but he couldn't tell why. She seems to have been a sort of enigma. (32)

The echoes with Enfield's inability to describe Hyde to Utterson are clear: '"I can't describe him. And it's not want of memory; for I declare I can see him this moment"' (34). The revelation of what Helen is comes at the end of Machen's narrative; but before that, in a chapter titled 'The Suicides', the police's bafflement at the causes for these high-society suicides is contrasted with the investigation into the killings of Jack the Ripper. It is noted that 'not even the mere ferocity which did duty as an explanation of the crimes of the East End, could be of service in the West', because 'Each of these men who had resolved to die a tortured shameful death was rich, prosperous, and to all appearance in love with the world' (51). This effectively turns Helen into a serial killer.

Helen is an outsider to the high-society world of London that she infiltrates and attacks. She is ontologically different, but also different in class and national terms, as we see her progress from rural Wales to an upper-class cosmopolitan London.[22] Hers is a demonic narrative of social progression that exposes what lies beneath civilisation, in an implicit echo of Strahan's view that 'true' suicide is distributed across classes, although requiring an agent to activate (or to resurrect, in Villiers' terms) such inherent proclivities. The civilised body is where, for Machen, we find the presence of corruption. Herbert informs Villiers that she had '"corrupted my soul"' because he had '"seen the incredible, such horrors that even I myself sometimes stop in the middle of the street, and ask whether it is possible for a man to behold such things and live"' (26). The question is, *what* is it that Herbert, and indeed the other men, have seen? The answer appears at the end, in Dr Matheson's account of Helen's death, when she is confronted by her crimes and forced to commit suicide. Her death struggles provide an evolutionary recapitulation of life. Matheson, who dies of an 'apoplectic seizure' (68) shortly after recording this event, notes,

> Here ... was all the work by which man has been made repeated before my eyes. I saw the form waver from sex to sex, dividing itself from itself, and then again reunited. Then I saw the body descend to the beasts whence it ascended, and that which was on the heights go down to the depths, even to the abyss of all being. The principle of life, which makes organism, always remained, while the outward form changed. (70)

Helen's death points towards life, but it is a version of life which includes within it the sense of an ending that Foucault, in *The Order of Things*, had regarded as troubling for the nineteenth century. Foucault provides a context for this sense of an ending, which he saw as articulated within an emerging nihilism. He argues that 'Rather than the death of God – or, rather in the wake of that death and in a profound correlation with it – ... Nietzsche's thought heralds ... the end of the murderer.'[23] The age is anti-idealistic, and this is reflected in Machen's focus on Villiers' claim that he has lost his 'body' and 'soul' because both have become corrupted. Indeed, it is a form of corruption that seems to overcome duality as it suggests that the evolutionary narrative shown to Matheson has no room for souls. The significance of Helen's dissolution had been suggested in an early scene in the novella when Clarke, a main focaliser of the narrative, has a dream just before the experiment on Mary which leads to her impregnation. Clarke recalls that in the dream he remembers a woodland walk from fifteen years previously, in which

> an infinite silence seemed to fall on all things, and the wood was hushed, and for a moment of time he stood face to face there with a presence, that was neither man nor beast, neither living nor dead, but all things mingled, the form of all things but devoid of all form. And in that moment, the sacrament of body and soul was dissolved, and a voice seemed to cry 'Let us go hence', and then the darkness beyond the stars, the darkness of everlasting. (11)

The description evokes Genesis, and the impregnation of Mary by a 'great god' functions as a blasphemous reworking of the creation of the universe and the birth of Christ. The relationship between body and soul is 'dissolved' because the differences which distinguish them become erased in 'all things mingled'. The dream prefaces Helen's conception, and it reappears at her moment of death in Matheson's quasi-scientific account of her suicide. Her death thus incorporates the sense of an ending that seemed to be epistemologically confirmed through scientific studies in biology.

Self-destruction in the period is not just a matter of disposition; it is also a matter of knowledge. The principle of life shaped through Machen's Nietzschean 'darkness of everlasting' implicates the void that also appears in *Jekyll and Hyde* as a self-generated boredom that produces a Hyde who alleviates both ennui and the circumstances which generated it. For Machen, there is 'the form of all things but devoid of form', and in *Jekyll and Hyde*, Jekyll recalls 'the shocking thing [was] that what was dead and had no shape, should usurp the offices of life' (95). Both Hyde and Helen are troubling shape-shifters who are seemingly blasphemous but who in reality possess a capacity to physically transform, which suggests that their vitality destroys older, more stable, conceptualisations of the self. The debate about the relationship between body and soul provides a key marker of these changes. Religious discourse is not so much challenged in these Gothic texts as reworked and redirected for secular considerations of an epistemology of life and death. Wilde's *The Picture of Dorian Gray* addresses these issues of body and soul via a metaphysical approach which is couched within a quasi-scientific framework.

Lord Henry Wotton, contemplating his influence over Dorian Gray, reflects on the relationship between the body and the soul:

> Soul and body, body and soul – how mysterious they were! There was animalism in the soul, and the body had its moments of spirituality. The senses could refine, and the intellect could degrade. Who could say where the fleshy impulse ceased, or the physical impulse began?[24]

As they would be in Machen, opposites become conflated and a new version of the self is developed within this erosion of binary terms. Wotton's train of thought at this point is focused on Dorian, but what he does not know, and indeed cannot know at this stage, is that Dorian has no soul and so the terms of his deliberation are technically redundant, even whilst they theoretically model a version of the self which is similar to that proposed by Stevenson and Machen. This points towards a tension in the novel between science and art that appears to constitute an unresolvable dialectic. Wotton uses an art-for-art's-sake rhetoric that moulds Dorian as Wotton channels the gnomic decadent manifesto of the Preface into the novel itself. However, although Wotton may speak a language of aesthetics, he thinks scientifically; and to that end he implicitly regards Dorian as the product of a Frankenstein-like experiment in which 'To a large extent the lad was his own creation' (65), leading him to conclude:

> It was clear to him that the experimental method was the only method by which one could arrive at any scientific analysis of the passions; and certainly Dorian Gray was a subject made to his hand, and seemed to promise rich and fruitful results. (66)

The experiment is a quite specific one focused on the psychology of love, in which Dorian's 'sudden mad love for Sibyl Vane was a psychological phenomenon of no small interest' (66). The experiment, of course, goes wrong, as Sibyl becomes bad art when she is unable to *act* being in love whilst she *is* in love. The passions, as Wotton would have it, are therefore of a different order, or intensity, than art, so that the subject, psychologically understood, needs to be looked for elsewhere. Dorian provides a connection to a potentially different model of the subject which is closer to Darwin than to models of psychology. Dorian, as part of his 'intellectual development', for a season ... inclined to the materialistic doctrine of the *Darwinismus* movement in Germany, and found a curious pleasure in tracing thoughts and passions of men to some pearly cell in the brain, or some white nerve in the body, delighting in the conception of the absolute dependence of the spirit on certain physical conditions, morbid or healthy, normal or diseased. (147, italics in original)

Agency thus becomes transformed into the type of hereditary tendency that was reworked in theories of degeneration.

The Picture of Dorian Gray appears to balance three types of theory, centring on art, psychology and physiology, against each other. These are kept in tension because Wotton distinguishes between art and psychology by assigning art a privileged place which is beyond human experience (as witnessed in his account of Sybil's suicide which focuses on her as lost art). Physiology is of a different order of knowledge than psychology or that provided by seeing the world (and your place in it) through aesthetics. Dorian's brief fascination with Darwin implies an engagement with teleology that was apparent in both Stevenson and Machen. The soulless body is, at one level, made so because the inner life of the spirit is replaced by an inherent tendency that in turn shapes 'the spirit', or the idea of selfhood. This biological inheritance cannot be subtracted from the subject, whereas the soul, through renunciation, can – so that the past inevitably shapes the present:

[Dorian] used to wonder at the shallow psychology of those who conceive the Ego in man as a thing simple, permanent, reliable, and of one essence. To him, man was a being with myriad lives and myriad sensations, a complex multiform creature that bore within itself legacies of thought and passion, and whose very flesh was tainted by the monstrous maladies of the dead. (157)

The echoes of *Jekyll and Hyde* are clear, and the image of the 'complex multiform creature' anticipates Dr Matheson's view of Helen's dissolution in *The Great God Pan*. The suggestion that the 'very flesh' harbours within it a 'monstrous' inheritance is also developed in theories of degeneration and in Strahan's application of natural selection to 'true' suicide, although Wilde's novel ultimately, in keeping with the fin-de-siècle Gothic, challenges such theories even whilst it appears to give them credence.

As noted earlier, theories of art in *Dorian Gray* seem to be of a separate order to the claims of physiology and psychology, but there is an implication that Wotton's aesthetic theory imports an amorality that he has gleaned from science. Michael Davis has noted that

Wilde's commonplace book, which he kept whilst a student at Oxford, reveals Wilde's awareness of theories of the mind, developed by W. K. Clifford, James Sully and William James, which suggested a possible relationship between mind and matter; in the novel, this is developed through a theory of atoms that Dorian uses to account for why the portrait degrades: 'Was there some subtle affinity between the chemical atoms that shaped themselves into form and colour on the canvas, and the soul that was within him?' (106).[25] Later, this leads him to questioning whether 'If thought could exercise its influence upon a living organism, might not thought exercise an influence upon dead and inorganic things?' (118). A type of idealism might appear to be shaped here, but it is one which is defined by its relationship to the material world, implying a connection between the living and the dead.[26] This new subject requires that the older version of the self, which is ontologically coherent, self-present and fundamentally bourgeois rather than spiritual or physical, be cast off in an act which reclaims suicide as a positive trope for the necessity of a cultural self-murder that liberates this new subject.

It is noteworthy that *Jekyll and Hyde*, *The Great God Pan* and *The Picture of Dorian Gray* emphasise the importance of birth as a means of heralding the arrival of this new subject. Hyde is a being who grows throughout the novella: physically, he progressively fits Jekyll's clothes more comfortably than he did at the beginning, and towards the end it appears that it is his voice which takes over the text. At one level, it suggests that the apparent 'evil' that Hyde represents has gained ascendency, but at another (as we have seen in the ambivalent ending) it indicates that the forces of social and psychological repression have been broken through. Hyde might superficially appear as degenerate, but he is a figure whose radical vitality is created from within and who can only be released at the point of Jekyll's death. He is, like Helen Vaughan, impossible to describe, because he represents a model of subjectivity that does not exist other than as a trope for the teleological epistemological changes of the time which indicate the emergence of a new sense of an ending, and so a new way of thinking about the fin de siècle. Helen's dissolution also suggest these new developments, as her dying morphological changes recapitulate a model of evolution which also implies a model of the end, rooted within a Darwinian version of the subject – one which H. G. Wells would explore in *The Time Machine* (1895), where Wells' time traveller also witnesses the end of the evolutionary process.[27] That life implicates the presence of death, and death suggests a new type of life, is developed by Wilde as a tension, scientifically available at the time, between outer and inner worlds, between the material and the spiritual. Dorian is also a childlike figure, born 'premature', who decides to hide the degenerating painting in 'a play-room [used] when he was a child', a room built by his grandfather who 'had always hated' Dorian (135). For Dorian, 'it seemed horrible to him that it was here the fatal portrait was to be hidden away' (135). The links between an unhappy childhood and a self-destructive adult life are emphasised in the use of 'fatal'. As with Hyde and Helen Vaughan, he has been born for this end as a type of experiment, which for Wotton goes wrong. Ultimately, Dorian destroys himself when he stabs the portrait because 'It had been like conscience to him. Yes, it had been conscience. He would destroy it' (245). Thus, Dorian dies in body and soul in a moment which graphically echoes the merging of mind and matter that had scientifically framed Dorian's thinking about the subject, and so he overcomes 'the living death of his own soul' which the portrait represents.

The wider question raised by these texts concerns whether death should be considered tragic and if suicide represents a particularly transgressive death. The religious context would seem to provide a prohibition on self-murder. Marshall, however, stresses that there is no biblical sanction against suicide and that 'Nobody objected seriously to suicide in the old days', although the Church had subsequently 'filled up that chasm in the Bible' so that suicide acquired 'a mixed character of mutiny, stupidity, and horror'.[28] Strahan also notes this lack of biblical prohibition and additionally argues that 'suicide is sufficiently common among the clergy, and even among the dignitaries of the Church, to prove that religious sentiment is no protective against the suicidal impulse'.[29] The problem of defining the new self that the fin-de-siècle Gothic explores through the trope of suicide is related to visibility – to how the indescribability of Hyde, or the eeriness of Helen Vaughan, or even the portrait of Dorian suggest a problem with how to represent this new self, one which kills off the older, seemingly more civilised (ostensibly stable) bourgeois model of the subject. This problem of visibility is one that Marshall, interestingly, relates to the word 'suicide'. Whilst suicides can be found in all periods, the term itself was not coined until the eighteenth century. Marshall correctly attributes the term to the Abbé Desfontaines (1685–1745) and argues that its late coinage reflects an 'unconscious disavowal of it' and asserts that 'Silence is an argument' which has made suicide 'an outcast from speech'.[30] This outcast term is reflected in the Gothic outcasts of the fin de siècle which are used to explore new models of the self which have been fashioned in Darwinian and post-Darwinian models of evolution. In this process, these texts embrace the alterity of the Gothic villain to conduct an implicit form of intellectual interrogation of how this new subject can only be born by casting off the old.

Suicides in the fin-de-siècle Gothic texts discussed here do not represent the negative forms of cultural self-destruction that we witness in theories of degeneration. The Gothic radically reappropriates suicide as a space in which to investigate how the older order can be destroyed and so release the new vitalities suggested in this emerging model of the fin-de-siècle self.

Notes

1 R. L. Stevenson, *The Strange Case of Dr Jekyll and Mr Hyde*, in *Dr Jekyll and Mr Hyde and Other Stories*, ed. and Intro. Jenni Calder (Harmondsworth: Penguin, 1984), pp. 27–97, at p. 70. All subsequent references are to this edition and are given in parentheses.
2 Edwin Ray Lankester, *Degeneration: A Chapter in Darwinism* (London: Macmillan, 1880), p. 33.
3 See H. G. Wells's 'Zoological Retrogression', *Gentleman's Magazine*, 271 (1891), 246–53, where he satirically critiques Lankester's use of the Ascidian as an example of degenerative decline.
4 Max Nordau, *Degeneration* (Lincoln, NE and London: University of Nebraska Press, [1895] 1968), p. 19.
5 Frederick Marshall, 'Suicide', *Blackwood's Edinburgh Magazine*, 127 (June 1880), 719–34, at 719. All subsequent references are to this edition and are given in the text.
6 *Ibid.*, 732.
7 S. A. K. Strahan, *Suicide and Insanity: A Physiological and Sociological Study* (London: S. Sonnenschein, 1893), pp. 82–3. All subsequent references are to this edition and are given in parentheses.
8 *Ibid.*, p. 83.
9 *Ibid.*, p. 85.
10 *Ibid.*, p. 174.
11 *Ibid.*, p. 173.
12 *Ibid.*
13 See Michel Foucault, *The Order of Things* (New York: Pantheon Books, 1974), p. 385.
14 Linda Ray Pratt, 'Empedocles, Suicide, and the Order of Things', *Victorian Poetry*, 26:1/2 (1988), 75–90, at 85.
15 Strahan, *Suicide and Insanity*, p. 66.

16 *Ibid.*, pp. 68, 219.
17 Barbara T. Gates, *Victorian Suicide: Mad Crimes and Sad Histories* (Princeton, NJ: Princeton University Press, 1988), pp. 119–20.
18 Strahan, *Suicide and Insanity*, p. 145.
19 R. L. Stevenson, *The Suicide Club* (New York: C. Scribner's Sons, 1896).
20 Strahan, *Suicide and Insanity*, p. 145.
21 Arthur Machen, *The Great God Pan*, in *The Great God Pan, The Shining Pyramid, The White People* (Cardigan: Parthian, 2010), pp. 3–76, at p. 24. All subsequent references are to this edition and are given in parentheses.
22 This social and national travel echoes that of Machen, who moved to London after having been raised in Wales, in the former Roman fort town of Caerleon. The drama of that move is reflected in the disorientations of the would-be author, Lucian Taylor, in Machen's *The Hill of Dreams* (1907).
23 Foucault, *The Order of Things*, p. 398, See Pratt, 'Empedocles, Suicide, and the Order of Things', 85.
24 Oscar Wilde, *The Picture of Dorian Gary*, ed. Peter Ackroyd (Harmondsworth: Penguin, 1985), p. 65. All subsequent references are to this edition and are given in parentheses.
25 See Michael Davis, 'Mind and Matter in *The Picture of Dorian Gray*', *Victorian Literature and Culture*, 41 (2013), 547–60.
26 Spiritualism would be another place in which these ideas are addressed. F. W. H. Myers, *Human Personality and Its Survival of Bodily Death* (London: Longmans, 1903), discusses these matters within a quasi-scientific context which also emphasises the presence of a divinely ordained evolutionary model of the human spirit. Myers appears critical of suicide, but his appendices to the abbreviated 1907 Second Edition indicate that he had corresponded with R. L. Stevenson on the topic of duality. See F. W. H. Myers, *Human Personality and Its Survival of Bodily Death*, Second Edition (London: Longmans, 1907), pp. 356–9.
27 H. G. Wells, *The Time Machine* (London: Heinemann, 1895).
28 Marshall, 'Suicide', 720, 721.
29 Strahan, *Suicide and Insanity*, p. 162.
30 Marshall, 'Suicide', 735.

Graeme Pedlingham

'To be mistress of her own fate': suicide as control and contagion in the works of Richard Marsh

> The remarkable prevalence of suicide in England this summer brought the painful question of self-destruction prominently before the public.[1]

So wrote S. A. K. Strahan, a prominent member of the Medico-Psychological Association, in the Preface to his 1893 work *Suicide and Insanity*. This is a title that illustrates Strahan's accordance with the predominant medical view that the two do not necessarily coincide, this being what is often referred to as the 'standard' theory. Indeed, this 'painful question' was the source of much consternation and rumination towards the end of the Victorian period, amidst growing and oft-expressed anxieties that suicide was a burgeoning epidemic. We find this view expressed, for instance, by William Knighton's much republished 1881 article for the *Contemporary Review* entitled 'Suicidal Mania', in which the author claims, based on the statistical work of Bertillon and Morselli, that 'men everywhere are becoming more weary of the burden of life', and therefore that 'suicides are annually becoming more common, not in England only, but all over the civilized world'.[2] Such anxieties regarding an emerging threat to the sustainability of society are, famously, encapsulated in *Jude the Obscure* (1895) by the Doctor's apocalyptic suggestion that 'Father Time' represents 'the beginning of the coming universal wish not to live'.[3] Hardy is far from being alone in expressing such bleak philosophies or in evoking the apparent normalisation of suicide, which can be seen throughout European cultural productions in the latter half of the nineteenth century and into the twentieth. Indeed, James

Thomson's 1874 poem 'The City of Dreadful Night' reflects sombrely on life in London to the point of implying that death may be preferable to the death-like existence of so many of its inhabitants.[4] This disturbing idea of suicide as an ordinary, everyday, even expected occurrence is central to the shocking quality of Manet's *Le Suicidé* (c.1877–81), in its decontextualised and unnarrated realism. Similarly, we need only think of the nonchalant reaction to a presumed suicide represented in Vasily Perov's *Die Ertrunkene* ('Drowned') (1867) or George Grosz's *Selbstmörder* ('Suicide') (1916) – albeit responding to very different historical moments – to appreciate how the trope of prevalent suicide often became culturally equated with fears over a loss of meaning, a loss of humanity and a declining civilisation.[5] A perceived increase in rates of suicide may have seemed to be evidence for a society that had lost faith in itself.

It is this context, and this rich vein of anxiety, that Richard Marsh (1857–1915), as an author of popular fiction, clearly taps into. Representations of, or allusions to, suicide appear frequently throughout his *oeuvre*. Marsh was a prolific writer, publishing around eighty novels and short-story collections between 1881 and 1915, and, despite his relative obscurity today, contemporaries compared him favourably with Edgar Allan Poe, H. G. Wells, Bram Stoker and even Charles Dickens. Indeed, one of his publishers (Answers Library) felt able, in 1910, to claim for Marsh the title of 'most popular living author'.[6] Although he is certainly best known for his Gothic fiction, most notably his highly successful 1897 novel *The Beetle*, Marsh's work spans an impressively wide range of genres, including detective fiction, comedies, romances, war stories and boys' adventures. It has been suggested that this protean capacity was a consequence of Marsh's 'writing career [being] driven not only by his love of storytelling but also by financial and professional incentives'.[7] As Minna Vuohelainen argues, 'Marsh targeted a number of such communities [of taste] through genre fiction, never relying solely on the support of a solitary, potentially fickle, niche audience.'[8]

Marsh clearly adapted astutely to prevailing cultural trends and anxieties throughout his career, and so it could be suggested that he similarly uses suicide in his work to heighten its dramatic (and perhaps pecuniary) potential. However, suicide is a matter of more personal reflection for Marsh, and not so easily conceptualised as being merely instrumental. Indeed, given the low periods of his life, with his father's very public and scandalous bankruptcy as well as his own time in prison, suicidal thoughts or even expectations may well have been a feature of Marsh's family story. The extent of these reflections is evidenced by a manuscript in the Reading University Archives for an undated – and hitherto unpublished – essay, written by Marsh at some point between 1891 and 1910, and simply entitled 'Suicide'.

The essay strikes a tone, characteristic of Marsh, somewhere between the ludicrous and the tragic. But added to the remarkably black humour which we find here is a fierce social commentary that is quite out of keeping for the writer. We can read this tension in the typically provocative opening suggestion that 'there may be something to be said even in favour of suicide'.[9] This is a statement that Marsh will interpret in various ways throughout the essay, but in it we may hear the echo of David Hume's divisive argument from *On Suicide* (1755; published 1783) that 'no man ever threw away life while it was worth keeping'.[10] Marsh's essay seems to correspond with Hume's in some of its thinking, but also provides a kind of *ad absurdum* critique. Hume claims that 'both prudence and courage should engage us to rid ourselves at once of existence when it becomes a burden. It is the only way that we can then be useful to society' (10–11), whilst Marsh, I would suggest, implicitly interrogates this idea of 'usefulness' through questioning how and by whom it is defined. For much of the essay, Marsh answers this with a certain whimsical audacity, by taking the task upon himself and using this theme of suicide for the social good as a means of satirising some of his favourite targets.

So, after noting, and rather exaggerating, the custom of reciprocal honour-suicides in particular countries (France, Japan, China), Marsh goes on to suggest in 'Suicide' that it might be something of an improvement if journalists and critics were, on the self-slaughter of those that they critique, obliged to kill themselves in turn. Or, 'if the Liberal had to die every time that a Conservative took it into his head to slaughter himself on his front door step, what martyrs for their country would arise!' (1–2). In each of these cases, there is an emphasis on reciprocal suicide, on an obligation to kill oneself if another commits suicide in one's presence. Whilst Marsh's discussion of this is rather frivolous here, it is one for us to hold in mind for the time being: the implications of witnessing suicide will become an important idea to Marsh's treatment of it in his fiction.

From here, Marsh goes on to expand the remit of the socially 'burdensome' even further, including those whom one has a personal grievance with or distaste for: 'Every one of us must be acquainted with, at least, some persons who would perform a positive service, not only to ourselves, and to their friend, but to the world at large, by taking themselves out of it' (2–3). In 'Suicide', we find descriptions of Jones, of Brown ('objectionable'), of Smith ('ill-mannered') – all appellations that together serve as shorthand for 'everyman' – suggesting that anyone can be defined as a 'social burden', given the right criteria. Again, Marsh lampoons the line of thinking that Hume represents. For instance, Hume puts forward a marginal social benefit case: 'Suppose that my life hinders some person from being much more useful to the public: in such cases, my resignation of life must not only be innocent, but laudable' (9). But Marsh parodies this position in 'Suicide' through recourse to an, admittedly rather cynical, subjectivism: 'It is easy enough, when, as has been observed, you come to think of it, to see that there is something to be said in favour of suicide in the case of others' (3–4). If Marsh is sceptical about arguments advocating or encouraging suicide on the grounds of social utility – he is, after all, well attuned to the unreliability of a fickle 'public' – what of those who do end, or are prevented from ending, their lives? 'But', asks Marsh, 'how about ourselves?' (4).

In his unpublished essay's cataloguing of 'reasons why human beings have voluntarily deprived themselves of the mystery of mysteries, life' (4), Marsh proceeds through a series of supposed cases, framed as sardonic extremes. These are generally not, it must be said, some of Marsh's most progressive moments. Examples include 'the lady who "handed in her checks" because her lover sent her pink roses instead of red' (7) and the 'Women in England [who] have taken poison because somebody or other would not take them to a certain ball' (7), or the 'lady – a sane woman as women go! – [who] threatened to throw herself off the pier … by way of winding up a discussion which had commenced with the expression of her desire to become the possessor of a certain pair of shoes' (7).

However, these reductive and gendered examples are sandwiched, structurally, between more credible (although still gendered) causes of suicide. In 'Suicide', we find allusions to rape (through referencing Lucretia), destitution, starvation and fear of the loss of physical beauty. We find that 'women have destroyed themselves because they have had too many children, and women have destroyed themselves because they have had none' (7). All of these Marsh identifies as being actual causes of suicide, amongst women but also 'men, in emerging numbers', which he has knowledge of.

The causes of suicide that Marsh lists here, I would suggest, are strongly connected with questions of control. Specifically, there is a sense that the individual is impelled towards suicide by social and cultural forces outside his or her control; that he or she is not in control of his or her fate. This is perhaps clearest with the victims of crime, of poverty, of biology, of social prejudice. But even the more frivolous examples that Marsh notes have this element to them. For example, the desire to possess 'a certain pair of shoes' has echoes of Durkheim's 1897 inference that 'superfluous consumption', of the kind enabled and encouraged by the rise of globalised consumerism, produces a 'thirst for novelty, for unknown indulgences and sensations that are as yet unnamed, but which lose all their appeal as soon as they have been experienced'.[11] The 'hypnotic', 'addictive' qualities often ascribed to luxury consumerism at this time (and since), especially in connection with the emergence of the department store as a new experience in consumption, can be seen to feed this 'unslakable thirst [which] is a perpetually renewed source of suffering' and may have the effect of increasing incidents of 'anomic suicide'.[12] Our 'certain pair of shoes' could then be interpreted as a kind of metonymic acknowledgement of this condition, which may have been a particularly familiar one to Marsh's milieu given that, according to his grandson Robert Aickman, he spent much of his time enjoying the pleasures of the London metropolis.[13]

In his essay, Marsh makes brief mention of mental illness as a cause of suicide, and follows a similar line of thinking to Strahan, Durkheim and the 'standard model':

> I am tolerably certain that not all suicides are mad ... If, with her own hand, she summons death, & insists upon his presence at her side at once, is she a coward, – or mad? She simply desires to be mistress of her own fate. (10)

There is no causal link between suicide and insanity here, and clearly no sense of suicide being a form of madness. Indeed, for Marsh, those who study the causes of suicide, whether social or psychological, are the more likely to be mad: as the essay states, 'There is, I apprehend, no stranger subject for the student of a morbid, if not of a pathological, turn of mind' (4).

We are given a profusion of causes for suicide in Marsh's essay, from those with a certain tragic inevitably to the apparently random and implausible - a profusion so multitudinous that Marsh acknowledges himself that it 'would be easier to point out the reasons which have induced men and women not to commit suicide, than the reasons which have' (5). Suicide seems to take on a disturbing replicative capacity; it 'has a tendency to become a fashion' (4), Marsh tells us. It 'is apt to become a sentiment' (4). Allied to this we find the unsettling sense that everyone has the innate potential to commit suicide, seemingly with little provocation. 'Most of us', Marsh says in 'Suicide', 'have morbid tendencies, of some sort or other, in the direction of *felo de se*. Undeveloped, fortunately, in the vast majority of cases, but, in the germ, still there' (9). The self takes on an alien quality here, an uncontrollable quality, with the ever-present threat of being overwhelmed by suicidal mania. It is 'opportunity alone', Marsh argues in 'Suicide', that is so often the only missing factor. Given this potentiality, Marsh comes to reflect that 'the wonder, perhaps, is, not that there are so many suicides, but that there are so few' (7–8).

After considering reasons, and supposed reasons, for contemporary suicide, we find Marsh returning to his theme of suicide having its benefits, but in a much more sombre sense in relation to those who are prevented from ending their lives. In doing so, Marsh comes closer to the position that Hume articulates in arguing that 'whenever pain or sorrow so far overcome my patience, as to make me tired of life, I may conclude that I am recalled from my station in the clearest and most express terms' (7). Marsh is no utilitarian, but, like Hume, he is most certainly an advocate of liberty and autonomy.

Towards the end of 'Suicide', Marsh reflects on the condition of those that 'long for death' due to ill health, but are denied it by law. He presents a strongly pro-'right to die' case, as he opines,

> the doomed man and woman, who are rotting in our hospitals, enduring suffering which no horse ever knew, or was ever allowed to know ... we actually go out of our own way to keep them in it ... One may fancy that there will come a period in the history of the world when men will look back, and say, that this was not to show humanity. (10)

Again, for Marsh, the issue here is one of control, but in this case it is an inability to *commit* suicide, rather than an inability to *resist* it. In this more polemical aspect of the essay, such a position is found to deny self-control to an individual who 'simply desires to be mistress of her own fate'.

Suicide comes to occupy a dual status here. It *threatens to take control* of an individual by actualising his or her 'morbid tendencies'; the cause can seem slight or substantial, but for Marsh if the opportunity is presented any individual can be possessed by such an idea and compelled towards death. However, suicide is also depicted as *a means of taking control* over this one part of life, over the manner and timing of its end.

This structure of duality is a familiar one in Marsh's literary *oeuvre*, and it is unsurprising to find him exploring a similar point of tension here. In Marsh's Gothic works, for which he is best known, individual control or self-control is frequently undermined by an 'alien' or external force. This becomes a significant locus of anxiety in these Gothic texts. *The Beetle* (1897), for instance, involves a polymorphous Egyptian human-beetle creature travelling to London to enact revenge by using its mesmeric powers to control others. Individual autonomy is lost in this violation, an experience described by one early victim (Robert Holt) as 'something was going from me – the capacity, as it were, to be myself'.[14] This deeply disturbing discovery, that one is unable to exercise authority over oneself, as Victoria Margree notes, 'is to suffer a humiliating loss of the right to self-determination and self-governance'.[15] For Margree, it is a dynamic that plays out at multiple levels in Marsh's work, with imperialist anxieties also being expressed through a sense of ambivalent control 'equated with the potential loss of a nation's right to self-governance'.[16] But when it comes to representations of suicide in his fiction, issues of control become rather hazier.

Marsh has a remarkable predilection for making his characters kill themselves, although this occurs most often in his crime novels and those concerned with criminality. It is one of the many ironies in Marsh's treatment of suicide that, generally speaking, it is only the criminal (that is, predominantly, the murderer) for whom suicide acts as a means of controlling one's fate, and this as a means of escaping the judgement of the law. For instance, in the resolution of *The Crime and the Criminal* (1897), murderer Reggie Townsend dupes the police officer in charge of his custody into allowing him access to his handkerchief, cunningly laced with hydrocyanic acid, for just such an eventuality.[17] We find another case in the final acts of *A Spoiler of Men* (1905), when the illicit chemist and 'zombie-maker' Cyril Wentworth similarly 'escapes' apprehension by having 'slipped a capsule into his mouth'[18]; and another with ingenious killer Ralph Hardwicke, in *The*

Mystery of Philip Bennion's Death (1897), who re-enacts Bennion's murder on himself using the same poisoned smoking pipe; and so on.[19] The criminals in these narratives not only control their own *dénouement* but also, as Marsh positions them, seem to assume control of the narrative itself. For novels of crime and detection, there is no further development possible: no trial, no punishment, no restitution. The narrative ceases in all cases in short order, giving a sense not only of self-control through this final act, but also control over the metanarrative itself and the experience of the reader.

Whilst we could read these suicides as a form of redemption or absolution, Marsh clearly subverts this. Not only does he criticise the notion that suicide can be interpreted in this way, something that he identifies in 'Suicide' as being particular to the French who 'are apt to think that sins ought to be forgiven them, because they crowned them, by what, in the eyes of some folks, was the greatest sin of all' (4), but he also presents the suicide of each of these novels' antagonists as an affront to justice. Townsend, in *The Crime and the Criminal*, on successfully killing himself, triumphantly exclaims, 'Done you! Hurrah!'[20] Likewise, Wentworth's final sense of self-satisfaction seems designed to provoke indignation at its contempt:

> 'It's no good, Mr Wentworth', said one of them; 'we've got you'.
>
> He smiled at them.
>
> 'Pardon me', he replied, in his soft, pleasant voice and inevitable air of being completely at his ease, 'I assure you, you are wrong; you haven't'.[21]

In these texts, suicide serves as a means of control, in a way that becomes tragically ironic if we take a comprehensive view of Marsh's work on the subject: only the criminal can determine his or her own fate here and, to Marsh's criticism, the law would make criminals of those that acted similarly even if they be, as 'Suicide' suggests, 'agonised wretches'; 'men and women to whom existence means death, and worse than death' (10).

We do, however, find an exception to this mode of representing suicide in Marsh's *Mrs Musgrave – and Her Husband* (1895) and *A Master of Deception* (1913), which together engage explicitly with the tensions around suicide as a means of either exerting or submitting to control in rather more complex ways, through their treatment of heredity. Early in *Mrs Musgrave*, Hereward Musgrave makes the somewhat surprising discovery that his new wife, Ethel, has concealed from him the fact that her father, Edward Gardner, was hanged for murder. Edward was hanged on the testimony of the celebrated specialist in mental illnesses, Dr Byam, who perjured himself in testifying that the accused was sane, thereby ensuring his execution. As Byam goes on to relate, his reason for doing so was to prevent Gardner from having children, in the belief that his homicidal insanity would be passed from one generation to the next. However, Gardner did have a daughter, the eponymous Mrs Musgrave. Byam confronts Ethel, threatening to reveal her past to Hereward (neither being aware that Hereward knows it anyway by this point). Ethel kills him. What is kept ambiguous is whether she killed him in self-defence, Byam having inappropriately propositioned her, or whether she simultaneously took revenge for her father and ensured Byam's silence. Either way, Hereward refuses to believe anything to his wife's detriment, claiming, in overtly religious – indeed blasphemous – language, that she 'has attained perfection ... She is to me the Alpha and Omega; the beginning and the end'.[22] In his eyes, she epitomises conventional ideals of Victorian womanhood, a view strengthened by her giving birth to their daughter during the course of the novel, and he even kills to protect her (whilst simultaneously protecting his idealisation of family life). However, Mrs Musgrave in fact mirrors Byam in her resolute belief that she carries the hereditary 'taint' of murderous insanity. Whether she is actually insane or not is really an open question: whilst seemingly a bastion of security throughout, for Hereward at least (who exhibits a remarkable capacity to disregard her crimes and her possible madness, even as he acknowledges them), she certainly exhibits signs of insanity towards the end of the novel. This may be a temporary insanity, potentially puerperal, possibly brought about by her belief that her 'blood-guilt' has infected her husband, making of him a murderer too; or it may indeed be hereditary and have been there all along. The key point here is her belief that she has inherited both the guilt and the potential for homicidal insanity from her father. And Hereward's descriptions of her in fact often reinforce this: she is almost obsessively described as 'a child', a 'precocious child', insisting to the reader her definability as her father's daughter (42). She may be presented as a 'modern artist's *fin de siècle* ideal black-and-white study of "Innocence"', but at the same time we are also constantly reminded of her status as inheritor to a troubling and troubled ancestry (6).

The inevitability of hereditary here, following both Dr Byam and Ethel Musgrave's understanding, can be brought under the control of the individual only through suicide. And not just Ethel's suicide, but also Hereward's, and the infanticide of their daughter. Ethel effectively destroys herself twice over, both physically and in her status as a mother. Through this, she performs the action necessary to end the hereditary 'taint', which Byam, the symbol (albeit a questionable one) of medical authority, was unable to. She is thus, within the paradigm of hereditary theory, performing a responsible action in killing herself and her child. Whilst suicide here represents a form of control, there is also an element of compulsion, of being controlled, as suicide is the only 'socially responsible' choice open to Ethel: without her own intervention, there is no guarantee that her existence and 'contamination' will be ended by the law (in similar circumstances, it required Byam's perjury to ensure this outcome with Ethel's father); without the infanticide that destroys herself-as-mother, her 'corrupted' lineage may continue.

This paradigm of hereditary inevitability is, however, questioned in various ways, both in *Mrs Musgrave* and, I would suggest, to a greater extent in Marsh's later novel, *A Master of Deception* (1913). Near the beginning of this text, the dapper, murderous anti-hero, Rodney Elmore, is informed that his father committed suicide:

> Never was son more like his father, in all things ... Rather than face the music, he committed suicide ... Rodney was aware of a sensation of actual physical pain as he listened, as if sentence had not only been pronounced, but punishment also begun.[23]

Whilst this scenario of the criminal committing suicide to determine his or her own fate is a familiar one from Marsh's earlier works, this later work is more interested in the effects of this on subsequent generations: 'He, the son of a lifelong rogue, who had only escaped the penalty of his misdeeds by self-destruction!'[24] We can see that receiving this information has a tangible, physical effect on Rodney, emphasising its transformative power. Rodney's internalised sense that he is now to be 'punished', evoking a higher or even supernatural judgement on him, may have echoes of Ethel Musgrave's belief that her fate is sealed by her heredity and seems liable to become one of the novel's several self-fulfilling prophecies.

The narrative seems to move progressively towards Rodney repeating his father's final act, as his multitude of plots begin to unravel and the noose of suspicion closes around him, particularly if we are familiar with Marsh's earlier works. However, Rodney manipulates any such expectation, assuming control by feigning his own suicide. In the process of doing this, he subverts any claim to inevitability that may be predicated on a theory of heredity. Rodney is not compelled towards suicide by his genetic inheritance, nor does he resort to this as a means of 'escaping' the legal ramifications of his crimes, yet he is able to control his own destiny through exploiting the belief of those around him in the inevitability of this paradigm (as well as, potentially, the expectations of the reader). As the titular 'master of deception', Rodney goes so far as to 'deceive' his own apparent biological determinism. Similar to Ethel Musgrave's case, the sense of controlling one's fate through voluntarily ending one's life is shown to be a matter of belief, rather than necessity: for Ethel, her belief in a theory of heredity propounded by Byam made suicide a means of control, but also the only 'moral' choice available to her. Rodney's disavowal of this paradigm breaks the tension between taking control and being controlled, as he essentially refuses to be compelled towards suicide but retains its function as a means of self-determination. For Marsh, who, I would suggest, presents Rodney Elmore with a certain affection, there may well have been personal motivations for resisting notions of hereditary criminality, given both his and his father's experiences of the law.

We find external influences such as theories of biological determinism, which seem to control the individual and compel him or her towards suicide, being subverted in these texts, reinforcing the individual's ability to resist such discourses. So, it is all the more notable that the more abstract, psychological (but not pathological) influences that Marsh introduced in his essay 'Suicide', such as 'morbid tendencies', suicide's capacity to become a 'fashion' and, most particularly, the inciting effects of 'opportunity', seem to be significantly greater threats with the potential to influence anyone, no matter social status, lineage or circumstance.

Whilst we may have an absence of actual suicide in *A Master of Deception*, it is perhaps surprising to note that we also have a relative absence of the act of suicide throughout Marsh's fiction. Suicide is, in fact, descriptively almost invisible, being reduced to offhand statements of fact, such as 'a faint transparency of smoke issued from his lips. And he fell dead', from *The Mystery of Philip Bennion's Death*, or 'as he spoke, he reeled, and fell – dead', from *A Spoiler of*

Men.²⁵ In comparison with the explicit, often grotesque, detail that Marsh frequently uses in describing murder (with bodies convulsing, twitching, faces turning purple, 'eyes ... bulging out of their sockets', etc.), the images of suicide that we are given seem curiously empty, and often ambiguously referred to only as 'it' or 'that kind of thing'.²⁶

One possible reason for this is suggested by Graham Patterson, who becomes Rodney Elmore's unfortunate victim in *A Master of Deception*, when he thinks that Rodney means to commit suicide rather than murder: '"You – you're not going to make away with yourself before my eyes?"'²⁷ This fear of witnessing murder returns us to the rather more frivolous examples of reciprocal suicide referred to earlier in Marsh's essay on 'Suicide'. But there seems to be a consistent anxiety that, in witnessing suicide, the impulse may be transferred; that it may instil a proclivity towards imitation; in effect, that it may become contagious. And it is this apparent potential for representational contagion that, I suggest, Marsh structures his narrative to contain. Indeed, this is quite in keeping with common assertions regarding the relationship between cultural representation and suicide, such as Strahan's claim that 'even the representation on the stage, of suicide under conditions appealing forcibly to sympathy and imagination, has often been known to be followed by imitative self-destruction'.²⁸ Indeed, Durkheim makes note of the commonality of this view in the late nineteenth century whilst refuting it as a cause significant enough to warrant a response (such as censorship): 'Certain authors, ascribing to imitation a power it does not possess, have demanded that the printing of reports of suicides and crimes in the newspapers be prohibited.'²⁹ However, even Durkheim supports the sense that suicide can be self-replicative, to a limited degree: 'In short, certain as the contagion of suicide is from individual to individual, imitation never seems to propagate it so as to affect the social suicide-rate.'³⁰ So, Marsh is certainly in keeping with contemporary thinking here, but suggests that there is a more significant threat posed by imitative suicide than many others, and seems to take precautionary action in his work by effectively eliding it. Marsh's narrative structures, therefore, can come to support a sense of suicide as self-replicating, insinuating and in need of representational control.

This sense is reinforced by the almost miraculous foresight of Marsh's characters to provide in advance the means and opportunity for doing away with themselves. Whether this be Hereward

Musgrave's collapsible poisoned tube that he carries with him always, or Reggie Townsend's handkerchief laced with hydrocyanic acid, or Ralph Hardwicke's 'bewitched meerschaum pipe', all are available for use at the opportune moment. The technical/chemical knowledge or the outlandishness of many of the devices used for suicidal purposes throughout Marsh's fiction reinforce his narrative strategy of avoidance and protection: the reader is not confronted with easily replicable scenarios. However, this strategy of elision and obscurity, in some ways, has a contrary effect, by suggesting that there is a need for protection; that we as readers need to be guarded, ultimately, from ourselves.

Marsh's work establishes an ambivalence in his conception of suicide, but one that is centred on a single issue: control. Suicide may function as a means of controlling one's own fate but also threatens to take control through its constant liability for epidemic proliferation. This latter threat, for Marsh, takes a dizzying array of forms outlined in his unpublished essay 'Suicide', leaving an image of a world in which suicide is an ever-present spectre. However, Marsh's treatment of causal factors becomes less stable in his literary work: we find characters who are at the mercy of scientific and social paradigms (such as heredity) which compel them towards suicide, but also characters who resist such discourses, even using them to assert their self-determination. That the characters who 'succeed' in using suicide as a means of ensuring self-control are inescapably defined as criminal represents a critique of both the force of social compliance and expectations, as well as laws around suicide that invariably conflate ending one's own life with criminality. However, for Marsh the locus of anxiety around suicide is most explicitly in the 'germ' of the idea that, he argues, rests within us all; it is in the constant potential for the self to rebel against its own survival. Ideas for Marsh are infectious, and he leaves us with a sense that none is more so than the suicidal impulse. For Marsh, the two most threatening factors in this context are representational contagion and availability of opportunity, for their capacity to produce an undifferentiated epidemic of suicide. It is these that have to be controlled for his readership, through a strategy that serves (intentionally or no) to heighten anxiety: the threat of the suicidal impulse becomes a threat founded in the unknowability of ourselves, and in this Marsh speaks to wider contemporary concerns that the self in the late nineteenth century is increasingly discovered to be disturbingly other.

Notes

1. S. A. K. Strahan, *Suicide and Insanity* (London: S. Sonnenschein, 1893), p. v. E-book, available online at Internet Archive. https://archive.org/details/suicideandinsan00stragoog, accessed 20 April 2017.
2. William Knighton, 'Suicidal Mania', *Contemporary Review*, 39 (1881), 81.
3. Thomas Hardy, *Jude the Obscure*, ed. P. Ingham (Oxford: Oxford University Press, 1985), p. 411.
4. J. Thomson, 'The City of Dreadful Night', in *The City of Dreadful Night* (London: Watts, 1932), pp. 5–6.
5. Édouard Manet, *Le Suicidé* ('The Suicide', c.1877–81), Oil on canvas, Foundation E. G. Bührle, Zurich; Vasily Perov, *Die Ertrunkene* ('Drowned', 1867), Oil on canvas, Tretyakov Gallery, Moscow; G. Grosz, *Selbstmörder* ('Suicide', 1916), Oil on canvas, Tate Liverpool, Liverpool.
6. Answers Library, Richard Marsh Advertisement, *Daily Mirror*, 25 May 1910, p. 2.
7. Minna Vuohelainan, '"Contributing to Most Things": Richard Marsh, Literary Production, and the Fin de Siècle Periodicals Market', *Victorian Periodicals Review*, 46:3 (2013), 401–22, at 401.
8. *Ibid.*, 411.
9. Richard Marsh, 'Suicide' (Essay MS, c.1891–1910), p. 1. Papers of Richard Marsh, RUL MS 2051/3. Reading: University of Reading Special Collections. Further references to this unpublished manuscript are given in parentheses in the body of the text.
10. David Hume, *On Suicide* (London: Penguin, 2005), p. 10. Further references are to this edition and appear in parentheses.
11. Émile Durkheim, *On Suicide*, trans. R. Buss (London: Penguin, 2006), p. 281.
12. *Ibid.*, p. 270.
13. Robert Aickman, *The Attempted Rescue* (Leyburn: Tartarus Press, 2001), pp. 9–12.
14. Richard Marsh, *The Beetle: A Mystery*, ed. M. Vuohelainen (Kansas City, MO: Valancourt Books, 2008), p. 22.
15. Victoria Margree, '"Both in Men's Clothing": Gender, Sovereignty and Insecurity in Richard Marsh's *The Beetle*', *Critical Survey*, 19:2 (2007), 63–81, at 68–9.
16. *Ibid.*, 69.
17. Richard Marsh, *The Crime and the Criminal* (London: Ward, Lock, 1897), pp. 342–3.
18. Richard Marsh, *A Spoiler of Men*, ed. J. Högland (Kansas City, MO: Valancourt Books, 2010), p. 198.
19. Richard Marsh, *The Mystery of Philip Bennion's Death* (London: Ward, Lock, 1897), p. 169.
20. Marsh, *The Crime and the Criminal*, p. 342.
21. Marsh, *A Spoiler of Men*, p. 198.
22. Richard Marsh, *Mrs Musgrave – and Her Husband* (Memphis, TN: General Books, 2012), p. 27. Subsequent references are to the edition and are given in parentheses in the text.

23 Richard Marsh, *A Master of Deception* (1913), Project Gutenberg E-book 2011, available online at www.gutenberg.org/files/38161/38161-h/38161-h.htm, accessed 9 March 2018 (unpaginated: references given by chapter), ch. 3.
24 *Ibid.*
25 Marsh, *The Mystery of Phillip Bennion's Death*, p. 169; *A Spoiler of Men*, p. 198.
26 Marsh, *A Master of Deception*, ch. 8.
27 *Ibid.*, ch. 9.
28 Strahan, *Suicide and Insanity*, p. 143.
29 Durkheim, *On Suicide*, p. 140.
30 *Ibid.*, p. 141.

Bridget M. Marshall

Suicide as justice? The self-destroying Gothic villain in Pauline Hopkins' *Of One Blood*

This chapter explores how the villains in classic Gothic novels by Ann Radcliffe and Charles Brockden Brown used suicide to evade justice, and how this 'suicide solution' is later reworked by Pauline Hopkins in her 1903 Gothic novel *Of One Blood*. While the suicides of Radcliffe's and Brown's villains demonstrate their disregard for justice and judicial processes, Hopkins radically revises the possibility of justice through suicide. In these examples, suicidal Gothic villains present the reader with a complex moral quandary about how to achieve justice, showing how the Gothic engages in legal and ethical questions about free will, and with our evolving understanding of mental illness.

Ann Radcliffe created two villains who seek to avoid execution by the justice system by taking their own lives before their death sentences can be carried out by the state. At the end of *The Romance of the Forest* (1791), on the day the villain (the Marquis de Montalt) is supposed to appear in court to be tried for the murder of his own brother, he takes his life by drinking poison. The narrator explains that 'convinced he had nothing to hope from his trial, he had taken this method of avoiding an ignominious death'.[1] Montalt successfully avoids prosecution (and a likely inevitable conviction and execution), yet he still summons the justice system: just prior to his death, he calls for a priest and two notaries, to confess his crimes in both a religious and a legal form. Montalt is thus redeemed, at least partially, through his confession: his religious confession allows him reconciliation with the Church, while his legal confession aids in establishing the legal facts of his case. Nonetheless, Montalt's act of suicide immediately following the confession would be considered a mortal sin in the eyes of the Catholic Church. The legal status of Montalt's suicide is complicated by Radcliffe's somewhat vague (and frequently anachronistic) setting. Montalt's act of 'self-murder' occurred in France, likely sometime in the latter half of the 1600s; starting in 1670, a French law established that 'every convicted suicide should forfeit his goods and be drawn on a hurdle to a profane grave',[2] which would leave Montalt's family penniless and his body desecrated – surely a terrible outcome for all. However, in France in the year 1791 (notably, the same year *The Romance of the Forest* was published), 'suicide was decriminalized completely'[3]; it would seem that Radcliffe has applied the laws of her contemporary time, since Montalt's legally documented deathbed depositions fully reinstate the heroine Adeline's true identity and restore her fortune and family name, which she had lost when Montalt murdered his own brother, who was also Adeline's father. Montalt's suicide spares Adeline the considerable trauma of his trial for the murder of her father, which Adeline has sought to avoid:

> Though justice demanded the life of the murderer, and though the tenderness and pity which the idea of her father called forth urged her to avenge his death, she could not, without horror, consider herself as the instrument of dispensing that justice which would deprive a fellow being of existence. (347)

Thus, Montalt's suicide becomes a final act that is simultaneously villainous (sinful in the eyes of the Church and illegal in the eyes of the law) but also perhaps redemptive, since he saves his victim further grief and the expense of a trial with an inevitable verdict requiring state-sanctioned execution.

Radcliffe would employ this solution again a few years later in *The Italian* (1797), which ends with the murder-suicide of two co-conspirators. The monk Schedoni avows to his confessor that he has poisoned both his sometime accomplice Nicola di Zampari (who revealed Schedoni's misdeeds) and himself; Schedoni proudly proclaims, 'I have destroyed him, who would have destroyed me, and – and I have escaped an ignominious death.'[4] Both Montalt and Schedoni use the same phrasing – they seek to avoid an 'ignominious death' – yet it does not seem that their deaths by suicide are in fact less ignominious than death by judicially sanctioned execution. While Montalt and Schedoni face a stark choice between a trial (and likely conviction and execution) or suicide, they do not appear to be in emotional distress; these men make their choice after careful thought, calculation and planning (including procuring the poison). They are not madmen in these moments, but clear-eyed, shrewd men: they take control of their narratives, make confessions and regulate the means and timing of their deaths. Their suicides can be read as the apotheosis of their villainy, their final acts of defiance against both human and divine law.

Radcliffe's precedent-setting villain suicide solution was quickly carried to the American Gothic by its forefather, Charles Brockden Brown, who employed the same method in two of his Gothic novels: *Wieland; or, The Transformation, An American Tale* (1798) and *Edgar Huntly; or Memoirs of a Sleep Walker* (1799). In Brown's first novel, *Wieland*, Theodore Wieland is convicted in court for the murder of his wife and their five children, but he insists, 'I will not accept evil at their [the jury's] hand.'[5] Still in the throes of madness, he escapes prison and makes an attempt on his sister's life; when he discovers that he has been under a delusion, and fully realises the horror of the deeds he has committed, he abruptly stabs himself in the neck with a penknife. Wieland's act is sudden and violent, showing none of the premeditation or contemplation of Radcliffe's villains. Further, his suicide does not provide any solace to his victim; instead, his sister, the innocent Clara, witnesses the act and is devastated. She describes her horror thus: 'For a spectacle like this was it my fate to be reserved! ... These images have not, for a moment, forsaken me. Till I am breathless and cold, they must continue to hover in my sight' (171). Wieland's suicide is an impulsive and violent act committed by a man in extreme anguish; indeed, it is possible that in this moment of suicide, he is labouring under yet another delusion. Wieland's suicide intensifies rather than mitigates the suffering of his surviving victim, and does not resolve questions in the way that the suicides in Radcliffe's novels did.

Brown again employs the figure of the suicidal villain at the very end of *Edgar Huntly*. Sarsefield explains how Clithero (who he refers to as 'the lunatic') 'threw himself overboard', and when he was about to be rescued, 'he forced himself beneath the surface, and was seen no more'.[6] Clithero is presumed dead, and Sarsefield suggests that this is for the best for him, since 'he has saved himself from evils, for which no time would have provided a remedy, from lingering for years in the noisome dungeon of an hospital' (194). Both Clithero and Wieland are accused of (and know that they have committed) the murder of a family member (whether biological or adoptive). Both men have been under a great deal of mental stress and angst, and it is possible that they are not in full control of their mental faculties at the time of either their murders or their suicides. Both of Brown's suicidal villains act rashly, in the heat of the moment, apparently without consideration and possibly gripped by madness. This presents a stark contrast with Radcliffe's calm, shrewd suicidal villains, who turn to suicide only after they have been imprisoned and their conviction and execution by the court is nearly guaranteed.

Radcliffe's and Brown's 'suicide solution' is taken one step further in Pauline Hopkins' novel *Of One Blood; or, the Hidden Self*, originally serialised in *Colored American Magazine*, 1902–03. *Of One Blood* is difficult to categorise, but many of its features – haunted houses, family secrets, ghosts and incest, just to name a few – indicate its place within the Gothic tradition. Several critics have remarked on its Gothic characteristics: Yogita Goyal describes the novel as having 'a particularly Gothic twist'[7]; Eugenia DeLamotte notes that it is filled with 'Gothic mysteries' and provides 'great Gothic insight'[8]; Walter Benn Michaels refers to the novel's 'amazing Gothic plot'[9]; Laura Doyle describes Hopkins' novels as 'sentimental fiction with strong gothic accents' and *Of One Blood* as her 'most pessimistic, and most gothic novel'[10]; and Deborah McDowell's introduction to the novel also discusses the Gothic features of the text.[11]

In 'The Wind of Words: Plagiarism and Intertextuality in *Of One Blood*', Geoffrey Sanborn calculates that 18 per cent of Pauline Hopkins' *Of One Blood* consists of directly transcribed passages from other texts,[12] which he proposes shows the way that Hopkins 'is locating herself within various existing traditions of popular writing'[13]; one of those popular traditions is certainly the Gothic. Sanborn notes that many of the directly transcribed passages are copied from 'travelers' or historians' accounts of Africa' or 'melodramatic fictions of African travel'[14] that figure prominently in the second half of the novel, which is set mostly in Africa. In the second half of the book, Hopkins deploys classic 'Imperial Gothic' in the tradition of Rider Haggard's *She* (1887); her novel features all three of Patrick Brantlinger's suggested 'imperial Gothic themes of regression, invasion, and the waning of adventure'.[15] Even as the characters cross a desert in Africa, they survey an oddly Gothic landscape as they spy 'a cliff, looking, in the distance, like a half-ruined castle, which the Arabs believed to be enchanted'.[16] In Africa, the specific hazards they encounter further suggest other classic Gothic texts, as when Reuel Briggs, while trapped on a precipice, encounters a leopard about to spring upon him in a scene that uncannily resembles Charles Brockden Brown's panther scene in *Edgar Huntly*. (Both Briggs and Huntly focus in particular on the eyes of the predator cats, and both Huntly and Briggs kill the cats with well-aimed head shots.) The novel demonstrates a perfect vision of Anglo-American fears central to imperial Gothic when the narrator intones that a city on the horizon appears to be incredibly beautiful and charming, yet

> it is the eternal enchantment of the cities of the Orient seen at a distance; but, alas! Set foot within them, the illusion vanishes and disgust seizes you. Like beautiful bodies they have the appearance of life, but within the worm of decay and death eats ceaselessly. (509)[17]

The novel portrays both the African continent and the United States as sources of Gothic horrors. The plot follows the intertwined lives of three children of a black slave mother (Mira) and her white plantation master, none of whom knows their true parentage or that they are siblings: Aubrey Livingston, switched at birth with a dead white child, believes himself to be white; Reuel Briggs knows he is black but passes for white; and Dianthe Lusk at first knows she is black and lives as a black woman (singing with the Fisk Jubilee Singers) but falls into a mesmeric trance, loses her identity completely, is re-named 'Felice Adams' and is welcomed into a white family. Mira's three children are the product of her rape by her plantation master, who is also her own half-brother. With its tangled family tree and slow revelation of the kinship relations among the main characters, the novel drives towards a terrible tragic ending that reflects the horrors of the heritage of American slavery. In the face of these horrors, Hopkins' characters (and not just the villains) turn to suicide as a solution, suggesting motives for suicide that are beyond either cold calculation or the impetus of madness: in Hopkins' novel, supernatural intervention and mesmerism can motivate (or even inhibit) suicidal acts.

On the very first page of the novel, Reuel Briggs, a Harvard medical student in Cambridge, asks 'Is suicide wrong?' (441), setting up the character's (and the novel's) dark perspective on the world. Briggs is not a villain; his suicidal thoughts do not lead to a suicidal act, and are motivated by his melancholy, his poverty and his ongoing need to keep his racial identity a secret to pass as white. The knowledge of his mother's enslavement and rape weighs on him; as Maisha Wester suggests in her reading of the novel, 'the slave mother's silence is inherited by and destructive to later generations'.[18] Reuel's contemplation of suicide is motivated not by any act he has committed, but by the psychological pain he experiences as a result of dealing with both his racial identity and the racism of the society in which he lives. He has in fact been contemplating suicide 'for months' (442) at this point, but 'courage was yet wanting for strength to rend the veil' (442). He ultimately does not make an attempt at suicide, but he notices 'voices and hands seemed beckoning him all day to cut the Gordian knot' (442). Here, Hopkins makes the first suggestion that there could be supernatural forces involved in Reuel's contemplation of suicide. Although the 'voices and hands' may only be in Reuel's mind, or used metaphorically, ghosts and mesmerism feature prominently throughout the novel, so it is possible that this is a supernatural intervention and not merely a metaphorical description of Reuel's ruminations.

Reuel again considers suicide after he arrives in Africa, where he has gone to seek a fortune to support his wife, Dianthe Lusk (aka Felice Adams); the trip was actually arranged by the conniving Aubrey Livingston, who plans to have Reuel killed so that he can have Dianthe for himself. None of the three know that they are all 'of one blood' – siblings who have been separated since birth. After being told that Dianthe is dead (although she is not), Reuel takes his gun, leaves a note and departs for the pyramids: 'he had no purpose, no sensation ... His love was dead: – that was the one fact that filled his thoughts at first. Then another took its place. Why should he live?' (542). Reuel's suicidal thoughts and preparations are motivated not only by his general melancholy, but by his grief over the loss of his beloved; however, these thoughts are immediately undermined when he falls into a sepulchre and hears 'a low, distinct hiss' (452), presumably of a poisonous snake – immediately 'he who had been desirous of death but an hour before obeyed the first law of nature' (543). His terror in this moment propels him with a new desire to live; significantly, no snake ever appears, and the source of the hiss is never identified, possibly suggesting again some kind of supernatural intervention. Reuel vacillates on the act of suicide, feeling that he cannot continue living, but finding that he cannot go through with the act; he never ultimately commits suicide, despite (or perhaps because of) either supernatural or serendipitous interventions by voices or threatening noises.

Reuel's beloved Dianthe also contemplates suicide: when she discovers that her husband Reuel is still alive, and that Aubrey (who is now also her husband) deceived her by hiding Reuel's letters to her and forging a letter stating that Reuel was dead, 'the very heavens beckoned her to commit a deed of horror' (600). She instead attempts to murder Aubrey, but he catches her leaving a poisoned glass of water for him and demands that she drink it instead. He does not exactly physically force her to do this, and although she delays, she does not exactly resist. Dianthe at this point is described as 'a mind unbalanced', and the narrator suggests that she feels 'guilt' (610), perhaps indicating her own suicidal thoughts. Although she begs for mercy and is 'shrinking ... on her knees', Aubrey simply repeats his command that she drink (610). She complies with his demand thus: '"To Reuel!" gasped Dianthe, and set the glass down empty' (610). Her final exclamation honouring Reuel suggests a self-sacrificing suicide, an act that she commits intentionally and in honour of him. Although her action is certainly compelled by the physically more powerful Aubrey (and we cannot underestimate the power of mesmerism that repeatedly affects Dianthe), he never physically hurts her. Dianthe actually drinks from the glass – which she herself had prepared – in an act that could be read as a suicide, though indeed one compelled by Aubrey, and for which Aubrey is certainly responsible.

This rather curious chain of events – a character compelling another to take her own life – plays out in another variation with Aubrey's death at the very end of the novel. Once the details of Aubrey's crimes are revealed (he caused the death of Molly Vance, attempted to kill his brother Reuel, deceived his sister Dianthe into a sexual relationship and then killed her), Reuel Briggs, along with a cohort of African people he has brought back with him from the kingdom of Telassar to Cambridge, confront Aubrey in his study. Ai, prime minister of Telassar, puts Aubrey into a sort of trance; Ai later explains, 'Justice will be done' (620), and shortly thereafter, Aubrey's body is found floating in the Charles River, the same place where the body of Molly Vance was found. The narrator explains that '"death by thine own hand", [was] whispered in [Aubrey's] ear while [he was] under hypnotic influence' (620); essentially, he was forced to commit suicide. This act – in which he is compelled in a trance state to take his own life – is remarkably parallel to the way that he forced Dianthe to take her own life with the poison. Prior to the mesmeric trance-setting by Ai, Aubrey has indicated no interest in taking his own life; indeed, he apparently feels no guilt for his actions, and has engaged 'shrewd and active lawyers' (618) to defend him against the charges. When Ai and company arrive to do their justice, Aubrey does not even speak; he is silent and 'did not change countenance' (619) through the whole ritual. Maisha Wester rightly points to Aubrey's status as a 'typical Byronic hero', who eventually 'descends into pure villainy'.[19] That his life ends through suicide – even if it is not quite a standard suicide – fits with the Byronic hero/villain trope, and his suicide provides a parallel and perhaps just end, when paired with his forcing of Dianthe (his sister) to commit suicide earlier. Unlike Radcliffe's villains, who commit suicide because they seek to avoid the humiliation of a trial, Aubrey is in fact eager to prove himself in court, and it is only through supernatural, mesmeric intervention that he takes his own life, subverting the need for further legal proceedings in Cambridge.

The narrator ultimately explains that according to the laws of Telassar – the imagined ancient kingdom in Africa that is the setting of half of the novel – men 'became their own executioners when guilty of the crime of murder' (620). But these men are no longer in Telassar; they are in Cambridge, which makes this extra-judicial resolution a bit more complicated. The means of inflicting death in cases where the judiciary has deemed a crime worthy of the death penalty has always been fraught with concern; in some ways, Telassar's edict – under which villains 'become their own executioners' – makes a certain amount of sense. In *Residues of Justice: Literature, Law, Philosophy*, Wai Chee Dimock argues that many nineteenth-century texts display ambivalence about the solutions provided by the justice system; Dimock observes 'the sense of mismatch, the sense of shortfall, that burdens the endings of these texts',[20] and indeed the justice meted out through the suicide of the villain in Brown's, Radcliffe's and Hopkins' novels falls short of resolving the terrible events that have happened. The 'suicide solution' causes mixed reactions among the survivors of Aubrey's crimes. After Ai informs the group that 'Justice will be done', Charlie Vance replies, 'Then I am satisfied' (620); however, 'Reuel spoke not one word' (620). Charlie, whose sister Molly was murdered by Aubrey, is satisfied with this justice, but Reuel, whose beloved wife/sister Dianthe was murdered by Aubrey, is apparently less sanguine. Having the laws of the imagined Telassar implemented in Cambridge might seem to provoke legal concerns about appropriate jurisdiction; however, curiously, the Cambridge native (Charlie Vance) seems satisfied with this resolution, and no further legal action occurs in the novel.

By the end of the novel, all three children of Mira – Reuel, Dianthe and Aubrey – have contemplated, attempted or committed suicide, with varying reasons and with varying degrees of control over their thoughts and actions. The prevalence of mesmerism throughout the novel, and the particularly curious self-execution under hypnosis, reveal considerable anxiety about whether acts of suicide occur with the full consent and power of the one committing the act. The notion that someone committing suicide is not fully in control of his or her actions is a troubling one. Contemporary research in this field shows that those contemplating suicide are often deeply ambivalent about whether or not they want to go through with the act, sometimes even in the moment of taking the action.[21] Historically, since the early modern period in England, juries considering cases of suicide could specify a verdict of either *felo de se* ('a felon of himself') or *non compos mentis* ('not of sound mind'), indicating that there has always been some understanding (even if limited) that mental illness (or an unsound mind) plays a role in suicide.[22] Hopkins goes a step beyond the notion that mental illness might be in play, suggesting that supernatural powers (mesmerism and trances) may be at work as well.

Hopkins had previously treated suicide in her fiction in 'The Mystery within Us', a short story that appeared in the very first issue of *Colored American Magazine* in May 1900.[23] In that tale, a character named Tom Underwood, a doctor, describes how he once contemplated suicide:

> I raised the bottle [of prussic acid] to my lips with the intention of draining it. Halfway there my arm lost its carrying power, and I sat upon the edge of my couch startled into momentary forgetfulness of my project as I mentally analyzed the condition of the arm. Again I essayed to raise the member, but although my mind was more active than it had been for some time, I found that my entire body had lost the power of volition![24]

Underwood's loss of control over his body, despite his mental desire to cause himself harm, seems similar to the mesmeric trances that appear in *Of One Blood*; however, while his trance prevents him from committing his planned act, Aubrey's trance made him commit the act he had not considered. Awestruck at his inability to complete the deed, Underwood soon experiences another paranormal phenomenon: he describes a 'Presence' that '*seemed* to speak' (capitalisation and emphasis in original), who questions why he would take the life that God has given him (24). Underwood identifies the presence as the ghost of Dr Thorn, a man of great repute in the medical profession who has recently died, who tells him that he is destined to carry on his medical work. On awakening from his dream/trance, Underwood notes that the bottle of poison has disappeared, and instead, he discovers the manuscript of a medical treatise, which he then publishes as his own and which makes him famous (and saves many lives). Aside from its outcome, the averted suicide scene has remarkable parallels with the completed suicides that appear in *Of One Blood*. In all of these scenes, the person attempting suicide is not fully in control of his or her body. In Dianthe's case, she is compelled by Aubrey, and in Aubrey's case, he is compelled by some manner of mind control exerted by Ai. While these two characters are compelled to take their own lives via some manner of external intervention, in Underwood's case, he is prevented from committing the act by that supernatural intervention.

Underwood's case is perhaps most clearly paralleled by that of Reuel, the character who is the first to contemplate suicide, but who (unlike both his siblings) never goes through with it. Reuel has been contemplating suicide for months; however, as noted earlier, 'the courage was yet wanting for strength to rend the veil' (442). In his dreamy state, after pondering his reading, like Underwood, he sees the outline of a figure (in his case, that of a woman) and finds that he is unable to move his body. Like Underwood, Reuel 'stared about him in a bewildered way like a man awakening from a heavy sleep ... The vision was gone ... [he was] conscious of an odd murmur in his head, which seemed to control his movements' (446). Reuel, like Underwood, does not follow through with his contemplated suicide because of a supernatural intervention. Thus Hopkins' mesmerism saves some from death by their own hands, while it actually enables (or even compels) others to complete the deed.

In all of these examples from Hopkins' fiction, a supernatural intervention makes the final determination of the suicide – either forcing it or preventing it. While there are certainly supernatural (or possibly supernatural) elements in Radcliffe and Brown, they are never involved in suicides. In Radcliffe, suicides are committed by villains, and carried out methodically and apparently by men of sound mind, who have made conscious decisions to choose death by suicide over presumed execution by the justice system. In Brown, suicides are committed by villains in acts of extreme fury, without forethought or planning, suggesting that they are rash acts of passion, but have the same effect of sparing the villain from any official judicial process. But Hopkins' suicides all involve a supernatural intervention; none of the suicidal characters are fully responsible for their suicidal acts (or their choice not to complete the act). This depiction of suicide is unusual in the genre of the Gothic. It is also somewhat unexpected when compared to typical twentieth-century portrayals of suicide, which most frequently, as Julie-Marie Strange explains, were framed as being the result of 'a weak moral character'.[25] Between the 1790s of Radcliffe and Brown, and the early twentieth century of Hopkins, there was a revolution in the understanding of suicide, led in large part by Émile Durkheim's 1897 monograph, *Suicide*. But while Durkheim's work applied social scientific methods to the study of suicide to gain a greater understanding of the causes of suicide, it still remained a mysterious and typically dreaded topic. Hopkins' supernatural interventions in her portrayals of suicide suggest that an individual contemplating suicide is not merely 'weak-willed', nor is he coldly calculating nor in frenzied madness; instead, Hopkins seems to suggest that forces larger than the individuals are in play. While this portrayal may be far from the increasingly scientific approach to understanding mental illness, it does begin to capture the notion that suicide is not merely about an individual's emotions or will, but about larger forces around them, whether those forces are explicitly supernatural, or perhaps the forces of race, class and other structures of social order that impact on an individual's ability to survive in the world.

The suicides of Hopkins' characters, who are African American and only a generation or two removed from the conditions of slavery, must also be read specifically in relation to the history of the transatlantic slave trade and American chattel slavery. Historians have documented numerous accounts of African people who chose suicide rather than be taken into slavery.[26] As historian William D. Piersen explains, 'many slaves believed death in Africa was preferable to the unspeakable horror that awaited across the Atlantic'[27]; Piersen discusses numerous historical cases of men and women on slave ships refusing food and water, or jumping into the ocean to take their own lives. Both fictional and non-fictional stories about slavery frequently feature scenes of suicide by individuals who choose to take their lives rather than be taken into or returned to slavery; Olaudah Equiano's *Narrative* (1789) mentions slaves who 'jumped into the sea' as they 'prefer[red] death to slavery',[28] and William Wells Brown's 1853 novel *Clotel; or, The President's Daughter* includes two women (Clotel and Ellen) who choose suicide over being sent into slavery. In Hopkins' time, and in the primary setting of *Of One Blood*, slavery was no longer the present reality; however, segregation, lynching and the terrorising of African American people continued to inflict deep psychic wounds in both communities and individuals.

Hopkins' African American characters' suicides are in large part motivated by the history of slavery and their lived experiences of racial injustice. Reuel, Dianthe and Aubrey are each deeply affected by slavery; their mother was raped, and they were denied basic information about their own identities and family connections. Although Aubrey is the novel's villain, he is also a victim of slavery and systemic racism, and his suicide is quite different from those of the villains in Radcliffe and Brown; he is neither calculating nor crazed. Aubrey is not in control of the choice to commit suicide; rather, he is forced to commit the act by a powerful external force. For the typical suicidal Gothic villain, suicide offers both self-determination and an escape from judicial systems and punishments; for Aubrey, his compulsory suicide is not truly self-determined, and in effect, it serves as the judicial system's punishment. Hopkins' novel re-deploys the Gothic villain suicide trope to portray the circumscribed options of African Americans in the early twentieth century. *Of One Blood* suggests that suicide is not simply the result of an individual's defiant choice and rebellious action against society; it may also be the product of unseen forces, whether supernatural or social, that can overtake and control individuals.

Notes

1 Ann Radcliffe, *The Romance of the Forest*, ed. Chloe Chard (Oxford: Oxford University Press, 1999), p. 353. Subsequent references are to this edition and are given in parentheses in the text.
2 Mark Williams, *Suicide and Attempted Suicide: Understanding the Cry of Pain* (New York: Penguin, 1997), p. 14.
3 *Ibid.*
4 Ann Radcliffe, *The Italian, or the Confessional of the Black Penitents: A Romance*, ed. Frederick Garber (Oxford: Oxford University Press, 1986), p. 403.
5 Charles Brockden Brown, *Wieland and Memoirs of Carwin the Biloquist*, ed. Jay Fliegelman (New York: Penguin, 1991), p. 201. Subsequent references are to this edition and are given in parentheses in the text.
6 Charles Brockden Brown, *Edgar Huntly; or Memoirs of a Sleep Walker*, eds Philip Barnard and Stephen Shapiro (Indianapolis, IN: Hackett Publishing, 2006), p. 194. Subsequent references are to this edition and are given in parentheses in the text.
7 Yogita Goyal, *Romance, Diaspora, and Black Atlantic Literature* (Cambridge: Cambridge University Press, 2010), p. 36.

8   Eugenia DeLamotte, 'White Terror, Black Dreams: Gothic Constructions of Race in the Nineteenth Century', in Ruth B. Anolik and Douglas L. Howard (eds), *The Gothic Other: Racial and Social Constructions in the Literary Imagination* (Jefferson, NC: McFarland, 2004), pp. 17–31, at pp. 28–9.
9   Walter Benn Michaels, *Our America: Nativism, Modernism, and Pluralism* (Durham, NC: Duke University Press, 1995), p. 59.
10 Laura Doyle, 'Double Crossings: Black Yankees, Pauline Hopkins and the Atlantic World', in Daniel Maudlin and Robin Peel (eds), *The Materials of Exchange between Britain and North East America, 1750–1900* (New York: Routledge, 2016), pp. 53–64, at pp. 59–60.
11 Deborah E. McDowell, 'Introduction', *Of One Blood; or, the Hidden Self* (New York: Washington Square Press, 2004), pp. v–ix.
12 Geoffrey Sanborn, 'The Wind of Words: Plagiarism and Intertextuality in *Of One Blood*', *J19: The Journal of Nineteenth-Century Americanists*, 3:1 (2015), 67–87.
13 *Ibid.*, 73.
14 *Ibid.*, 72.
15 Patrick Brantlinger, *Rule of Darkness: British Literature and Imperialism, 1830–1914* (Ithaca, NY: Cornell University Press, 1990), p. 253.
16 Pauline Hopkins, *Of One Blood. The Magazine Novels of Pauline Hopkins*, ed. Hazel B. Carby (Oxford: Oxford University Press, 1990), p. 515. Subsequent references are to this edition and are given in parentheses in the text.
17 All of Hopkins' Gothic-infused descriptions of Africa cited here are nearly direct (unattributed) quotations from stories in *Frank Leslie's Popular Monthly* and *Scribner's*; see Sanborn for specifics.
18 Maisha L. Wester, *African American Gothic: Screams From Shadowed Places* (New York: Palgrave Macmillan, 2012), p. 76.
19 *Ibid.*, pp. 93, 94.
20 Wai Chee Dimock, *Residues of Justice: Literature, Law, Philosophy* (Berkeley, CA: University of California Press, 1996), p. 10.
21 See Edwin S. Shneidman, *The Suicidal Mind* (Oxford: Oxford University Press, 1998), p. 133.
22 Michael MacDonald and Terence R. Murphy, *Sleepless Souls: Suicide in Early Modern England* (Oxford: Clarendon Press, 1990), p. 16.
23 Cynthia Schrager's work pointed me to this information and this story. See her article, 'The New Psychology and the Politics of Race: Pauline Hopkins and William James', in John Cullen Gruesser (ed.), *The Unruly Voice: Rediscovering Pauline Elizabeth Hopkins* (Urbana, IL: University of Illinois Press, 1996), pp. 182–209, at pp. 184–6. See also Thomas Otten, who suggests that this story 'may well be Hopkins's first published piece of fiction', in 'Pauline Hopkins and the Hidden Self of Race', *ELH*, 59:1 (1992), 227–56, at 235.
24 Pauline Hopkins, 'The Mystery Within Us', in Elizabeth Ammons (ed.), *Short Fiction by Black Women, 1900–1920* (Oxford: Oxford University Press, 1991), pp. 21–6, at p. 23. Subsequent references are to this edition and are given in parentheses in the text.
25 Julie-Marie Strange, *Death, Grief and Poverty in Britain, 1870–1914* (Cambridge: Cambridge University Press, 2005), p. 61.

26 For further discussion of suicides on slave ships, on recapture attempts and during and after slave rebellion attempts, see David Lester, 'Suicidal Behavior in African-American Slaves', *Omega: Journal of Death & Dying*, 37:1 (1998), 1–13.
27 William D. Piersen, 'White Cannibals, Black Martyrs: Fear, Depression, and Religious Faith as Causes of Suicide Among New Slaves', *The Journal of Negro History*, 62:2 (1977), 147–59, at 147.
28 Olaudah Equiano, *The Interesting Narrative of Olaudah Equiano*, ed. Vincent Carretta (New York: Penguin Books, 1995), p. 59.

7

Fiona Peters

Gothic influences: darkness and suicide in the work of Patricia Highsmith

Patricia Highsmith held very strong beliefs when it came to suicide. When Highsmith's friend Arthur Koestler committed suicide with his wife, due to his leukaemia and Parkinson's disease, she was both shocked and furious. Andrew Wilson describes a friend of Highsmith, Jonathon Kent, recalling his experience of this:

> 'The only time I ever saw Pat morally outraged was when she talked about the deaths of Arthur and Cynthia Koestler', says Jonathon Kent. 'She felt that Koestler had persuaded Cynthia to kill herself and that was immoral. As she talked about it her face blackened, and she was very angry. She said that she would never forgive him.'[1]

Patricia Highsmith's novels are murderous affairs: beyond the Ripliad (the five novels that feature her best-known, amoral and guilt-free and immoral serial killer, Tom Ripley), the rest of her other eighteen novels and numerous short stories often grapple with the implications of the protagonists' murderous and sometimes suicidal thoughts. In the non-Ripley novels, Highsmith's protagonists often feel what could be described as an overabundance of guilt over their crimes, both real and imagined. The author herself made a clear distinction between her more 'depressive' novels such as *Edith's Diary* and the Ripley novels (to which she turned to 'cheer herself up'), the latter presenting us with a hero who effectively managed without the human characteristics of conscience and morality: 'Ripley is funny, I hope. He's amoral, in a way he's a flexible sort of character. I consider him an adventurer; he came from an ordinary, rather limited background in the U.S., and took the plunge into Europe. He's amoral about murder – he does it and then he reasons it away.' Ripley, she says, is an exception in her books. Other characters are very much concerned with conscience. 'They're always chewing over their guilt, wondering how well they'll sleep at night with that on their conscience.'[2]

So Highsmith's twenty-three novels and many short stories address the act of killing in multiple ways, but notably it is what she perceives as the 'crime' of suicide that exercises and 'morally outrages' her. Suicide and premature death haunted Highsmith's life like a dark spectre. As Andrew Wilson documents, one lover, Allela Cornell, drank nitric acid, suffering a long and painful death in 1946. In 1953, Highsmith left another lover, Ellen Hill, to attempt suicide after a blazing row (Hill lapsed into a coma but survived).[3] Other lovers also committed suicide, including the woman on which Highsmith's lesbian novel *Carol* was based. In her 1954 novel *The Blunderer*, she portrays the attempted suicide of protagonist Walter Stackhouse's wife Clara in an unsympathetic and cold manner. This character is viewed as neurotic and unstable and is in part based on Ellen Hill, Highsmith's own lover.

She describes Clara's drug-induced coma in a manner close to her own experience with Hill:

> Walter could not escape the fact that he had known that she was going to take the pills. He could tell himself that he hadn't really thought she would take them, because she hadn't the other time, but this time had been different and he knew it. In a sense, he thought, he had killed her – if she died. And therefore he thought that he must have wanted to kill her.[4]

In this novel, Walter goes to the cinema and forces himself to sit through a movie knowing full well that Clara could be dying while he has absented himself from her. This is an almost direct transposition of Highsmith's own actions when she saw Ellen Hill take an overdose. It is symptomatic of her pragmatic approach to being expected to take responsibility for the extreme and self-destructive actions of another person in a way that she viewed as manipulative:

> Highsmith, sickened by the sight of her, left the apartment, called on Kingsley and her husband Lars, before going to have a supper of hamburgers with a friend. She arrived back at home at two in the morning to find Ellen in a coma. On the typewriter, Ellen's suicide note read, 'I should have done this 20 years ago. This is no reflection on you.' Coffee and cold towels were no good so Pat had to call the doctor, who tried to pump Ellen's stomach.[5]

Highsmith's escape from responsibility was temporary, but her absence could have led to Ellen's death. She viewed suicide as a selfish and romantic gesture – even though she herself considered it when caught up in yet another unhappy love affair: 'For the first time suicide has crossed my mind – I think only in a romantic way. It is generally selfish, which is my main objection to it.'[6] Many of Highsmith's 'heroes', while not committing suicide, self-obliterate instead through recourse to psychotic and obsessional behaviours that in effect render their social interaction with the everyday world impossible to sustain – in effect, suicide of the psyche and not the body. Several of Highsmith's novels touch on the theme of suicide and at the same time display Gothic tropes in their use of darkness, for example *Those Who Walk Away* (1967). In the setting of a dark, ghostly and sinister Rome, a father pursues a young man whom he believes drove his daughter, the young man's wife, to suicide. As mentioned already, *The Blunderer* explores the theme of suicide, revealing the author's personal attitude towards it.

This chapter could concentrate solely on themes of darkness, nature and other Gothic-related motifs, and it does cover these in respect of two of Highsmith's novels, *Ripley Under Ground* (1970) and *The Boy Who Followed Ripley* (1980). However, the intention here is to go a little deeper than that, bringing into play the psychoanalytic theorisations of the 'two deaths', 'the act' and the 'death drive', to explore why suicide cannot be viewed as a purely individual act because it also, by its very nature, reveals psychic traits of the uncanny, monstrosity and the borderline between life and death – themes utilised in many crime fiction texts as well as being a mainstay of Gothic fiction.

In general, discussions of suicide and literature tend to concentrate on the individual and the effects that the act has on those around them. This is central, of course, but nevertheless neglects articulations of 'psychic suicide' that have relevance, specifically for the Gothic text but more generally for much crime fiction, in relation to the idea of the living dead, or monstrosity. Suicide can be viewed as the result of individual struggle, often due to depression or terminal disillusionment with life – self-murder based on a decision to eradicate life as it exists in both its physical and psychic dimensions. Trauma can lead to deferred suicide, often in survivors of historical events such as the Holocaust, who stay alive to testify and then subsequently commit suicide: writers such as Tadeusz Bowowski and Primo Levi being well-documented examples. In some major respects, the question of experiences that are beyond representation relates to these instances of 'deferred suicide' in ways that echo through literary texts, most notably the Gothic, with its references to the sublime and 'undead' liminal spaces. Primo Levi describes as the 'muselmann' those prisoners in Auschwitz and other concentration camps who retain a physical life, albeit an emaciated, almost dead shell, while having withdrawn psychically from the world of intersubjectivity, or in other words having committed psychic suicide while still physically alive. In this situation, the suicide of the self is not, strictly speaking, a choice but, rather, the only way to escape the daily brutalisation; however, it demonstrates the ways in which suicide is not a clear and reasoned act and can, in fact, be virtually imposed by the will of others, as I will argue in the discussion of *Ripley Under Ground*. Giorgio Agamben, in *Remnants of Auschwitz: The Witness and the Archive* (2000), argues that survivors' reasons for staying alive in the camps, for not committing suicide, were related to the need to remain 'afterwards' (if any afterwards could be imagined) to bear witness. Agamben cites Hermann Lanbein: 'I firmly decided that, despite everything that might happen to me, I would not take my own life ... since I did not want to suppress the witness that I could become.'[7] Agamben also cites Wolfgang Sofsky, who stated,

> Naturally, I could have thrown myself on the fence, because you can always do that. But I wanted to live. And what if that miracle happens we're all waiting for? Maybe we'll be liberated, today or tomorrow. Then I'll have my revenge, then I'll tell the whole world what happened here – inside there.[8]

Raising questions of those driven into situations in which suicide becomes something to react *against* rather than the annihilation of self as an active choice can lead to a consideration of individual suicide, as Jared Stark argues in 'Suicide After Auschwitz':

> Indeed, the difficulty of comparing suicide inside and outside the camps is apparent from the difference between the questions and aims that motivate the study of one or the other: whereas conventional studies of suicide attempt to understand why suicide takes place at all, usually with a view towards reforming or healing the conditions that encourage or fail to discourage suicide, suicide in the camps begin, explicitly or implicitly, with the question of why it did *not* take place (or not on a massive scale) under conditions that should have been particularly generative of suicide.[9]

Slavoj Žižek interprets French psychoanalyst Jacques Lacan's notion of 'the two deaths' in a way that is useful here and can be linked to his theory of 'the act', which I would argue can apply to the 'act' of murder and the 'act' of suicide in ways that are applicable to both Gothic and crime fiction representations within literary texts. The concepts of guilt and shame are applicable here also. Žižek argues that the usual binary between life and death can be subverted insofar as it is possible to exist both in a living death or a deathly life. The point here is that we can die not just once, but twice. Death in the real, the disintegration of our actual bodies, but also a Symbolic death:

> This does not involve the annihilation of our actual bodies, rather it entails the destruction of our Symbolic universe and the extermination of our subject positions. We can this suffer a living death where we are excluded from the Symbolic and no longer exist for the Other.[10]

The other, in this instance, is our Symbolic framework in which we are considered human by those around us – not an individual other but the social network that includes us as 'human'. For Žižek, going mad or being excluded from society are two possibilities for the deathly life, and it seems that the extremity of social exclusion (whether the self-exclusion of the potential individual suicide or the traumatised prisoner) means that the gap between the two can manifest in representations of the monstrous and uncanny, perfect within the Gothic framework but also included in crime fiction. Central to Lacanian theory (on which Žižek bases much of his own arguments) is the argument that the space between the 'two deaths' is filled not with desire that is excluded but with an unconditional and repetitive demand to do or tell what cannot be represented. By this, he means that the notion that there is any direct recourse to biological essentialism (whether in respect of sexual difference or to provide a stable identity that exists outside identification and language) is false. If that is the case, then the human subject can cease to exist within the Symbolic and revert to previous *imagos* of the pre-Symbolic Imaginary body: 'These are the images of castration, mutilation, dismemberment, dislocation, evisceration, devouring, bursting open of the body, in short, the *imagos* that I have grouped together under the apparently structural term of the *imagos of the fragmented body*.'[11] Slavoj Žižek utilises Lacan's notoriously opaque style and takes this further and into popular culture with its representations of the 'hollowed out' human subject in his work *Looking Awry: An Introduction to Jacques Lacan Through Popular Culture*, when he describes the 'two deaths' as 'the fantasy of a person who does not want to stay dead but returns again and again to pose a threat to the living'.[12]

There is a strong link between this aspect of Lacanian theory and Freud's conception of the death drive as first articulated in 'Beyond the Pleasure Principle' (1920). This much-maligned speculative piece is without doubt the most important Freudian paper in respect of suicide, insofar as it problematises his previous conception of the pleasure principle. Through his observations of the effects of psychic trauma in the First World War and other events, Freud developed the term 'traumatic neurosis' which led him to acknowledge that his previous belief that dreams acted as the fulfilment of a wish was not necessarily the case. He goes on to introduce his concept of repetition compulsion through the medium of play as a way that a small child learns how to cope with the absence of its mother, what Freud calls a great cultural achievement:

> the instinctual renunciation (that is, the renunciation of instinctual satisfaction) which he had made in allowing his mother to go away without protesting. He compensated for this, as it were, by himself staging the disappearance and return of the objects within his reach.[13]

However, rather than acting as a protection against loss, Freud argued that repetition compulsion can lead to the repetition of unpleasurable thoughts and feelings, instead of being a process of working through towards an end result in which the unpleasant experience becomes expunged.

The concept of the death drive develops when Freud tries to reconcile the impetus towards self-destruction by unpleasurable repetition (often turned outwards from the self into aggressive tendencies) by positing an opposition between the ego or death instincts and the sexual or life instincts. He does not view the death drive as necessarily a flight towards suicide as much as a tendency towards a pre-birth – an inorganic state, free from the vicissitudes of the traumatic and destructive nature of everyday life. But of course suicide is the extreme manifestation of the death drive unchecked and, while vigorously contested by some, has been adopted as a central aspect in our understanding of self-destructive behaviour. Jacques Lacan views it as an essential component of every human drive, while Žižek uses the concept in much of his work on popular culture, theorising it as a kind of zombie drive and thus linking it to areas directly relevant to pleasure as represented in Gothic and crime fiction.

This chapter argues that Patricia Highsmith's novels reflect the ways in which she approaches the question of suicide in her personal life and beliefs and that they also articulate in literary form the psychoanalytic theories I have briefly outlined. The Gothic continues to inflect crime fiction with its themes of terror, frightening and overwhelming feelings, evil and horror. Highsmith is renowned for the often unique ways in which she addresses the psychological in her novels – she seduces the reader to identify with human beings trapped in situations where death is inevitable, whether through murder, suicide or psychotic acts. The chapter examines how suicide or self-murder, perhaps the darkest of acts, accesses the Gothic in ways not usually considered within the context of crime writing. Emphasis will also be placed on the ways in which the theme of suicide both foregrounds crime fiction's debt to the Gothic *and* provides an interdisciplinary presence that binds the two genres together. It could be argued that by approaching the necessary darkness of suicide, classic Gothic tropes emerge, conscious or otherwise.

Crime fiction is viewed, naïvely perhaps, as the genre that must incorporate murder (although the crime at the heart of arguably the first full-length crime fiction text, Wilkie Collins' *The Moonstone* [1868], is in fact a theft). This is generally represented as murder of the other, not self-murder. If we use the concept of self-murder to describe the act of suicide, then it is perhaps easier to articulate within the parameters of crime and thus crime fiction. A key difference between crime fiction and the Gothic is of course that in crime fiction the protagonist or victim, once dead, cannot re-emerge later in any vampiric or other manifestation – once dead, within crime fiction, then dead forever. It could be argued that within the loose generic category of crime fiction, death is something that is both central and at the same time irreversible. The consequences of death by murder or self-murder (suicide), and the ongoing investigations that arise, are key.

It is my contention that the genres of the Gothic and crime fiction of the late twentieth and early twenty-first centuries are of particular importance at this point in time. Crime fiction is gaining in popularity year on year, and one of the reasons is the ways that it addresses key issues of human experience, cross-culturally and in a global sense. It is clear that crime fiction is currently reworking and subverting certain fundamental conventions of its 'traditional' generic categorisation, as is the Gothic. Crime fiction, while often adhering to convention and thus offering a form of reassurance in an unstable world, has, I argue, increasingly projected a radically de-stabilised perspective on the world. It is well documented that Patricia Highsmith's work has been a prime mover in these developments.

Environment, place, has long been at the forefront of literary texts, and of course both crime fiction and the Gothic cannot be understood without recourse to the ways in which environment plays its part in creating the atmosphere and conditions conducive to the action that occurs. Aligned with that, the destabilising use of otherness through 'outsiders' stretches back at least to Agatha Christie's Hercule Poirot. Themes regarding place that crime fiction plunders the Gothic tradition to utilise and expand include seeming ghosts, vampires, werewolves and other key stock of the Gothic tradition. As the Gothic genre itself twists these tropes and reinvents itself through time, so crime fiction picks up and plays with myth and legend. Through the figure of the flesh-and-blood detective, readers can be led to identify, confront and overcome deep-seated anxieties that within the Gothic tradition have been written through a preoccupation with the fragility of the border between life and death. As mentioned previously, in crime fiction, key figures within the narrative, while able to occupy liminal spaces to some extent, must ultimately situate themselves on one side of the line between life and death. Suicide has long been utilised in literary texts that include elements of the Gothic – such as Goethe's *The Suffering of Young Werther* (1774) (a text that Mary Shelley has Frankenstein's Creature read) and Robert Louis Stevenson's *Strange Case of Dr Jekyll and Mr Hyde* (1886). A major theme in crime fiction, like the Gothic, represents the city as modern, rational and logical and at the same time nightmarish, dark and uncanny. The city is a place both of safety and of threat, disturbing the notion of 'home' as stable, replacing it with a Freudian sense of 'unheimlich'.

Neil Gordon argues that Highsmith, like Richard Yates, is a Gothic novelist who has

> worked with a very limited palette of human emotions, one that most notably excludes joy or love, connection or harmony, completion or satisfaction, differentiated from the classically defined Gothic by the fact that the horrors they describe are not supernatural and exist largely in an interior landscape, from which they haunt their characters' always subjective and often liquored-up experience of reality.[14]

This quote highlights the ways in which Gothic elements including the horrific and the sublime are adopted by writers such as Highsmith, and interiorised through character and dissociation with reality. While she does refer to suicide in some short stories it is, however, through two of her 'Ripliad' series, the second, *Ripley Under Ground* and the fourth, *The Boy Who Followed Ripley*, that I intend to approach the topic here. The character that displays most clearly the characteristics picked up by Neil Gordon in the previous quote is the anti-hero (and, according to some critics, psychopath) Tom Ripley. He certainly displays a restricted palette of human emotions which allows his creator to have him act in ways that most people would abhor. Highsmith created the character of Tom Ripley in 1954 when, while in Italy, she spotted a young man walking alone on a beach in Positano at 6.00 a.m.:

> Then I noticed a solitary young man in shorts and sandals with a towel flung over his shoulder, making his way alone along the beach from right to left … I could just see that his hair was straight and darkish. There was an element of pensiveness about him, maybe unease. And why was he alone?[15]

The first and best-known Ripley novel is *The Talented Mr Ripley* (1955). In this text, Tom Ripley, a young American man who had been living on the fringes of upper-class New York society while committing small acts of petty crime, chances on an opportunity to travel to the 'old world' of Europe to bring back the son of a wealthy businessman whose family believe he is wasting his life as a dilettante, painting in Italy when he should be taking up his role in running the family business. Tom eventually murders the young man, Dickie Greenleaf, temporarily taking on his identity until he has ensured that Dickie's income will go to him, Tom Ripley, as beneficiary of his will.

In Highsmith's second Tom Ripley novel, *Ripley Under Ground*, Tom Ripley is married and living a bucolic existence, having bought a bourgeois country house in a small town south of Paris. He has benefited from Dickie Greenleaf's money, but to make a little income alongside indulging his penchant for transgression of the legal and moral law he has become involved with an art forgery ring. A painter, Derwatt, committed suicide on a beach in Greece, a fact known only to his inner circle who spread the false information that he is living as a recluse in Mexico. Among Derwatt's friends is another talented painter called Bernard Tufts who continues painting in the 'Derwatt' style, producing works that sell for ever-increasing prices. When an American private collector, Murchison, visits the London gallery that represents Derwatt and questions the change in his use of colour, this sets him on a trail to try to discover if someone has been forging Derwatts, Tom is brought in to impersonate the dead artist. The unconvinced

Murchison then visits Tom Ripley (as himself, a collector of the paintings) at his home in France, where he meets an untimely death when Tom kills him in his wine cellar using as a weapon a particularly good bottle of Margaux. After this, Bernard Tufts visits Tom in France and is enlisted into helping him to dispose of Murchison's body. Highsmith utilises this task to represent the differences in attitude and sensibility of the two men in the moments after they dispose of the body, with Tom happy and content while Bernard vomits at the side of the road: 'Tom felt sorry for him. Himself so merry and well, and Bernard sick at his stomach. Bernard stayed two minutes, three, four, Tom thought.'[16]

Bernard is a depressive who threatens Tom with exposure of the forgery ring and eventually hangs a dummy from the cellar in Tom's house in an act of fake suicide. Tom's wife finds the 'body', and as Tom himself ventures down to the cellar he reflects on this, to him, excellent solution: 'At least this was suicide, Tom thought: That ought to be provable. It wasn't murder' (150). A note from Bernard reads,

> I hang myself in effigy in your house. It is Bernard Tufts that I hang, not Derwatt. For D. I do penance in the only way I can, which is to kill the self I have been for the last five years. Now to continue and try to do my work honestly in what is left of my life. (152)

After twice attempting to murder Tom in his home and making the decision to stop forging Derwatts, Bernard leaves for Salzburg. Tom realises that Bernard is contemplating suicide and, after looking for him in Greece and Paris, eventually tracks him down in Salzburg. An extremely strange and dangerous game begins as Tom stalks Bernard through the city but does not reveal himself to Bernard except insofar as he allows him a glimpse of himself at strategic moments. Thus Bernard's anxiety increases since he thinks he has seen a ghost, believing that he was successful in his second attempt to murder Tom: 'Tom realised that that was exactly what Bernard had thought he had seen, a ghost. A ghost of Tom Ripley, the man he had killed' (230). Soon after this Gothic moment, one that Tom finds funny, Bernard tries to escape from 'the ghost', leaving the town on foot and heading up into the foothills of the surrounding mountains. He does not set off immediately though, leaving Tom plenty of time to confess that he is in fact not a ghost and still alive and well. If his intention was to deter Bernard from committing suicide then this behaviour does not work, as it clearly has the opposite effect. Tom instead bides his time, allowing Bernard to become more and more distressed despite his reassurances to himself that he is going to, he wants to and he must, help Bernard. This contradiction between action and intent thus confuses the issue as to whether Tom is, in fact, driving Bernard to suicide (as my reading argues) or holding back because he does not know what to do. In typical Ripley fashion, the moments when Tom sees Bernard are bland and lacking in psychological insight – however, the reader is left in no doubt that Tom will not help Bernard as it is clearly not in his own interest: 'Each glimpse of Bernard sent a weird pain through Tom: it was as if he were seeing someone already in the throes of death, yet walking about' (234).

Knowing Bernard to be suicidal, Tom follows him at a distance as he walks out of town and up the hill: 'He was going to kill himself, Tom realised. Maybe not this instant. Maybe he would walk around and come back in an hour, in two hours. Maybe this evening' (235). During Bernard's route up the mountainside he stops at a small bar for a glass of wine, and at this crucial moment Tom steps into the bar and reveals himself to Bernard then quickly, without speaking, exits the bar backwards. After continuing to follow Bernard some eight kilometres up into the mountains from Salzburg while keeping hidden from view, Tom again reveals himself to Bernard, terrifying him and causing him to leap to his death. Tom rationalises his actions to himself, twisting the narrative to show himself in the best possible light:

> Tom began to realize that he had willed or wished Bernard's suicide, while at the same time, since he had known Bernard was going to kill himself, Tom could hardly accuse himself of forcing suicide upon Bernard. On the contrary, Tom had shown himself pretty clearly alive – several times unless Bernard preferred to see a ghost. (240)

After some abject and macabre passages where Tom attempts to cremate and bury the body, trying to make it appear that the body is that of Derwatt while destroying evidence that it is in fact Bernard's, Tom frees himself of the art forgery allegations, enabling him to continue to lead the good life to which he has become accustomed. This novel contains multiple Gothic themes throughout; both mountains and the domestic home space are utilised to evoke the terrors both of the chase and the homely, the sublime and the domestic. The uncanny similarities to *Frankenstein* (1818), of chase, creation and destruction, dominate the novel.

In *The Boy Who Followed Ripley*, the representation of suicide is quite different. This book finds Tom Ripley again in residence at his

French home *Belle Ombre* ('Beautiful Shadow'), still peripherally involved with the London gallery that was established with the sale of fake Derwatts, and content in his aesthetically pleasing life. By this, the fourth Ripley novel, Tom is settled into a contented lifestyle that suits him. The third and previous Ripley novel *Ripley's Game* (1974) demonstrates Tom's interfering side. In this novel he influences a terminally ill local man to become involved in Mafia killings with him, mainly out of boredom. In *Ripley's Game*, Tom's unique moral code is foregrounded as he dispatches members of the Mafia to rid the world of vermin, as he sees them, rather than from expediency in his previous killings and his hounding of the depressed Bernard to death in the mountains in *Ripley Under Ground*. While Tom remains free of guilt, and his murders go unpunished both in respect of the law and his own physical stability, the suicide in *The Boy Who Followed Ripley* goes further into affecting his life than the other texts in the Ripliad.

The Boy Who Followed Ripley begins with Tom Ripley's feeling that he is being followed as he goes about his daily business in *Belle Ombre*. One evening, as he returns home from his local village bar, he feels that somebody is following him in the dark. Instead of being scared by the possibility of being mugged or worse, Tom invites the boy into his home, arriving from the unlit darkness of the outside lanes into *Belle Ombre*, a well-lit sanctuary that reflects its name:

> 'You're welcome to come in for a beer, if you like.' The boy's dark brows frowned a little, he bit his underlip and looked up dismally at Belle Ombre's two front turrets, as if whether to come in were a big decision.[17]

The Boy Who Followed Ripley is in some ways a complete reversal of the way the 'act' of suicide is activated and instigated in *Ripley Under Ground*. In that novel, Tom stalks Bernard and almost terrifies him into suicide. Bernard has reached the point where his existence is detaching from the Symbolic universe, and Tom finds it easy to tip him over the edge, both metaphorically and literally. In *The Boy Who Followed Ripley*, the boy of the title, Frank Pierson, is a sixteen-year-old American who, we discover, has murdered his wealthy wheelchair-bound father by pushing him over a cliff. Tom recognises something of himself in Frank and sets out to help him after he is kidnapped and a ransom payment demanded.

While Tom sees himself in Frank, there are substantive differences that he fails to take account of or recognise, such as the guilt that

Frank experiences about his patricide. The final section of the novel takes place at Frank's family home in Maine when Tom returns him to his family, who are ignorant about Frank's actions. The two walk in the dark towards the edge of the cliff where the murder occurred:

> *So here is where it happened,* Tom thought, then he saw Frank walking past him, hands in the back pockets of his jeans, to the edge of the cliff, and he saw the boy look down. Tom had an instant's fear for Frank, because it was so dark, and the boy seemed so near to the edge, even though the edge did slope up a little, Tom could now see. (301)

Frank had told his mother that his father had committed suicide, and while his extended family were unsure if it had been suicide or an accident, no suspicion was explicitly laid at Frank's door (except by Susie, an elderly housekeeper). For Tom Ripley, this meant that Frank should be able to put it behind him and live his life without regret or guilt, as he himself had done since his killing of Dickie Greenleaf, in *The Talented Mr Ripley*.

Shortly after he visits the cliff's edge with Frank, Tom sees him there again, alone: 'The boy looked down. But mostly he looked at the sea, and he seemed, to Tom, to take a deep breath and to relax. Then he stepped backward' (318). In this instance, Tom manages to distract Frank at the last moment and saves him, but he soon tries again when alone and this time succeeds. Tom discovers the body:

> He did not even breathe for several seconds, until he realized that he was shaking, and in danger of falling off the cliff himself. The boy was dead, and there was no use of anything, of trying anything by way of saving him. (322)

To conclude, *The Boy Who Followed Ripley* and *Ripley Under Ground* both demonstrate Gothic themes in the most obvious way, including tropes such as darkness, cliffs and mountains, all imbued with a sense of the sublime, unlike the domestic, rather sordid attempted suicide that so appalled Highsmith when her girlfriend tried it – with its base level attention-seeking behaviour, as Highsmith saw it. On a deeper level, Frank in *The Boy Who Followed Ripley* can be viewed as living in the state, theorised by Lacan and often illustrated by theories of collective trauma, of the two deaths – in his case, that of a dead psyche in a still living body. Similarly, Bernard in *Ripley Under Ground* is virtually stalked to his physical annihilation by Tom Ripley (in a direct reversal, he tries his very best to save Frank). As an anomaly, a guilt-free human being functioning in a Symbolic universe of other people whom he can relate to only on a surface level (Frank is an exception here), Tom can recognise that Bernard is suicidal anyway, has given up on the project towards life and again, is a dead psyche in a living body. The 'act' of suicide represents a particularly Gothic sensibility in these instances that has resonance beyond the obvious and can lead to further discussion on life and death in both crime fiction and Gothic.

Notes

1 Andrew Wilson, *Beautiful Shadow: A Life of Patricia Highsmith* (London: Bloomsbury, 2003), p. 396.
2 Hugh Herbert, 'Maid a'killin', Review of *Ripley's Game*, *Arts Guardian*, 18 March 1974. From Fiona Peters, *Anxiety and Evil in the Writings of Patricia Highsmith* (London: Routledge, 2011), p. 146.
3 Wilson, *Beautiful Shadow*, p. 184. See also Andrew Wilson, '"Instantly I Love Her": The Affairs that Inspired Carol', www.telegraph.co.uk/film/carol/true-story-patricia-highsmith-lesbian affairs/, accessed 21 May 2018.
4 Patricia Highsmith, *The Blunderer* (London: Penguin, 1988), p. 54.
5 Wilson, *Beautiful Shadow*, p. 184.
6 *Ibid.*, p. 248.
7 Hermann Langbein, *Auschwitz, Zeugnisse and Brichte*, eds H. G. Adler, Herman Langbein and Ella Lindens-Reiner (Frankfurt: Athenäum, 1988), p. 186, quoted by Giorgio Agamben, *Remnants of Auschwitz: The Witness and the Archive* (New York: Zone Books, 2002), p. 15.
8 Wolfgang Sofsky, *The Order of Terror: The Concentration Camp*, trans. William Templar (Princeton, NJ: Princeton University Press, 1997), p. 340, quoted by Agamben, *Remnants of Auschwitz*, p. 15.
9 Jared Stark, 'Suicide after Auschwitz', *Yale Journal of Criticism*, 14:1 (2001), 93–114, at 94.
10 Tony Myers, *Slavoj Žižek* (London: Routledge Press, 2003), p. 106.
11 Jacques Lacan, 'Aggressivity in Psychoanalysis', in *Écrits: A Selection*, trans. A. Sheridan (London: Tavistock, 1977), pp. 8–29, at p. 15.
12 Slavoj Žižek, *Looking Awry: An Introduction to Jacques Lacan Through Popular Culture* (Cambridge, MA: The MIT Press, 1992), p. 22.
13 Sigmund Freud, 'Beyond the Pleasure Principle', in *Penguin Freud Library Vol 11: On Metapsychology*, trans. J. Strachey (London: Penguin, 1981), p. 285.
14 Neil Gordon, 'Murder of the Middle Class', *The Nation*, 13 September 2001, www.thenation.com/article/murder-middle-class/
15 Cited in Wilson, *Beautiful Shadow*, p. 195.
16 Patricia Highsmith, *Ripley Under Ground* (London: Vintage, 1999), p. 121. Subsequent references are to the edition and are given in parentheses in the text.
17 Patricia Highsmith, *The Boy Who Followed Ripley* (London: Penguin, 1980), p. 12. Subsequent references are to the edition and are given in parentheses in the text.

8

Xavier Aldana Reyes and Rachid M'Rabty

Better not to have been: Thomas Ligotti and the 'suicide' of the human race

Thomas Ligotti, who commanded the attention of horror aficionados in 1989 after his first collection of short stories, *Songs of a Dead Dreamer*, was picked up by the major American publishing company Carroll and Graf, has experienced a minor revival in the second decade of the twenty-first century.[1] Ligotti's scant writing in the twenty-first century, especially after he started taking medication for his bipolar disorder, has had little impact on his growing critical and popular appreciation.[2] First, horror publisher Subterranean Press, who had already collected previous material for *The Shadow at the Bottom of the World* (2005), offered Ligotti the opportunity of updating and rewriting his first three short story collections, which appeared in limited and 'definitive' editions in 2010, 2011 and 2012.[3] In 2011, another collection, *The Agonizing Resurrection of Victor Frankenstein and Other Gothic Tales* (1994), was similarly revised and published in an exclusive signed limited edition by Centipede Press. Beyond the nostalgic world of horror cultdom, where Ligotti has over the years received due acknowledgement, the author has grown in popularity. His pessimistic vision of the world as expounded in his non-fiction piece *The Conspiracy against the Human Race* (2010) found clear echoes in the critically acclaimed first series of HBO's *True Detective* (2014).[4] Finally, his first two collections, *Songs* and *Grimscribe: His Lives and Works* (1991), were re-published in a single volume by Penguin Classics in 2015, a canonising move comparable to the Library of America's controversial inclusion of a volume of H. P.

Lovecraft's stories, *Tales*, in 2005.[5] It seems there is something about Ligotti's writing and his advocacy of the desirable extinction of the human race that resonates with the underlying sense of melancholy and impending catastrophe of our Gothic present.[6]

Ligotti's Gothic horror belongs firmly in the traditions of Edgar Allan Poe and Lovecraft in its foregrounding of madness and altered (hallucinogenic) states of mind, and its expression of existential crises provoked by revelations about the nature of life as we understand it. Although the odd classical monster finds her/his way into some of his stories – the vampires in 'The Lost Art of Twilight' (1986); the rewritings of works by Bram Stoker or Mary Shelley, among others, in *The Agonizing Resurrection of Victor Frankenstein* – Ligotti's supernatural beings tend to be Hoffmannesque dummies, clowns and living puppets, or else obsessive, deranged experts in 'putrid arcana', as the narrator in 'The Sect of the Idiot' (1988) puts it.[7] Events normally take place in a geography left deliberately ambiguous to create a sense of pervasive universality and total spatial decentring: Ligotti's world is recognisably our own, yet is rendered thoroughly uncanny by a de-anchoring process that refuses to, for example, acknowledge nationalities or mention commercial brands. More interestingly for someone who has been strongly connected to Lovecraft, his stories are, with very few exceptions – most notably, 'The Last Feast of Harlequin' (1990) – devoid of aeon-old intergalactic creatures. This is because Ligotti's horror stems from his dark vision of humanity, and is driven by the scary reality of suffering and of the nonsensical nature of existence. Since the 2000s – especially in *My Work Is Not Yet Done* (2002) and in some of the stories in *Teatro Grottesco* (2006) – these nightmarish scenarios have been tinged by a critique of Kafkaesque capitalist microsystems, although these are largely used to facilitate metaphorical readings about the wider, and largely futile, human impulse to apply ordering systems to a universe ruled by chaos.

In this chapter, we consider the implications of Ligotti's complex beliefs, attributed to his ingrained pessimism, namely, his thoughts on suicide and his argumentative defence of antinatalism. Ligotti's perception of the role and value (or lack of it) of human existence permeates his fiction; his position is that it would be better not to have been than to live with the prospect of suffering. The 'horror of consciousness', as he calls it, has implications for the role that ecocide, the extinction of the human race as a collective decision, plays in the Ligottian universe. In it, the cessation of conscious life is both the optimal state of (non-)being and an inevitability, and it leads to the embrace of one's own decay (and that of the world). This profusely dark and melancholic vision of a species-wide suicide is one of the author's main contributions to the Gothic.

Antinatalism and the horror of consciousness

Ligotti's Gothic horror is one where the claustrophobia so often external in first-wave Gothic fiction, with its emphasis on, for example, female captivity, is interiorised, but not necessarily through the psychological landscapes well-developed by Victorian and fin-de-siècle fictions. In the latter, psychosis or other illnesses may stand in for pervasive hauntings of the mind. For Ligotti, Gothic horror is internal because consciousness is inescapable and, worst of all, the source of all our discontents; it has led us, most dramatically, to the knowledge of the certainty of our deaths. Unless severely mentally impaired, human beings are conscious of the inevitable end that awaits them and, if pessimists, of the fact that any joy or pleasure gained in this world is ultimately illusory and must succumb under the duress and strain of pain and fear as one comes closer to death.[8] In the introduction to *The Conspiracy against the Human Race,* Ligotti posits the idea that consciousness is, in fact, the 'parent of all horrors', a concept explored via the work of Norwegian philosopher Peter Wessel Zapffe – especially his 'The Last Messiah' ('Den sidste Messias') (1933) – who proposed that human existence is essentially a tragic incident in the development of organic life.[9] This key evolutionary change estranged humans from the rest of organic life, condemning humanity to a search for meaning in a nonsensical universe. Pain and fear of death, as well as survival and procreative instincts, have kept human beings alive thus far, so it is natural that they are inherent parts of the process of living.

According to Ligotti's reading of Wessel Zapffe, the realisation that these two negative constants in life – pain and the fear of death – are the only two universal principles by which human existence is organised is ultimately too crushing for most people to uphold constantly or seriously, so societies have found distracting mechanisms that either ignore the problem (entertainment, hedonism) or else counterbalance its negative aspects (religion, belief in a better afterlife). These strategies are, however, little more than illusions belying what, for Ligotti, is the unimpeachable truth that 'human life moves in only one direction – towards disease, damage, and death'.[10] Hence the 'biological paradox' of humanity: 'beings that cannot live with [their] consciousness and cannot live without it', their tragedy that of seeking transcendence from the petty and visceral baseness of life.[11] Because 'we feel shortchanged if there is nothing else for us than to survive, reproduce, and die', we are forced into the quixotic position of 'striving to be unself-conscious of what we are – hunks of spoiling flesh and disintegrating bones'.[12] Coping strategies include anything from substance abuse and its literal alteration of consciousness to the negation or occlusion of reality in ideology. The best example of the latter is the focus on the positive aspects of existence and the decision that overall, life is worth the suffering, or that it is definitely better than not having existed at all. For Ligotti, this state of affairs places humans in an intermediate stage between living and not living, and is what leads him to present them as live dummies or puppets, as believers in self-possession bloated with a laughable sense of self-importance. Relying on work in neurophilosophy by the likes of Thomas Metzinger, Ligotti also proposes that achieving a sense of self is essentially impossible and just as chimerical and pointless a process as teleology or the search for humanity's origins.[13]

The parameters outlined in the previous passages allow Ligotti to divide up the world into optimists, who choose to hang on to the positive aspects of life and decide that it is all worth the trouble, and pessimists. At the heart of pessimism lies the horrific proposition, a philosophical truism in essence, that, all things considered, it would be better not to have been, since existence is 'basically undesirable' and the world 'MALIGNANTLY USELESS'.[14] The logical reasoning behind this, and a rationale that cannot be totally proven or disproven, is that, because life involves suffering on a permanent basis – from the pangs of hunger to illness – it is indefensible. Ligotti's is not a vindictive position, but a mostly rational and intellectual one; as a pessimist, his 'primary concern is eliminating suffering', rather than further entrenching it.[15] Nobody can not be and have been or be at the same time, so arguments will differ on whether life is worth the hassle. Even then, because nothingness means no pain, non-being presents a much healthier and honest option in purely philosophical terms.[16] How or why this should be transposed into a series of actions is less clear, for direct suicide – a recurring suggestion and the only way out of consciousness – is not really an option most pessimists would consider. Not only is fear of death not overcome through suicide, but the prospect of the pain the process may cause, as well as its utter pointlessness (it does not change the fact that existence is essentially nonsensical), makes it less appealing than those opposing fundamental pessimism might otherwise entertain.

Insofar as Ligotti has a 'special plan for this world', his answer is antinatalism, the conscious decision by the entire human race to stop reproducing, which would lead to the extinction of the human race – its effective suicide.[17] Let us consider this proposal as Ligotti has presented it:

> Antinatalism is based on the principle that suffering of whatever kind or degree should not be caused or perpetuated, and that human existence necessarily entails suffering that we can neither escape nor justify, least of all by experiencing pleasures. Thus, the only way to end all suffering is to cease producing beings who suffer. In the abstract, I hold to that principle and believe that those who do not hold to it are simply of a different mindset. In everyday life, I live for the most part as a deluded individual except when I sit down and recall what I believe in principle.[18]

Two crucial points develop from even this brief exposition. The first is that the motives behind Ligotti's defence of antinatalism are not sadistic or intended to generate suffering in others. Crucially, antinatalism should not constitute the imposition of mass suicide by force or ideological brainwashing. On the contrary, Ligotti understands antinatalism as the least painful option for future generations, an idea in keeping with his insistence that he is also a 'socialist'.[19] Second, antinatalism does not seek to evangelise; its ultimate purpose is not to transform or radicalise non-believers. Antinatalism, for Ligotti, is a thought experiment that reflects his own beliefs about the pointlessness of human existence and, as he has made clear on various occasions, is a proposition he does not think stands any chance of catching on, given that it goes against everything that has kept the fabric of human life alive for thousands of years. Antinatalism is more than a simple opinion, however, for 'while no one can prove that there is any praiseworthy incentive to reproduce, there are cases in which most would agree there are indeed praiseworthy, or at least not blameworthy, incentives *not* to reproduce'.[20] The latter, naturally, includes the contribution – the creation – of a human being who will ineluctably feel pain and suffering, and will inevitably die.

As he has spelled out, *The Conspiracy against the Human Race* is also a treatise on how the horror of existence operates in supernatural horror. While Ligotti does not exactly make a case for its purpose or real-world value, he does attempt to explain how supernatural horror connects to a wider philosophy of the world. As someone who believes, at a personal level, that authorial voice is the most important thing about – in fact, inextricable from – the literary experience of a given text, Ligotti's vision permeates his fiction. The intertwinement between practice and philosophy is not a novelty in his *oeuvre*. His early 'Notes on the Writing of Horror: A Story' (1985), for example, proposed and exemplified what he considers are the three basic techniques of horror writing (the realist technique, the traditional Gothic technique and the experimental technique), only to then argue for another style, his, where 'readers would be distressed not by [an] isolated catastrophe ... but by the very existence of a world where such catastrophe is possible'.[21] In another piece, 'Professor Nobody's Little Lectures on Supernatural Horror' (1985), passages from which ended up in *Conspiracy*, Ligotti lays down the cathartic qualities of supernatural horror as a form of self-mockery for the pessimist, as a way of 'indulging in cruel pleasures against ourselves and our pretensions', of delighting in 'the Cosmic Macabre'.[22]

Ligotti's doom and gloom – or brave and realistic assessment of reality, depending on one's view – thus translates quite differently into his fiction. The encounter with the weird in Lovecraft, an encounter that pits humanity's insignificance against a vast chaotic cosmos (cosmic horror), is replaced with a clash with reality in which the world we know (understood in Ligotti as evil and horrific) is glimpsed via strange artefacts like special lenses or music boxes. Similarly, characters in stories such as 'The Spectacles in the Drawer' (1987) or 'Flowers of the Abyss' (1991) are afforded glimpses into 'a far-off realm of secret truth whose gateway is within the depths of our own blood', into 'the madness of things that to [their] mind[s] form ... the very foundation of existence'.[23] Significantly, however, these newfound dimensions are not so much alternative universes as they are a more faithful rendition of ours – the 'real' world superimposed on to the one in which we choose to believe. The latter is othered in Ligotti's fiction, rendered an 'unearthly realm' where only madness and/or death await, and thus works metaphorically and provides the desired weird effect, a 'subjective sense of strangeness'.[24] As Ligotti claims in his appreciation of weird fiction, weird experiences in fiction resonate with real life because an 'experience of the weird is a fundamental and inescapable fact of life'; 'like all such facts, it eventually finds its way into forms of artistic expression'.[25] In this respect, Ligotti's and Lovecraft's visions are contiguous, if their inflections sometimes differ representationally. Although the nightmarish revelations of a perennial darkness at the heart of all things in 'The Shadow at the Bottom of the World' (1991) or 'In the Shadow of Another World' (1991) are not intrinsically dissimilar to the 'abysses of clouds and smoke and lightning' in some of Lovecraft's more abstract horror tales, Ligotti's interest lies in the inherently hallucinatory experience of existence.[26] Both Lovecraft and Ligotti stage a chance confrontation with a world that cannot be comprehended, but Ligotti's characters are drawn by a species of death-drive to these revelations.

While both Lovecraft and Ligotti aim to create nightmarish scenarios, there is an impression of inevitability and mild conformist comfort in the latter. Nowhere is this double bind better articulated than at the end of 'The Night School' (1991), where darkness and the 'disease of the night' incarnated by one Instructor Carniero end up pervading the body of the narrator.[27] His final monologue is worth quoting in full:

> My desire to know something that I was sure was real about my existence, something that could help me in my existence before it was my time to die and be put into the earth to rot, or perhaps to have my cremated remains drift out of a chimney stack and sully the sky – that would never be fulfilled. I had learned nothing, and I was nothing. Yet instead of disappointment at my failure to fulfil my most intense desire, I felt a tremendous relief. The urge to know the fundamental things was now emptied from me, and I was more than content to be rid of it.[28]

While the encounter with utter darkness, the 'real' aspect of reality, often presented in a state of liquefying decay, is destructive for the human ego, it also offers some solace in its attack on self-deception. This is crucial both to Ligotti's conception of the world and to his literary output: there is no real earth-shattering instant, or if there is, this is portrayed metaphorically. The moment of horror occurs when we begin to see, through an awareness of our own decay and the impending inevitability of death, the world and humanity for what they are: meaningless, worthless and evil (insofar as intent is projected on to the endurance of pain without purpose).

Ligotti is not a fundamental nihilist, precisely because he does not believe in the concept of values; consciousness and free will are evolutionary mistakes that humans are unfortunate enough to have to live with. Despite an aesthetic and ethical engagement with nihilism throughout his fiction, Ligotti rejects any possibility of a positive outcome, hence his dismissal of Nietzschean nihilism and his vocal advocacy of extreme pessimism.[29] As a result, Ligotti's fiction undermines any impression that life, as experienced through egocentrism, hegemony or philosophy, can be overcome or transformed into anything other than an even more abstract and self-destructive experience. Ligotti's suicidal pessimism rejects any romantic or didactic belief in salvation. As in the fiction of his Gothic precursors, the sublime – albeit a perverse version that forgoes any sense of pleasure – is transposed on to decay and death, and it is only through the embrace of these, namely, the realisation of the true nature of existence as nightmarish, that one can achieve anything close to satisfaction. In his words,

> Crumminess and decay are actually qualities. ... To my sensibility, they don't feel like stages on the way to blackness. One can lose oneself in places and conditions of crumminess and decay. They're a refuge in which self-annihilation can take place without the terrors of death.[30]

To confront decay is to apprehend the horror of existence and thus to begin to imagine self-annihilation. If, as Ligotti writes in 'The Medusa' (1991), 'we may hide from horror only in the heart of horror', so, too, we may reduce existential anguish by embracing it in fictional terms.[31]

Imagining suicide and extinction

Against such a moral and aesthetic backdrop, the embrace of decay and suicide surface as the only viable means of alleviating the tragedy of conscious existence. Ligotti's is, of course, a fiction where no one is afforded the affirmation or relief that, philosophically speaking, suicide should bring, as this would be tantamount to a utopian ending, impertinent to the singular trajectory of existential misery of the author's vision. Instead, his horror is marked by uniquely bleak hallucinations of humankind's perpetual descent into disintegration. It is safe to say that Ligotti imagines, and has imagined, the willing ending of individuals and of communities, and that this is, as we have suggested, his most original contribution to the Gothic mode. Supernatural horror fiction, in its ability to probe the limits of reality as we understand it (or do not understand it), appears as the main vehicle for artistic expression through which to extend antinatalism.

It is important to note that, while suicide only appears in places in Ligotti's work, an undercurrent of pessimism and apathy permeates his entire *oeuvre*. Suicide, where it does appear, offers an imaginative opportunity to explore the implications of non-existence, and becomes a buffer zone for how suicide may be rethought as relief from pain. The dark veneer Ligotti sees in the shiny version of the world we sell ourselves is transmuted into the physical decay and ruination of places and communities, both of which hold a fascination for characters and lead to their downfalls.

Of the numerous short stories in which decay features significantly, 'Suicide by Imagination' (1994) is perhaps one of the most disturbing. Much like the society of which he is a reluctant part, the narrator of the story builds a life around a fundamental lie. For years, the man leads his friends to believe that his home is a grand setting, a fantasy impossible to sustain once the deterioration of the actual building becomes pronounced. This pyrrhic battle reflects the process whereby, as a species, humans have built a narrative of the world to obfuscate their plight with illness and, eventually, nothingness. The realisation of a suppressed reality drives the unnamed narrator to confront, imagine and feel his own death to the point where his projection of the absurdity of this state consumes him: 'And now he imagined the feeling of death as one previously beyond his imagination. This feeling was simply that of an eternally prolonged itching sensation.'[32] The trauma of the discovery of his rotting corpse by friends is only matched by their surprise at the state of ruin of their friend's home.[33] This scene is allegorical because it reflects humankind's masking of its terminal predicament; it lays bare the distracting spectacle, premised on self-delusion, which humans prefer to entertain. The confrontation with the decay that festers at the heart of all organic things is particularly troubling for the narrator's friends, so much so that each year, during autumn and winter – the seasons wherein vegetation struggles to survive, animals hibernate, nights grow longer – the trauma of what has been witnessed overcomes them in the form of a prolonged, malignant and persistent itch.[34] In light of this existentialist horror, self-harming (here brutal scratching) and suicide become the only viable prospects. The re-awakening to the 'real' in this story turns into a literal itch that will not scratch.

Death and decomposition also feature prominently throughout Ligotti's novella *My Work Is Not Yet Done*. The narrator, Frank Dominio, a man who suddenly finds himself dismissed for no obvious reason from the company where he works, begins to question the fairness of society and the kindness of others. Although we suspect he has always been a pessimist, working in this company has helped him notice that fellow colleagues and other persons are 'human detritus'.[35] But his realisation of the corruption of systems has many cognates in the story. Frank also enjoys spending time seeking out sites of ruin in the city, places that expose the cracks and fissures of the world at large. These spaces serve as a metaphor for human lived experience, as they make visible 'the fate of everything that ha[s] ever been and await[s] everything that w[ill] ever be'.[36] Decaying neighbourhoods, ruined buildings and dismal, corrupt and degenerate people eventually stir Frank towards suicide. As it does for the man in 'Suicide by Imagination', the possibility of not being comes as a relief from the sustained delusions of human egoism. The fantasy of suicide is the fantasy of a philosophical reprieve, a pessimistic assertion that life is suffered – agonised over – and that the most logical course of action remains the self-aware discontinuation of ourselves and, to break the chain of pain, of our species.

'As long as we have to live in this world, what could be more sensible than to want yourself and others to suffer as little as possible?', asks Ligotti.[37] Such noble, even ethical, desires, however, are never so simple in practice. While Ligotti's narrators, as has been argued, 'consistently express revulsion at humanity's role in a conspiracy of malignity', there seems to be little respite from such subordination to misery.[38] Death by suicide, particularly a blissful or an anaesthetised one that negates or bypasses the pain associated with death, is, on a number of occasions, teased as an impossibility because it ignores the most fundamental aspect of existence: suffering itself. When, in 'The Strange Design of Master Rignolo' (1989), Rignolo seeks the cessation of his life through a coming together in heady union with the Earth itself, he is punished for it by being buried alive, whereupon he is overcome by more agony and fear. Rignolo 'wanted out of this life without the pain and the fear', but, as his companions insinuate afterwards, the conspiratorial powers behind the universe could not allow him to succeed because that would 'set an example' that cannot be tolerated.[39] In Ligotti's world, the great conspiracy against humankind is that we must suffer both in this life and for this life, whether that is in our ceaseless expenditure of some form of excessive or excremental value that keeps the wheels of capitalist society moving, or else as a consequence of our perpetual state of decay as organic, sentient and cognisant creatures. Rignolo's attempt to anaesthetically end things on his own terms leads only to torture at the hands of unseen and brutal forces.

Significantly, suicide in Ligotti is tantamount not necessarily to the end of existence, rather to the cessation of the ego. In this way, suicide becomes something much more profound, namely, the annulment of human consciousness. For Frank, the troubled narrator of *My Work Is Not Yet Done*, life is a manifest delusion in which we are born out of nothing and kept alive despite ourselves. When Frank kills the cockroach to whose life-force his own is linked, what he feels is a modicum of relief, one for which the narrator lusts time and again.[40] Looking upon his own comatose body from a spectral position, he

> can only hope to know that feeling to its fullest when the moment comes and the river rushes in to drown [him] in its blackness. ... [He] cannot wait to tear into the tender flesh of [his] last victim, and with a single slash kill two. [He] cannot wait to be dead.[41]

Rather than the result of the ravings of a murderous maniac, suicide in this novella can in fact be read as a humanitarian attempt to abolish the suffering and fear of everyone on Earth. As becomes evident, Frank's death alludes to the wider act of ecocide for, 'by killing [him] self [he] felt that [he] would also be killing all of you ..., every swinish one of us in this puppet show of a world would be done with when that bus made contact with me'.[42] Naturally, that Frank feels humanity to be swinish in essence does somewhat colour his words, so that an act of compassion may be read as one of coercion or threat. If we follow Ligotti's (and, in this case, Frank's) thinking, however, the society in which we live, propounded by the wrong principles – those premised on prolonging and sustaining life – has bred 'swinish' behaviour. The act of terminal redemption, a true moment of messianic saving, is, however, cast as killing, for there is no way a pessimistic approach may be otherwise entertained by the general populace. Recasting heroism as an act of apparent villainy, or vice versa, also allows Ligotti to connect the ills of positivism with the profit-driven and incremental backbone of neoliberal capitalism. The enslaving systems of production of businesses and contemporary life thus mirror each other, and both are exposed as tyrannical, pointless and disingenuous. Suicide is fantasised about, imagined as panacea, as narrative *deus-ex-machina*.

Suicide in Ligotti can be actively endorsed, too, although this happens more rarely. In one of his last two published stories, 'Metaphysica

Morum' (2014), the narrator, overcome by visions and dreams of 'a whole new context' and no longer able to put up with things as they are, desperately craves suicide as a way out from his waking life.[43] However, as happens to painter Rignolo, the pain of death seems to outweigh that of continuance, and so he seeks an elusive painless end. Before committing suicide, the narrator feels it a 'moral right – real or irreal – to leave a suicide note expressing [his] ire to the unwitting doomed'.[44] Considering himself a 'fortuitous mutant', insofar as he seems out of sync with the rest of humankind, he sees the world as an inexplicable nightmare and human beings as receptacles for horror.[45] His suicide is the culmination of a 'redemptive demoralization', and by leaving a justification behind it, he seemingly hopes that his lament will serve as a catalyst for others. Suicidal pessimism is championed as the path to a future that 'longs for peace and freedom from suffering'.[46]

As we have argued, the moment of fear, for Ligotti, is that point where the falsity of the world, built on positivity and optimism, is revealed for what it truly is – a lie – and where we are forced to confront the inescapable decay of all organic life. This entails a form of awakening depicted artistically through an uncanny recognition of the unfamiliar that lies in the familiar. For Ligotti, 'ego-*life* is an illusion' to be undermined, so its annulment, via means of actual or metaphysical suicide, logically appeals to his hopeless subjects.[47] As it is better not to have been, Ligotti's sympathy towards suicide is pronounced. Yet, he concedes that the act 'resolves nothing'; the collective and existential suffering of humankind can only be alleviated through ecocide. Confronted with instances of existentialist horror, the possibility of total annihilation materialises for humans as the only real solution to the painful nightmare of consciousness. But Ligotti's antinatalist proposition remains largely an intellectual experiment, teased out to justify his standpoint to those who may otherwise deem him a miserable misanthrope; individual and/or collective suicide stays a projected fantasy of liberation, rather than a true ontological call to arms. This is not to say that his work lacks value, purpose or pleasure. As with other forms of Gothic horror, there is solace to be found in the process of exposing despair, of disentangling fascination from revulsion to show where these emotions imbricate. Ligotti's fiction is an imaginative extension of his philosophical vision of existence, a true *memento mori* that manages to overturn the world as we know it by positing extinction as desirable and the life of thought as the greatest tragedy. After Lovecraft, or even before him, Ligotti stands as the best cosmic pessimist of all time, and his modern Gothic horror as some of the darkest fiction to ever prod the illogic of life to its apparently natural suicidal endpoint.

Notes

1 The collection originally appeared in the United States in 1986 in a limited edition of 300 copies, published by Silver Scarab Press. The stories had been published in horror fanzines such as *Nyctalops*, *Fantasy Tales* and *Fantasy Macabre* throughout the 1980s.
2 In interviews throughout the years, Ligotti has spoken, sometimes at length and earnestly, about his various ailments, including panic-anxiety disorder, anhedonia and, more recently, a severe attack of diverticulitis, as well as of the effects these have had on his literary production. Mood stabilisers have had a noticeable impact on his capacity and desire to write, and he claims to have written most of his work during hypomanic phases. See Pål Flakk, 'Interview with Thomas Ligotti' (2012), in Matt Cardin (ed.), *Born to Fear: Interviews with Thomas Ligotti* (Burton, MI: Subterranean Press, 2014), pp. 207–33, at pp. 210–11.
3 We are quoting from the promotional material on the publisher's website. See *Subterranean Press*, https://subterraneanpress.com/store/product_detail/noctuary, accessed 1 September 2016.
4 The Ligottian echoes were such that a few fans questioned whether the television series had plagiarised his work. See Mike Davis, 'Did the Writer of *True Detective* Plagiarize Thomas Ligotti and Others?', *Lovecraftzine.com*, 4 August 2014, https://lovecraftzine.com/2014/08/04/did-the-writer-of-true-detective-plagiarize-thomas-ligotti-and-others/, accessed 1 September 2016.
5 Penguin Classics has gradually opened up to weird, Gothic and supernatural writers, with new publications in recent years of works by Clark Ashton Smith, Ray Russell, Charles Beaumont, Lord Dunsany and M. P. Shiel.
6 We are thinking, specifically, of the turn to apocalyptic narratives and zombie holocausts in the twenty-first century, from Robert Kirkman's *The Walking Dead* comic series (2003–present) and Max Brooks's *World War Z: An Oral History of the Zombie War* (2006) onwards. See Andrew Tate, *Apocalyptic Fiction* (London: Bloomsbury, 2017); Kyle William Bishop, *American Zombie Gothic: The Rise and Fall (and Rise) of the Walking Dead in Popular Culture* (Jefferson, NC: McFarland, 2010).
7 Thomas Ligotti, *Songs of a Dead Dreamer* and *Grimscribe* (London: Penguin, 2015), p. 205. For the sake of establishing a meaningful sense of chronology, we are using the first known publication date for the stories, rather than that of their reprinting in subsequent collections.
8 Thomas Ligotti, quoted in E. M. Angerhuber and Thomas Wagner, 'Disillusionment Can Be Glamorous: An Interview with Thomas Ligotti' (2001), in Cardin (ed.), *Born to Fear*, pp. 59–75, at p. 74. Logically, Ligotti's ideal world would be one where either the entire human race is anaesthetically euthanised

or else one where human beings 'ha[ve] experienced the annulment of [their] ego[s]': Thomas Ligotti, quoted in Matt Cardin, '"It's All a Matter of Personal Pathology": An Interview with Thomas Ligotti' (2006), in Cardin (ed.), *Born to Fear*, pp. 117–33, at p. 131.
9 Thomas Ligotti, *The Conspiracy against the Human Race: A Contrivance of Horror* (New York: Hippocampus Press, 2010), p. 15.
10 Thomas Ligotti, quoted in Thomas Wagner, 'Work Not Done? An Interview with Thomas Ligotti' (2003), in Cardin (ed.), *Born to Fear*, pp. 77–91, at p. 77.
11 Ligotti, *Conspiracy*, p. 28.
12 *Ibid.*
13 *Ibid.*, pp. 105–13.
14 *Ibid.*, pp. 43, 77 (capitals in original).
15 Thomas Ligotti, quoted in Tina Hall, 'The Damned Interviews: Thomas Ligotti' (2011), in Cardin (ed.), *Born to Fear*, pp. 175–81, at p. 179.
16 Thomas Ligotti, quoted in Geoffrey H. Goodwin, 'Thomas Ligotti Interview' (2009), in Cardin (ed.), *Born to Fear*, pp. 145–54, at p. 145.
17 The reference is to his short story 'I Have a Special Plan for This World' (2002).
18 Thomas Ligotti, quoted in Nathaniel Katz, 'Interview: Thomas Ligotti' (2011), in Cardin (ed.), *Born to Fear*, pp. 185–97, at p. 191.
19 Thomas Ligotti, quoted in Hall, 'Damned Interviews', p. 177.
20 Thomas Ligotti, quoted in Katz, 'Interview', p. 192 (italics in original).
21 Ligotti, *Songs of a Dead Dreamer* and *Grimscribe*, p. 102. Ligotti does make a point of establishing that this style is not uniquely his.
22 *Ibid.*, p. 188.
23 *Ibid.*, pp. 302, 314.
24 *Ibid.*, p. 318; Thomas Ligotti quoted in John B. Ford, 'The Grimscribe in Cyberspace' (2000), in Cardin (ed.), *Born to Fear*, pp. 53–7, at p. 57.
25 Thomas Ligotti, *Noctuary* (Burton, MI: Subterranean Press, 2012), p. 9.
26 The quotation is from 'The Music of Erich Zann' (1922). H. P. Lovecraft, *The Thing on the Doorstep and Other Weird Stories* (London: Penguin, 2002), p. 50.
27 Ligotti, *Songs of a Dead Dreamer* and *Grimscribe*, p. 401.
28 *Ibid.*, p. 402.
29 Thomas Ligotti, quoted in Hall, 'Damned Interviews', p. 177.
30 Thomas Ligotti, quoted in Geoffrey H. Goodwin, 'Thomas Ligotti Interview' (2009), p. 153.
31 Ligotti, *Noctuary*, p. 17.
32 *Ibid.*, p. 164.
33 *Ibid.*
34 *Ibid.*, p. 165.
35 Thomas Ligotti, *My Work Is Not Yet Done: Three Tales of Corporate Horror* (London: Virgin Books, 2009), pp. 38–9.
36 *Ibid.*, p. 38.
37 Thomas Ligotti, quoted in Hall, 'Damned Interviews', p. 177.
38 Jason Marc Harris, 'Smiles of Oblivion: Demonic Clowns and Doomed Puppets as Fantastic Figures of Absurdity, Chaos, and Misanthropy in the Writings of Thomas Ligotti', *The Journal of Popular Culture*, 45:6 (2012), 1249–65, at 1256.
39 Ligotti, *Noctuary*, p. 138.

40 Ligotti, *My Work Is Not Yet Done*, p. 111.
41 *Ibid.*, p. 138.
42 *Ibid.*, p. 136.
43 Thomas Ligotti, *The Spectral Link* (Burton, MI: Subterranean Press, 2014), p. 12.
44 *Ibid.*, p. 43.
45 *Ibid.*, pp. 43–4.
46 *Ibid.*, p. 44.
47 Ligotti, quoted in Katz, 'Interview', p. 191 (italics in original).

Jeffrey Andrew Weinstock

Vampire suicide

> 'You will make what haste you can', said the stranger, 'from the mountain, inasmuch as it is covered with sulphurous vapours, inimical to human life, and when you reach the city you will cause to be published an account of my proceedings, and what I say. You will say that you accompanied Varney the Vampyre to the crater of Mount Vesuvius, and that, tired and disgusted with a life of horror, he flung himself in to prevent the possibility of a reanimation of his remains.'
> Before the guide could utter anything but a shriek, Varney took one tremendous leap, and disappeared into the burning mouth of the mountain.[1]
> James Malcolm Rymer, *Varney the Vampire; or, The Feast of Blood*

So ends the inglorious career of terror practised for over two centuries by the antagonist of James Malcolm Rymer's sprawling 666,000-word penny dreadful, *Varney the Vampire; or, The Feast of Blood*, published serially from 1845–47. And while Bram Stoker's *Dracula*, published fifty years later, is generally considered to have established the 'ground rules' for how vampires act, Varney can take credit for one of the more curious recurring tropes of vampire narrative: vampire suicide. From Rymer's un-dead omnibus, considered the first full-length work of vampire fiction, to modern vampire narratives including films such as *Blacula* (William Crain, 1972), *Thirst* (Park Chan-wook, 2009) and *Only Lovers Left Alive* (Jim Jarmusch, 2014); television programs such as *True Blood* (based on the Southern Vampire Mystery series by author Charlaine Harris) and *Angel* (the *Buffy the Vampire Slayer* spin-off); and the literary works of authors such as Anne Rice and Kim Newman, vampires attempt suicide with relative frequency – and with a fair amount of success. This raises questions about why the immortal un-dead seek to be dead-dead, and what this tells us about the human creators that imagine them into being in the first place – because, as Jeffrey Jerome Cohen has famously asserted, monsters of all stripes are 'pure culture', inventions of the human imagination that reflect human anxieties and desires.[2]

Looking to the extensive body of vampire fiction and film that has developed since the early part of the nineteenth century, it becomes clear that vampires commit suicide for a variety of reasons, though these mostly fall into three broad categories: remorse, ennui and heroism. Taken together, the attempted or accomplished suicides undertaken by vampires function ideologically to bolster anthropocentrism, reaffirm conventional Judeo-Christian morality and undercut the appeal of immortality, particularly as the religious stigmatisation of vampires as inherently evil wanes. While it can often seem like a narrative representation of human 'sour grapes', vampire suicide frequently functions to affirm that immortality is as much a curse as a gift. Put differently, vampire suicide is a lesson for the living, as such narratives convey the message to envious humans to be careful what you wish for.

Interestingly, vampire suicidal tendencies can also be construed as representing a half-hearted attempt to recuperate the vampire genre from charges of immorality through a strategy of inversion. In folklore and in some popular culture texts, the punishment for the mortal sin of suicide is precisely to become a vampire. The consequence of the sin of hubristic unmaking is to become the embodiment of sin. Vampire suicide, particularly in instances of guilt or martyrdom, then, is a curious type of cleansing – purification achieved through the preferred means of self-slaughter: suicide by sunlight. As the creature of darkness waits for dawn or steps out into the midday sun, 'evil' transforms into a small pile of ashes. The second suicide then is the antidote for the first (or for the other sins that led to the transformation into a vampire). Narratives of vampire ennui are somewhat more complicated than those of vampiric regret; however, they nevertheless convey the message that the presumed pleasures of immortality and great power wear thin over the years as the world changes around the static vampire. In this way, narratives of vampire suicide are presented as cautionary tales: Evil (with a capital 'E') will be punished, life is a gift to be respected, the prospect of death gives life meaning, be satisfied with your lot and so on. This insistent reassertion of conventional anthropocentric morality (common to the Gothic overall) thereby functions as an alibi, allowing consumers of vampire narratives to 'have their cake and eat it, too' – that is, to take pleasure in and even identify with monstrous creatures that prey on human life while disavowing them in the end. Vampire suicide thus arguably becomes emblematic of the Gothic genre in general as the lewd and lurid middle gives way to the tidy conclusion and reassertion of conventional morality. We enjoy the bloody mayhem, and then the sun rises, the penitent monster turns to ash and order is restored.

Vampiric remorse

Literary narratives of vampire suicide as a consequence of remorse for crimes committed against humans and associated self-disgust originate with Varney and constitute the variant of the vampire suicide trope that most clearly depicts vampiric immortality as a curse rather than a gift. For a vampire to attempt suicide as a result of overwhelming guilt and regret requires several conditions. First and foremost, the vampire must come to consider feeding on humans as a transgression rather than a natural or permissible act; this entails both that the vampire subscribe to or retain a moral framework that distinguishes right from wrong and good from evil, and that the vampire construe vampiric predation on humans as the latter. The vampire thus experiences a form of cognitive dissonance as the requirements for its survival conflict with its own ethical principles. The vampire must either empathise or sympathise with its prey and retain a conscience that causes it to feel guilty. More succinctly, the vampire must at some point recognise its actions as *evil* and regret them, but be unable to stop because its continued existence depends on feeding on humans. It must come to appreciate its very nature as both evil and unchangeable – or at least conclude that its guilt is impossible to expiate in any other way.

Rymer's Varney, as a handful of commentators have observed, starts off monstrous and predatory, but becomes more conflicted and sympathetic as the narrative progresses. Bette B. Roberts explains that Varney 'indulges in repeated moments of self-pity for his loathsome, outcast experience', and notes Varney's weary questioning in Volume II, 'How long is this hated life to last?'[3] We learn in Volume III, prior to Varney's first unsuccessful suicide attempt, that Varney would gladly have been more human, and lived and died as those lived and died whom he saw around him. But being compelled to fulfil the order of his being, he never had the courage absolutely to take measures for his own destruction, a destruction that should be final in consequence of depriving himself of all opportunity of resuscitation. (650)

Varney then tries to drown himself in the ocean, but is revived, in keeping with the series' premise, by moonlight. The 'Varney' entry on the *Victorian Gothic* website characterises this as Varney's 'existential crisis', asserting that it is in the third volume that Varney 'develops into an increasingly reflexive, tormented character'.[4] In an extended overview of the series, the *Skulls in the Stars* blog similarly observes that

> Varney the vampire is a creature who does many evil acts, but is simultaneously haunted by those same acts and tormented by his own existence. As the epic progresses, Varney vacillates increasingly rapidly from monster and criminal to victim and even altruist, and one never quite knows what one will get from him! This sympathetic depiction of vampires is unmatched in other contemporary tales of vampirism and would not be reexplored until Anne Rice's *Interview with the Vampire* (1976).[5]

Roberts concludes that, at the end, the Varney we see 'is worn out and conscience-stricken, hardly the rebellious and indestructible symbol of evil'.[6]

Although Rymer's narrative is inconsistent concerning Varney's origins, one account offered by Varney is that his vampirism is divine punishment for murdering his son, resulting 'in his rebirth as a vampire; a wretched, unending existence as a parasite and a pariah' (2012). He considers his appetite 'horrible' and his repast 'terrible and disgusting' (627), and wonders when his 'weary pilgrimage' will end (681). Varney's existential crisis, initial suicide attempt and final completion of the act that culminates the series thus undercut the allure of eternal life by characterising the cost as unendurable. In doing so, *Varney* establishes a recurring trope – the benefits of being a vampire are not worth the ethical price that must be paid. Envy not the vampire, mortal readers (or viewers), for immortality is not worth the cost to one's conscience.

While Varney's suicide is an early example of the remorseful vampire taking his own life, the trope finds its fullest expression in late twentieth- and twenty-first-century vampire narratives. In some cases, vampire suicide as a refusal to accept the moral transgression of vampirism is relegated to minor characters who make clear that the option exists for the protagonist. This is the case, for example, in the Swedish film *Let the Right One In* (2008), in which the character Virginia (Ika Nord) survives the attack by the vampire Eli (Lina Leandersson) when the predation is interrupted by another character (Lacke, played by Peter Carlberg) and is taken to the hospital.[7] Aware of what she is becoming, Virginia asks an orderly to open the blinds to her room, and – vampires having become remarkably flammable in the intervening century and a half – she bursts into flames. This is similarly the case in Michael and Peter Spierig's science-fiction horror film *Daybreakers* (2009), in which the character Alison (Isabel Lucas) is forcibly turned into a vampire, but refuses to drink blood (apart from her own) and degenerates into a monstrous creature called a 'subsider' who is then put to death by exposure to the sun. Alison's refusal to drink others' blood is a conscious one that she knows will lead to hear death.[8]

The moral cost of being a vampire and the place of vampires within some kind of divine plan are issues frequently contemplated by Anne Rice's reflective vampires who often meditate on, and sometimes commit, suicide. While, as I discuss next, this is most frequently because their extended lifetime takes its toll and they can no longer adjust to a changing world, it is also occasionally a consequence of guilt and regret. This is the case for Rice's melancholic Louis de Pointe du Lac, a central character in the Vampire Chronicles. Although deeply conflicted about his vampiric existence – indeed, the first book in the series, *Interview with the Vampire* (1976), is essentially about Louis

9.1 The Combustible Vampire 1: Virginia from *Let the Right One In*.

9.2 The Combustible Vampire 2: Alison from *Daybreakers*.

trying to come to terms with his new identity – Louis's suicide attempt does not come until *Merrick* (2000), the seventh book in the series. Here, unable to resist the seductions of the eponymous Merrick, a powerful and attractive witch, he repeats the mistake he believes he made with Claudia – a young girl vampirised by Lestat and 'turned' by Louis in *Interview* – and transforms Merrick into a vampire. Having been manipulated by Merrick into betraying his principles, such as they are, Louis's intense guilt prompts him to expose himself to the sun at dawn, leaving him a charred and desiccated husk. Only the ministrations of David Talbot, a powerful vampire whose existence is linked to Lestat, prevent Louis from successfully ending his existence.[9]

While Louis's suicide attempt derives from his guilt over his implication in the creation and destruction of Claudia and then the transformation of Merrick, Rice's vampire Armand attempts suicide after a religious epiphany, making him in some ways similar to Varney. In *Memnoch the Devil* (1995), the fifth instalment in Rice's Vampire Chronicles, Armand is filled with religious fervour after hearing of Lestat's own religious revelation. Believing that Lestat has retrieved the mythical Veil of Veronica imprinted with the face of Christ, which seems to confirm the truths of the Christian Bible, Armand – now believing himself evil – makes an impassioned decision: "'I will bear witness. I will stand here with my arms outstretched" [...] "and when the sun rises, my death shall confirm the miracle"', he cries to his auditors. 'Bear witness, this sinner dies for Him!'[10] As with Louis in *Merrick*, Armand's attempt is unsuccessful (and, indeed, there is a good deal of doubt surrounding Lestat's visions). Nevertheless, the suicide attempt comes as a consequence of accepting a vision of the universe, at least temporarily, that places humanity at the centre of a cosmic contest between good and evil, with vampires aligned with the latter.

Perhaps the most striking iteration of the trope of the remorseful vampire committing suicide is Park Chan-wook's 2009 film, *Thirst*. As with Rice's melancholic Louis, the protagonist of *Thirst*, Sang-hyun (Song Kang-ho), does not seek to become a vampire, nor is his vampirism a consequence of divine retribution. Instead, Sang-hyun (whose name either by design or chance resonates with the English word 'sanguine', a blood-red colour) is a Roman Catholic priest who ironically becomes a vampire not as a result of evil action or reckless deed, but rather as a consequence of his selflessness – he has participated as a human guinea pig in a failed medical experiment seeking to develop a vaccine against a fatal disease.[11] Although infected with a deadly virus, Sang-hyun appears to make a miraculous recovery. He has not, however, been cured entirely and returned to 'normal' health; instead, he has become a vampire, and the virus in his system is only kept in check through the consumption of human blood – a condition that precipitates a moral crisis for Sang-hyun. Although endowed with super strength, dexterity and almost complete invulnerability, he nevertheless initially attempts to kill himself after finding himself unable to resist drinking blood from a comatose hospital patient.

Sang-hyun's transgressions, however, do not end with blood drinking, as he finds himself attracted to Tae-ju (Kim Ok-bin), the wife of his childhood friend Kang-woo (Shin Ha-kyun). Feeling liberated from social constraints and doubting the religious faith to which he had previously subscribed, Sang-hyun begins an adulterous affair with Tae-ju that culminates in the murder of her husband Kang-woo and the transformation of Tae-ju into a vampire. Tae-ju, to borrow from Rice's Vampire Chronicles, becomes the Claudia to Sang-hyun's Louis. Whereas Sang-hyun, conflicted about his vampirism and still retaining remnants of his human ethical code, has attempted to keep his vampirism in check and to avoid killing, Tae-ju transforms into a remorseless monster who revels in her supernatural abilities. Tae-ju not only takes pleasure in the kill but sadistically enjoys scaring her victims. In what is the film's goriest and most disturbing scene, Tae-ju viciously turns on three prior friends who have discovered her and Sang-Hyun's involvement in her husband's disappearance, stalking them through her apartment-turned-bunker. One friend survives only as a consequence of Sang-hyun's merciful deceit of Tae-ju, leading her to believe that he has killed the friend.

It is the massacre in the apartment that appears to convince Sang-hyun that vampiric existence is unethical to the point of being unbearable. He persuades Tae-ju that they must flee, and the two (together with Tae-ju's almost entirely paralysed mother) drive through the night, arriving much to Tae-ju's dismay at the edge of a cliff looking out over the ocean as dawn approaches. Sang-hyun has taken them to the end of the road – both literally and figuratively. With no apparent cover, Tae-ju attempts to hide from the sun in the car's boot and then beneath the vehicle, but each time is dragged out by Sang-hyun. Resigned to her fate, she then sits with Sang-hyun on the roof of the car, looking out over the sea. As the sun rises, their skin bubbles, smokes and burns and then, as they embrace in agony, they are reduced to blackened cinders – for them, sunrise is sunset.

9.3 The sole remains at the end of *Thirst*.

In each of these works, the suicide of the remorseful vampire is the solution to an existence construed as evil – and what is striking is that vampiric 'life' remains evil even in the absence of a conventional religious framework with God at the centre. The characters in the nineteenth-century *Varney* believe in the goodness of God, and Varney acts more or less within the context of the traditional Christian framework – his vampirism is a consequence of mortal sin and divine punishment. Having acted monstrously in life, he is punished by God and transformed into a monster (which then, curiously, preys on the innocent). Accursed, he performs the role of evil predator apparently assigned to him – even relishes it – until he can bear it no longer and, pricked by compunction, immolates himself in the crater of Mount Vesuvius. The logic, of course, defies close scrutiny – why would God punish someone by denying him death and presumably eternal damnation? Why would God transform a sinner into an almost indestructible monster who preys on the innocent? And why then would God allow that same monster to end his existence through suicide under particular conditions? Despite these vexing theological questions, however, the narrative framework constructs a familiar moral universe with God as arbiter of right and wrong, good and evil. The vampire is an abomination, a crime against nature, and the vampire's growing acceptance of this ultimately precipitates his self-destruction. God seems to demand – or at least sanction – the vampire's suicide.

Rice's Louis, in contrast, spends a lot of time fretting about God's apparent absence: indeed, a central scene in *Interview with the Vampire* has Louis attacking a priest at the altar. Holding the priest fast and compelling him to look at his vampiric face, Louis states rather than asks, 'Why, if God exists, does He suffer me to exist!' 'He was cursing me, calling on God at the altar', recalls Louis. 'And then I grabbed him on the very steps to the Communion rail and pulled him down to face me there and sank my teeth into his neck.'[12] Louis, transformed into a vampire by Lestat without his consent and searching for meaning, finds none in the Church, and is not punished for his heretical act. Although later instalments of the Vampire Chronicles call into question pronouncements concerning God's demise, the series, particularly in the first three books, nevertheless has vampires suffering existential crises and developing moral codes of conduct precisely in the absence of the spectre of divine reward and punishment. Louis's qualms about vampiric existence derive from a respect for human life. For a time, he will only feed on animals (so a vampire 'vegetarian' in the language of Stephenie Meyer's *Twilight* franchise) and later restricts his feeding to human evildoers. Nevertheless, he frequently meditates and at one point attempts to end an existence he perceives as cursed.

The situation for Sang-hyun in *Thirst* is the most ironic of all because he begins the narrative as a Roman Catholic priest who selflessly volunteers himself for a dangerous medical drug trial. What kind of a God, one could reasonably ask, would punish someone so devout and altruistic with vampirism? As in Rice's Vampire Chronicles, there is no sense in *Thirst* that vampirism is a divine punishment or that religious iconography holds any intrinsic power over the vampire. God is absent from the tale, and there is nothing to inhibit Sang-hyun or Tae-ju except their own residual moral scruples. In the end, Sang-hyun's suicide/murder – locked in an agonised embrace with Tae-ju, looking out across a sublime vista as the sun rises – constitutes a refusal to embrace a kind of feral post-human ethics that license bloodshed. Since God will not punish them, they must punish themselves – and their punishment confirms that human ethics remain the yardstick against which their actions must be measured. They are monstrous because they prey on humans, and suicide does not so much redeem them as relieve them (or at least delivers Sang-hyun) of the burden of vampirism, which acts as a blot on the human conscience in his vampire body. Put differently, when one transforms from human to vampire, the human superego goes along for the ride.

9.4 *Thirst* and the importance of sunscreen.

Vampiric ennui

Varney and Sang-hyun successfully commit suicide – and Louis attempts it – because of the weight of the guilt they bear. They increasingly feel the burden of having transgressed against God, turned against friends and loved ones and/or committed bloody and despicable acts, and reach a point where they can no longer 'live' with their bloody un-dead selves. While there are some vampires who assert that vampires are a superior species and should prey on humans without compunction – that humans are to vampires as animals are to humans – vampire narratives in large measure reject such thinking as evil, casting those vampires as antagonists and focusing instead on vampire protagonists who acknowledge the sanctity of human life. Perhaps if cows and chickens wrote novels, they might invent similarly conflicted human protagonists. The point of course is that such works function ideologically to reconfirm the human as the centre of the universe – they are 'pro-life'. And they need to be, because in many contemporary vampire narratives, vampires *are* the superior species: virtually immortal, able to fly or read minds, beautiful, strong, super-intelligent and so forth. Particularly in the absence of any God as arbiter of absolute morality, what would prevent mere mortals from envying and aspiring towards vampirism if not for quibbles about taking life? As vampires increasingly approximate superheroes, we can note a corresponding increase in suicidal vampires who cannot stomach the precondition for their continued immortal existence: the killing of humans. This is in some cases because God has commanded that 'Thou Shalt Not Kill' (Exodus 20: 13) and the vampires become religious converts; in other cases, it is because, even in the absence of God (or, from an existentialist perspective, perhaps precisely because of it), they still acknowledge the sanctity of human life. Conventional morality reasserts itself in the end, even as the lascivious middle licenses libidinal transgressions of all sorts. When the vampire commits suicide, it reminds us that the vampire is a monster and nice people do not wish to be monsters.

Although the vampire as murdering monster offers a compelling rationale for not aspiring to un-death, modern vampire narratives introduce an additional drawback: ennui. Immortality, it turns out, may become burdensome because vampires-née-humans are creatures of the world – and the world keeps on turning. Indeed, the passage of time confronts vampires with two challenges: to remain connected to an ever-changing world and to stay 'lively'. When literary and cinematic vampires as a consequence of longevity can no longer recognise the world through which they stalk, or when they can no longer find sources of excitement or interest, they begin to contemplate ending their existence.

This challenge faced by immortal creatures attempting to live a temporal existence is one developed extensively by Rice in her Vampire Chronicles. While Rice introduces a number of ancient vampires in her series, most vampires do not achieve great age, often because they cannot adjust to the changing conditions of a world they find increasingly bewildering. The *Vampire Chronicles* wiki explains that

> During their immortality, vampires will sometimes go into a kind of hibernation, either because they have become mentally unbalanced from knowing what they have become or because their surroundings have changed too much for them to cope with. ... Many vampires commit suicide if they continually exist in the world, leading to Marius [an ancient vampire] telling Lestat that he should live out one lifetime pretending to be human and watching the world change.[13]

Lestat's maker, Magnus, in *The Vampire Lestat* (1985), fails to heed this lesson and is presented as having been driven mad over the centuries by his vampiric nature and immortality. Having turned Lestat and imparted the rudiments of vampiric existence, he prepares to immolate himself. 'It's only mercy I ask', he says to Lestat, 'that I go now to find hell, if there is a hell, or sweet oblivion which surely I do not deserve. If there is a Prince of Darkness, then I shall set eyes upon him at last. I shall spit in his face.'[14] He then leaps into the fire.

Perhaps the most beatific representation of a vampire committing suicide as a consequence of the burden of extreme longevity appears in the HBO series *True Blood*. Introduced in the second season, the character Godric, played by Allan Hyde, is an ancient and powerful vampire who sired central *True Blood* characters Eric Northman (Alexander Skarsgård) and Nora Gainesborough (Lucy Griffiths). As revealed in the series, and summarised on the *True Blood* wiki, Godric is over 2,000 years old. For his first millennium, he was a 'violent, bloodthirsty savage with no regard for human life', and he passed along to his progeny his nihilistic view that 'there was no right or wrong, only survival, or death'. Then, finding that 'senseless killing had only left him feeling detached and empty', he had a change of heart, becoming gracious and compassionate towards humans.[15]

At the end of Season 2, Episode 9 – in what may well be the series' most poignant moment – Godric chooses to 'meet the sun'. 'Two thousand years is enough', he tells his offspring Eric, who is pleading for Godric to change his mind. 'Our existence is insanity. We don't belong here', he explains.[16] Commanding Eric to depart (a convention of *True Blood* is that vampires are subject to the commands of their makers), Godric turns to face the sun, accompanied by series protagonist Sookie Stackhouse. 'A human with me at the end, and human tears', he observes. 'Two thousand years, and I can still be surprised. In this, I see God', Godric concludes.[17] Then the sun rises and Godric burns. Christ-like, Godric hopes that his suicide will in some way inspire compassion in the radical members of both the human and vampire communities, each of which views the other with contempt.

Godric's suicide is presented as the culmination of a two-millennia-long process of self-scrutiny leading to enlightenment, which conveys two conclusions: compassion is preferable to nihilism, and immortality is more appealing in theory than in fact. Godric initially shared with Rice's Lestat a conception of the world as what Lestat calls throughout the series a 'savage garden', a place of beauty and danger without deeper meaning or divine guidance. Having been victimised himself and feeling unhindered by internal inhibition or external constraint, Godric allowed hatred and resentment to drive him, hunting humans for sport and 'passing on his disdain for the living to his progenies', Eric and Nora.[18] Godric, however, ultimately

9.5 Godric meets the sun.

rejected this nihilistic philosophy in favour of one founded on compassion, acknowledging his implication in the human hatred of vampires. The suggestion here is a kind of evolution of conscience that causes the reflective vampire to acknowledge the sanctity of human life and to reject his own existence – when your own existence is 'insanity', suicide becomes the logical resolution. Unlike Varney or Rice's Armand, however, Godric seems less guilt-ridden than simply tired. Despite his immense power, he concludes that his existence has run its course. To shuffle off his immortal coil and meet the sun is for him an act of purification that he hopes will inspire others to overcome prejudice and antagonism.

Less Christ-like than Godric and even more melancholic than Rice's Louis – if that is possible – is Adam (Tom Hiddleston) in Jim Jarmusch's 2013 art-house vampire film, *Only Lovers Left Alive*. Married for centuries to Eve (Tilda Swinton), but living on his own in his crumbling mansion in a desolate, depopulated Detroit, Michigan, Adam spends his time recording moody Goth songs he calls 'funeral music' on outdated studio equipment, collecting vintage musical instruments and lamenting the state of a world presided over by thoughtless human beings (which he refers to as 'zombies'). 'I'm sick of it – these zombies, what they've done to the world, their fear of their own imaginations', bemoans Adam to Eve during a video chat.[19] When Adam dispatches his lackey Ian (Anton Yelchin) to commission a wooden bullet, the familiar conventions of vampire narrative allow the viewer to understand that he is a vampire contemplating suicide.

Sensing his despondency long-distance, Eve travels from Morocco to join him in Detroit where the bulk of the minimal action takes place. Soon after she arrives, while Adam is out procuring blood (Adam's favourite, O-negative, which they get from an obliging doctor), Eve discovers the newly made wooden bullet and a small revolver. Confronting Adam on his return, Eve – who we understand is even older than Adam – berates him for his selfish introspection and despondency when the wonders of the world surround them and they have each other: 'How can you have lived for so long and still not get it? This self-obsession, it's a waste of living that could be spent on surviving things, appreciating nature, nurturing kindness and friendship. And dancing.' 'You've been pretty lucky in love, though, if I may say so', she adds wryly.[20]

9.6 A morose Adam holds a pistol to his heart.

Hell for Adam is not immortality but, to borrow from Sartre, other zombies. Adam despairs over what human beings are doing to their world, and the ways in which they have polluted their own blood. Adrift in an impoverished city that reflects and amplifies his sense of despondency, Adam feels cursed to be a bystander as human beings wreck the world and kill themselves in a kind of slow-motion (although rapidly accelerating) suicide of their own. Eve, in contrast, takes the long view, prognosticating that Detroit will rise again because it is situated by water, which will become a valuable commodity 'when the cities in the South are burning' – presumably a reference to climate change. But she also reminds Adam of the beauties and pleasures that the world holds for them. They are presented as lovers of art, culture and the natural world who have had centuries to hone and indulge their tastes. Eve loves literature, and her closest friend is Christopher Marlowe, revealed by the film to be both a vampire and the author of Shakespeare's works. Both are lovers of music who appreciate all forms from classical to R&B to alt rocker Jack White. And while Eve possesses encyclopaedic knowledge of plant and animal life, marvelling at mushrooms and urban coyotes (and using their Latin names), Adam seems to possess an intuitive knowledge of physics, having perfected a kind of dynamo that generates power from the atmosphere and explaining to Eve the sub-atomic 'spooky action at a distance' (a notion concerning 'entwined particles' that reflects the pair's relationship).[21]

Unlike Godric, Adam thus does not end up committing suicide. Instead, Eve's arrival lifts his spirits (as much as possible for the constitutionally morose Adam) as the two lovers comfort each other, dance to vintage R&B, enjoy frozen blood popsicles and tour Detroit at night in Adam's classic 1982 Jaguar XJ-S. As with human beings, for vampires to overcome ennui and enjoy existence requires companionship and a conscious effort at engagement with the world and its beauties. The irony of *Only Lovers Left Alive* is that the vampiric un-dead are the liveliest among us – from drug dealers in Tangiers to abandoned factories in Detroit, the slow suicide of the human race is a consequence of rapacious appetite and blunted sensitivity. In *Only Lovers*, the zombie human race is every bit as monstrous, bloodthirsty, destructive and suicidal as the vampires we create.

Vampire martyrdom

The inversion of conventional roles in contemporary monster narratives that cast monsters as sympathetic protagonists, and human society writ large – intolerant of difference, exploitative of the natural world – as the antagonist plays into one final category of vampire suicide: vampire martyrdom. These are narratives in which vampires perform heroic acts of selflessness to protect those they love or the world in general. In some cases, the vampires are action heroes who put their lives on the line, so to speak, to protect an unsuspecting public from insidious danger; in other cases, the vampires are monsters who surprisingly discover residual goodness lurking in their black souls.

There are a number of vampire superheroes who are prepared to martyr themselves in the service of protecting either humans or those they love from predatory monsters. The two most obvious as a consequence of the big-budget film franchises in which they star are probably Blade from the Blade series and Selene from the Underworld films. Neither, I should point out, consciously attempts suicide; however, both repeatedly jeopardise their leather-clad existence by confronting powerful forces that threaten the world. In the Blade films, the half-vampire, half-human (or *dhampir*) Blade (Wesley Snipes) is a vampire hunter who attempts to keep the vampire threat to the human race in check. In the Underworld franchise, Selene (Kate Beckinsale) is a 'Death Dealer' who hunts werewolves (Lycans). Neither feeds on innocent humans; both repeatedly are ready to martyr themselves for their noble causes.

More immediately connected to heroic vampire suicide are Eben in the American horror film *30 Days of Night* and Darla in the *Buffy the Vampire Slayer* spin-off, *Angel*. The plot to David Slade's 2007 American horror movie *30 Days of Night*, based on the comic-book miniseries of the same name, has an elegant simplicity to it: what better place for vampires than Barrow, Alaska – located above the polar circle – where the sun doesn't rise for thirty days straight? When vampires converge on Barrow for the month-long polar night feeding frenzy, the residents of the isolated town are forced into survival mode. Sheriff Eben Oleson (Josh Huston) and his estranged wife, Stella (Melissa George) almost last the month, but when the vampires begin burning down the town to destroy the evidence of the carnage that has transpired, Eben concludes that they cannot win without his making the ultimate sacrifice. Determining that to protect Stella he must fight fire with fire, Eben injects himself with tainted vampire blood and changes into a vampire. This gives him the strength and dexterity to confront the vampiric threat, and after Eben kills the lead vampire, Marlow (Danny Huston), the others disperse. Eben and Stella then watch the sun rise and share one last kiss before Eben's body turns to ashes in Stella's arms. His has been a double suicide – first un-dead, then dead-dead.[22]

The recurring character Darla (Julie Benz) in Joss Whedon's *Angel* meets her end by sacrificing her life not for her lover, but rather for her unborn child. Unlike Eben, whose purpose in *30 Days of Night* is that of a protector from the start, Darla's role in *Angel* is essentially to be an antagonist to the eponymous Angel (David Boreanaz), a vampire with a soul who in the spin-off series is dedicated to helping the helpless. After a sexual rendezvous with Angel (a strategic attempt to deprive Angel of his soul), Darla finds herself in the curious situation of being pregnant – vampires normally cannot conceive children through sexual intercourse and cannot give birth naturally to live offspring. Her

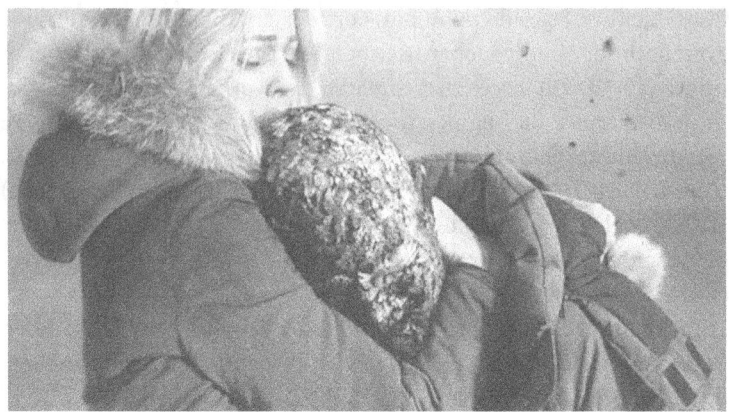

9.7 Eben bakes and flakes at the end of *30 Days of Night*.

pregnancy precipitates a reconsideration of her purpose as she begins to experience a new range of emotions, including love for the developing foetus; and, at the end of 'Lullaby', Episode 9 of Season 3,[23] she stakes herself, sacrificing herself for her baby who remains as she turns to dust – a 'final act of redemption to ensure the life of their son, Connor'.[24] Akin to Bella Swan in Stephenie Meyer's fourth Twilight instalment, *Breaking Dawn* (2008), who risks her vampiric life to bring a child into the world, Darla – with all the politically charged implications – concludes that the life of her child is more important than her own.

Conclusion: immortality hangs heavy over the heads of the un-dead

Narratives of vampire suicide clearly depict how monsters function to limn the human and naturalise a specific set of ideological values. When vampires attempt or commit suicide as a consequence of remorse, they comprehend themselves and convey to readers and viewers their own immorality. This may be as a consequence of accepting God's divine decree, or coming to appreciate the intrinsic value of human existence. These are ironically 'pro-life' narratives in which the suicide of the un-dead ensures the safety of the living and reaffirms a conventional good/evil dichotomy with human life at its centre: that which benefits humans is good; that which harms them is bad. No matter how superior or powerful vampires may be, human life is represented as sacrosanct.

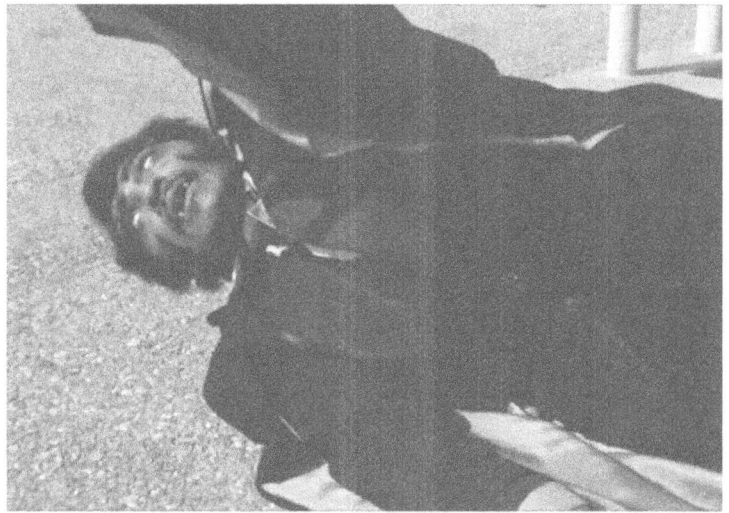

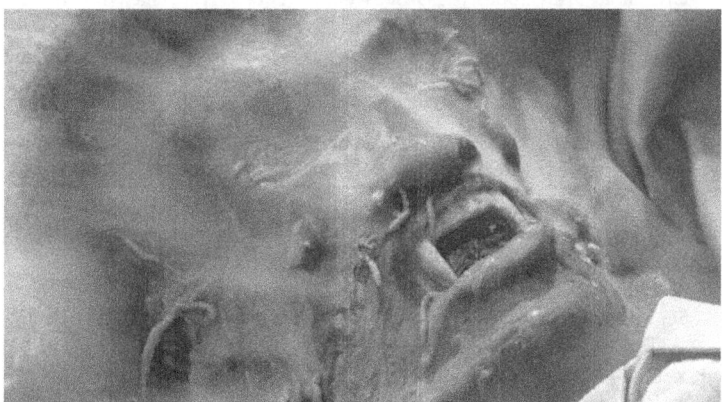

9.8 & 9.9 Blacula throws in the towel.

Narratives of vampire suicide as a consequence of ennui amplify the message that immortality is a curse rather than a gift. Far from being something to covet or aspire towards, immortality instead drains meaning from existence. Life is for the living, such narratives seem to say – and human beings have an obligation to cultivate an attitude receptive to the wonders of the world and to facilitate harmonious coexistence. Otherwise, we are committing a kind of suicide ourselves and are as good as dead already.

Narratives of vampire martyrs and vampire heroes prepared to sacrifice themselves for the good of others make the ideological 'stakes' of the vampire suicide narrative most immediately apparent, as they clearly affirm altruism over self-interest. To give one's life for others when one can never die takes the 'ultimate sacrifice' one step further. However, while one might perhaps be unlikely to question the nobility of a vampire soldier fighting on behalf of humanity or a vampire lover giving his life so that his wife may survive, what of the message that vampire women should be prepared to die so that their pregnancies can be carried to term? The unstated values informing such decisions make clear what is implicit in all narratives of vampire suicide – that the decision of the immortal creature to end its existence helps naturalise a set of values that foreground specifically human concerns.

Notes

1 James Malcolm Rymer, *Varney the Vampire; or, The Feast of Blood* (Crestline, CA: Zittaw Press, 2008), p. 759. Subsequent quotations are taken from this edition and appear in parentheses in the text.
2 Jeffrey Jerome Cohen, 'Monster Culture (Seven Theses)', in J. J. Cohen (ed.), *Monster Theory: Reading Culture* (Minneapolis, MN: University of Minnesota Press, 1996), pp. 3–25, at p. 4.
3 Bette B. Roberts, 'Varney, the Vampire, or, Rather, Varney, the Victim', *Gothic*, 2 (1987), 1–5, at 3.
4 Anon., 'Varney the Vampire; or, The Feast of Blood', *Victorian Gothic*, 1 March 2012, www.victoriangothic.org/varney-the-vampire-or-the-feast-of-blood/, accessed 19 March 2017.
5 Anon., 'James Malcolm Rymer's *Varney the Vampire*', *Skulls in the Stars*, 24 September 2008, https://skullsinthestars.com/2008/09/24/james-malcolm-rymers-varney-the-vampire/, accessed 9 March 2017.
6 Roberts, '*Varney, the Vampire*', 4.
7 Tomas Alfredson (dir.), *Let the Right One In* (EFTI, Sandrew Metronome Distribution Sverige AB, Filmpool Nord See, 2008).
8 Peter Spierig and Michael Spierig (dirs), *Daybreakers* (Lionsgate, 2009).
9 Anne Rice, *Merrick* (New York: Knopf, 2000).
10 Anne Rice, *Memnoch the Devil* (New York: Knopf, 1995), p. 297.
11 Park Chan-wook (dir.), *Thirst* (Moho Films, Focus Features Internationals, 2009).
12 Anne Rice, *Interview with the Vampire* (New York: Knopf, 1976), p. 114.
13 Anon., 'Vampire', *The Vampire Chronicles Wiki*, undated, http://vampirechronicles.wikia.com/wiki/Vampire, accessed 19 March 2017.
14 Anne Rice, *The Vampire Lestat* (New York: Knopf, 1985), p. 69.
15 Anon., 'Godric', *True Blood Wiki*, undated, http://trueblood.wikia.com/wiki/Godric, accessed 19 March 2017.
16 'I Will Rise Up', *True Blood*, Season 2, Episode 9, HBO, airdate 16 August 2009.
17 *Ibid.*

18 Anon., 'Godric'.
19 Jim Jarmusch (dir.), *Only Lovers Left Alive* (Recorded Picture Company, 2014).
20 *Ibid.*
21 *Ibid.*
22 David Slade (dir.), *30 Days of Night* (Dark Horse Entertainment, 2007).
23 'Lullaby', *Angel*, Season 9, Episode 3, WB Network, airdate 19 November 2001.
24 'Darla', *Buffy the Vampire Slayer: 20 Years of Slaying*, undated, http://buffy.wikia.com/wiki/Darla, accessed 28 February 2018.

10

Katarzyna Ancuta

Under the dying sun: suicide and the Gothic in modern Japanese literature and culture

The portrayal of Japan as 'the nation of suicide' is pervasive. In 1897, Émile Durkheim famously proclaimed that 'the readiness of the Japanese to disembowel themselves for the slightest reason is well known',[1] echoing the *bushido* tenet that 'the Way of the Samurai is found in death'.[2] The notion of suicide as an attribute of manliness is inscribed into Japanese culture, the cultural normalisation of and permissive attitude towards it explained through the country's religio-philosophical worldview, political ideology and collectivist social orientation. Throughout history, *seppuku* rituals, *kamikaze* deaths and *inseki jisatsu* responsibility-driven suicides of CEOs and politicians, but also economically motivated suicides of the elderly or entire families who do not want to be a burden to anyone, have been seen as 'altruistic suicides' committed by individuals who accept that their sacrifice is required 'for social ends'.[3]

In classical Japanese literature, suicides represented the two sides of the conflict between *giri* (social obligation) and *ninjo* (personal feelings). There were admirable suicides, committed out of a sense of moral responsibility, perhaps none so famous as those of the forty-seven *ronin* (master-less *samurai*) who rebelled to avenge the death of their lord and then collectively performed *seppuku* to atone for their transgression (based on the Ako incident that took place in 1703). Their story, known as *Chushingura*, was immortalised in dozens of *kabuki* and *bunraku* plays, the first one reportedly performed only twelve days after the men had died.[4] There were also suicides brought about by impossible love, like *The Love Suicides at Sonezaki*

(Chikamatsu Monzaemon, 1703) and its imitations which the shogunate attempted to ban on several occasions. Love suicide, a rather prolific literary theme during the Tokugawa period (1603–1868), was frowned on. Japanese men were expected to subdue their feelings in favour of obligation, and abandoning public duties because of love was denounced as egoistic. Suicide was meant to be 'well-thought through, thoroughly planned and emotionless ... a suicide committed spontaneously or in the heat of passion was believed to be unwise and was thus condemned'.[5]

In 2000, Henry J. Hughes made a case for the recognition of Japanese Gothic, as part of transcultural tradition, seeing that 'subversion of religious and social norms, an obsession with sex and death, and a fear of the supernatural or unknown ... are human qualities, not the province of one culture'.[6] His survey of Gothic moments in Japanese literature concluded with Japanese modernism, where 'the explosion of self into psychic collectivity becomes a quest for many Japanese Gothic heroes'.[7] One of the consequences of this is that suicide becomes an act of transgression rather than conformity. This chapter begins with a discussion of suicide in four modern Japanese novels – Natsume Soseki's *Kokoro* (1914), Kenzaburo Oe's *The Silent Cry* (1967), Haruki Murakami's *Norwegian Wood* (1987) and Tomotake Ishikawa's *Gray Men* (2012) – and concludes with a brief mention of Sion Sono's film *Suicide Circle* (2001) and its manga version, *Suicide Circle* (Furuya Ukamaru, 2002). In Gothic, suicide has been conventionalised as a declaration of guilt, a side-effect of madness, an extreme form of self-harm, the ultimate withdrawal from life and a reason for a ghostly return. In Japanese texts, suicide is at the same time civilised and barbaric, elegant and chaotic. It is a perfectly composed act of ascetic renunciation and achievement of a Buddhist ideal, as well as an unstoppable viral outbreak that threatens all life. It is an act of submission to societal norms, a cry of rebellion and a call to revolution; a choice of an individual, but also the play of karmic forces bound to be repeated. While proposing a familiar Gothic positioning of suicide in the context of depression, alienation, inertia, defiance against authority, dysfunctional relationships, death instinct or masochistic submission, the discussed texts, a testament to the convergence of Western and Eastern philosophies in modern Japan, invite us to revisit these Gothic conventions from a transcultural perspective.

Renunciation

Written in 1914 by Natsume Soseki, *Kokoro* (sometimes translated as 'the thinking and feeling heart') is an epitaph for the dying world, documenting the passing of the Meiji era, which transformed the deeply traditional and isolationist Japan and opened it up to Western influences. The young narrator recounts his intense relationship with an older man he calls Sensei (the master/teacher). Sensei appears to be a man of means, living a sheltered life without need for work or human contact. He has no family apart from his somewhat estranged wife, and his reclusive behaviour seems driven by a dark secret from the past. Though by no means menacing, with his brooding and oddly irrational behaviour, self-centredness and inability to talk of the past (hinting at a residue of guilt), Sensei exudes a subtle aura of a Gothic hero around him. The final section of the book contains Sensei's confession written as an elaborate suicide note. Sensei's misanthropic distrust in humanity is attributed to his uncle's betrayal, but is heightened because he found himself equally capable of betraying others and realised that 'evil does not so much exist without as within a man'.[8]

The core of Sensei's letter is his recollection of friendship with a young man called K. A son of a Buddhist priest, K. was adopted by a doctor's family and sent to Tokyo to study medicine. When he refused to do so, he was disinherited by both families and left to fend for himself. Impressed with his friend's ascetic discipline and religiosity, Sensei offered to share his lodgings with K., but was soon dismayed to discover that K. had become his love rival. Knowing his friend's strong views on spiritual purity, Sensei chastised him for straying off his path and quietly made arrangements to marry the girl himself. K.'s response was sudden and unexpected, as he took his life the same night, finding himself 'weak and infirm of purpose, and because the future held nothing for him'.[9]

K.'s death, the most elaborately described and consequential for the characters, is one of three suicides featured in the novel. It is set in comparison to the *junshi*[10] of General Nogi Maresuke, a historical figure who performed *seppuku* to follow Emperor Meiji to the grave and atone for a military mistake he had made thirty years before. It is also linked to the implied suicide of Sensei, whose decision to end his life is proclaimed in his final letter as the completion of an act of dying that began with his discovery of K.'s body. K.'s suicide speaks of his failure to reconcile emotional urges with strict philosophical and religious discipline. As Meredith McKinney observed, K. 'in many ways embodies the old world's strict code of values and ethics, which was coming into such painful conflict with the new Western concepts of individual rights and the primacy of the ego'.[11] K.'s death, therefore, 'foreshadows the ultimate death of that old world'[12] and everything it represents, his chosen method – slicing his throat open with a knife – as if mocking the ritual death of the *samurai* and anticipating General Nogi's gruesome tribute to his master.

General Nogi's ceremonial disembowelment invoked feudal traditions and stood in dissonance with the modern ideals of the Meiji era, and yet in a sense this anachronistic gesture expressed precisely the confusion of the generation torn between welcoming and resisting modernity. If Gothic texts are known to embrace the past, it is frequently to foreground 'the barbaric as opposed to the civilised; crudity as opposed to elegance'.[13] Since Japanese modernism coincided with the opening of the country, the excitement for the change was offset by the fear that Japanese traditions were threatened by the influx of potentially corruptive Western ideas. In this context, the cultural heritage invoked by this medieval ritual was simultaneously horrifyingly barbaric, as well as civilised and elegant.

Sensei's final suicide, which takes place off the pages of the book, is of most consequence for this discussion, as it offers a variation on a familiar Gothic trope of an alienated hero driven towards self-destruction. In Gothic texts, suicide is often attributed to what Eve Kosofsky-Sedgwick calls 'the poisonous effect of guilt and shame',[14] which may be of some importance here, but the Japanese cultural context calls for a different explanation. Wendy Jones Nakanishi argues that the desire for utter and complete annihilation 'either mentally, in the sublimation of his ego, or physically, in death, which may be in the service of a cause or simply as a means of ending an existence perceived as meaningless'[15] is characteristic of Japanese modernist heroes, who are usually portrayed as tragically lonely men at odds with their individuality, desperately seeking a greater whole they could lose themselves to.[16] Daniel Wright reads Sensei's death as an act of self-renunciation: 'a thoughtful and considered attempt by a troubled man to definitively and finally repudiate his own egoism' and 'be liberated from the dark and horrifying specters that haunt and corrupt the diseased soul of man'.[17] This, Wright explains, is the practical implication of the Zen philosophy that maintains that man can only understand and let go of the suffering associated with life through the epiphany of death.[18] It is neither death nor suicide that is seen as a Gothic moment in this context, but rather life, described by Wright as 'terror of Kafkaesque abyss'[19] beyond reason and morality, which the enlightened mind is capable of seeing and yearns to escape.

Sensei's suicide can be seen as the extreme form of reclusion, a series of withdrawals from society, family, friends and ideas one used to hold dear in life, culminating in the 'dissolution of the self into nothingness'.[20] Portrayed as the path to transcendence and liberation from earthly attachments, in Buddhist thought, reclusion is an admirable ideal. But perhaps it is also a failure, an inability to reconcile the tensions between one's ego and the group. Sensei's death signifies his refusal to accept the new and a choice to die with the old, where he believes he belongs. What then if the past is rejected together with the present?

Resistance

Kenzaburo Oe's *The Silent Cry* (1967) is rich in Gothic imagery of violence, disease and despair. The novel reflects its author's fascination with Bakhtinian grotesque, and yet for all its attempts at celebrating the carnivalesque ritual of destruction and renewal it remains surprisingly joyless.[21] The narrator/protagonist, Mitsusaburo, is introduced as the personification of the abject: curled up in a foetal position at the bottom of a septic tank pit, Mitsu meditates on the suicidal death of his friend who 'daubed his head all over with crimson paint, stripped, thrust a cucumber up his anus, and hanged himself'.[22] This grotesque hybrid – part human, part deity, part vegetable and ultimately (given its non-animated state) part object – is a battlefield of signifiers. The 'angry' red head evokes comparisons with the red-faced Shinto god Sarudahiko, popularly worshipped as the symbol of loyalty and masculinity. The vulnerable body stripped of its clothes resonates with images of surrendering Japanese soldiers removing the uniforms they dishonoured. The rope and the vegetable defiling the corpse, but also hinting at dark erotic play, additionally de-masculinise the subject. Moreover, while the text invokes the divine Sarudahiko who came down to bring order to Earth, it also draws attention to the creature 'who resisted in silence' (6), a sea slug whose mouth got slashed in punishment for defiance, locking him in an eternal silent cry.

The novel focuses on two Nedokoro brothers, Mitsu and Takashi, who return to the Shikoku valley of their childhood on a pretext of selling the family storehouse. This journey to their roots incites a struggle to claim ownership of memories which both men need to appropriate for their purpose, in particular those related to the 1860 uprising led by their great-grandfather's younger brother and the events of 1945 which saw their brother, S., beaten to death in retaliation for the earlier attack of the Japanese villagers on a Korean settlement in the valley. Hoping to recreate the 1860 rebellion, Takashi instigates the looting of the supermarket that belongs to the Korean 'Emperor of Supermarkets', who now wields economic power over the area, but the victory is short-lived, as the villagers soon return most of the stolen goods for fear of reprisals. Takashi then admits to raping and murdering a village girl (which may or may not have happened) and confesses to Mitsu that he committed multiple acts of incest with their mentally disabled sister and was instrumental in her suicide. This is followed by his own suicidal death, as he blows his head off with a rifle, the words 'I told the truth' scribbled on the wall as his testament.

Yasuko Claremont reads the novel as built around the double axis of evil and atonement, the rift particularly visible in the character of Takashi who feels torn apart by 'the desire to justify myself as a creature of violence and to punish myself for it' (211).[23] But while Takashi's 'telling the truth' can be seen as a confession of guilt, it also bears resemblance to Sensei's epiphany that all men are inherently evil and capable of violence, the revelation that is complete in the moment of death. It is 'the absolute truth which, if a man tells it, leaves him no alternative but to be killed by others, or kill himself, or go mad and turn into a monster' (157). Once again, if the truth implies the return of the haunted past, in Japanese texts time tends to be understood as cyclical, and past and present are frequently linked through karmic repetition. Unable to transcend their suffering, in Buddhist thought, sinners are doomed to repeat their sins in the hell of their own making.

The red-headed corpse of Mitsu's friend is an unrelenting reminder that 'monstrosity and grotesquerie merge in the hybrid forms that disrupt the borders separating what is acceptable within the categories of "human" and "non-human"'.[24] The array of characters – monstrous, human and animistic at the same time – hints at the possibility that life and death are also merged. Their grotesque bodies are monstrous because their human imperfections bring them closer to animistic spirits. Mitsu's missing eye turns him into an *oni* (a one-eyed demon); the Nedokoros' housekeeper, Jin, is a morbidly obese giant; the village leader resembles a sea urchin; and the 'resident madman', Gii, a draft-dodger who became a wild man, has 'merged' with a mythical monster, Chosokabe, that inhabits the forest. The characters are dehumanised by disease. Mitsu's child (a reflection of Oe's own) is reduced to an expressionless object after the removal of a brain tumour. Mitsu's wife is an alcoholic. His friend was institutionalised for prolonged depression resulting from physical trauma and sought solace in masochistic practices. Mitsu's older brother, S., exhibited symptoms of post-traumatic stress disorder after his return from war, and their sister is described as 'half-witted' (235). Even Takashi is initially infected with a sexually transmitted disease which he contracted from a black prostitute in America.

Grotesque bodies mingle with the imagery of race and an accompanying discourse of power. Takashi joins the anti-American student riots, where he occasionally switches sides to give and receive violence. A few years later, on a trip to America, he finds himself yearning for annihilation and enters the black ghetto hoping to get brutalised by 'savages'. When this does not happen, he returns to hire a black prostitute and pays her 'to act like she was a great black man raping a young Oriental girl' (214). The resentment of American occupation and economic domination in post-war Japan is offset by the imagery of oppressed American others – a political pamphlet with a photograph of a black man burnt alive, or the Native American tribal dress – the only item Takashi brings back from his trip. Americans are also seen as partially responsible for changing the balance of power within the Nedokoros' valley, where Koreans, brought to Japan as forced labourers, have embraced American-style capitalism and gained the upper hand over the compliant and impoverished Japanese farmers.

The novel opens and closes with the shocking imagery of suicide. The statement made by Mitsu's red-faced friend is matched by Takashi's half-dressed body with its skin 'torn and bloody as though studded with split pomegranates' (243) and an outline of a human head with its eyes 'blasted full of shot' (244) pencilled on the wall behind it. There is also the voluntary death of Mitsu's sister, a worthy Gothic heroine manipulated into an incestuous relationship by Takashi, rejected when pregnant, forced to undergo abortion and sterilised, whose victimisation led to guilt-driven suicide. Finally, the portrayal of S. becoming a willing sacrificial lamb to put an end to racial tensions in the village, but also to feed his drive to self-destruction brought about by the psychological damage he suffered during the war, has all the attributes of suicide through the renunciation of life. In *The Silent Cry*, however, this renunciation is split between the enlightened dissolution into nothingness and the rebellious cry of protest against the horrors of this world.

Ripple effect

If Oe conceptualises disease and suicide as the element of the grotesque, Haruki Murakami's *Norwegian Wood* (1987) offers an investigation into the relationship between grief, suicide and depression, a common theme in contemporary Gothic texts. The book acknowledges the fact that mental illness is a significant factor in a number of suicide cases in Japan, a situation which continues to this day. In fact, the National Police Statistics data for 2009 attributed 63 per cent of all suicide cases to health problems, out of which 41 per cent of suicides were linked to mental illness.[25] What makes this novel particularly susceptible to a Gothic reading, however, is Murakami's portrayal of narcissistic depression that revels in a discovery that 'the aim of all life is death'[26] and that life is driven by an instinct to return to the inanimate and inorganic state from which it originates.

The novel's narrator, Toru Watanabe, recalls his relationship with Naoko, a girlfriend of his best friend, Kizuki, who killed himself at the age of seventeen. This shared experience inevitably draws them together, but the budding romance is interrupted by Naoko's sudden withdrawal and her subsequent departure to a mountain retreat for therapy. While Toru's affection appears to fill her with hope of a recovery, eventually the conviction that her affliction is part of a genetic disposition takes over. Naoko's condition deteriorates; she is briefly hospitalised in a psychiatric institution, and finally commits suicide. Toru continues to struggle with grief and piece his life back together.

In narcissistic depression, Julia Kristeva argues, the afflicted persons 'do not consider themselves wronged but afflicted with a fundamental flaw, a congenital deficiency'.[27] Their sadness becomes the expression of the 'narcissistic wound' with which they form attachment. Their suicide is 'a merging with sadness and, beyond it, with that impossible love, never reached, always elsewhere, such as the promises of nothingness, of death'.[28] While Toru's depression is caused by the loss of his best friend and can be seen as grief-driven, Naoko seems to believe that suicide is 'in the blood'.[29] Naoko's sister killed herself at the age of seventeen, just like Kizuki. Several years before, her father's brother jumped in front of the train. None of them left a note, which made it impossible to identify a single cause. Toru replaces Kizuki with a new friend, Nagasawa, only to see history repeat itself, as his new friend's girlfriend, Hatsumi, kills herself as well. Her death fills Toru with sadness but seems not to have any deeper effect because he realises that since the day Kizuki died he has been trapped in 'a devitalized existence',[30] having learnt that 'Death was not the opposite of life. It was already here, within my being, it had always been there, and no struggle would permit me to forget that' (34).

Naoko and Toru represent two faces of the depressed narcissist, torn between the desire to satisfy their life and death instincts. Their behaviour is consistent with Kristeva's observation that 'the depressed person wanders in pursuit of continuously disappointing adventures and loves; or else retreats, disconsolate and aphasic, alone with the unnamed Thing'.[31] Toru moves on from one meaningless sexual encounter to another, while Naoko gradually loses an ability to communicate with the outside world. Ironically, Naoko's death has a liberating effect on those around her. Her roommate, Reiko, a long-term resident of the retreat following a failed suicide attempt, finds strength to face the outside world again. Toru makes up his mind to give a chance to his relationship with Midori, a girl whose will to live contrasts with Naoko's descent into death.

Midori is no stranger to death and favours quick dissolution over prolonged illness, when 'the shadow of death slowly, slowly eats away at the region of life, and before you know it everything's dark and you can't see, and the people around you think of you as more dead than alive' (104). One can only wonder whether this will turn into motivation to speed up the inevitable. In the final scene of the book, Toru reaches out to her but appears to be lost 'in the dead center of this place that was no place' (386), offering the reader no closure or resolution. The contagious and cyclical nature of depression portrayed in the novel suggests that nothing much will change for the protagonists, and a momentary glimpse of Toru's future in the opening paragraphs of the book confirms that he remains a melancholy character.

Among the suicides attributed to illness in Japan, depression is cited as the most common factor. It is also a contributing factor in the cases when suicides are seen as motivated by family problems, work or socio-economic conditions.[32] The reciprocal connection between suicide and depression is well documented. The novel's focus on the depressed narcissist, ravaged by pain but also addicted to that pain, is characteristic of contemporary Gothic. The connection between suicide and depression mirrors that between trauma and haunting – a past event (Kizuki's suicide) affects the present (Naoko's depression and suicide), and the present affects the future (Toru's melancholia). But the book also hints that Naoko was depressed long before Kizuki's death, which makes such a cause–effect pattern questionable. Suicide and depression become part of the ripple effect, with waves so immense that they obscure the centre.

Retaliation

Although statistics show that the majority of suicides in Japan are committed by older people,[33] there are also reports on the growing rate of suicides among the young. In 2014, suicide was the main cause of death among people aged fifteen to thirty-nine and accounted for almost half of the deaths among those aged twenty to twenty-nine (*Japan Times*). *Gray Men* by Tomotake Ishikawa singles out the young as the most vulnerable to suicide. The novel equates suicide with an act of violence committed by the state that sanctions inequality for the sake of profit. The main protagonist, Ryotaro, contemplates suicide as a result of bullying at work after he refuses to have sex with a rich client. His self-destruction is interrupted by the arrival of a man in a gray suit who recruits him for his cause of the 'redistribution of wealth'. The suited man, Gray, is set on a personal vendetta against Japanese society, which he sees as marred by corruption on every level and functioning as a mechanism of oppression serving the needs of the rich. How degenerate these needs can be is fully demonstrated through the existence of The Tower, a criminal organisation procuring underage girls for the gratification of the sadistic urges of rich men and auctioning them to be killed on camera for the erotic pleasure of the highest bidder. Gray and his army of averted suicides carry out bold robberies to secure the funds, set up a fake company that convinces the rich to invest in imaginary raremetal mining rights, hack computers to retrieve sensitive information that can be used to blackmail people into compliance and collect evidence to cause political scandal and topple the government. The redistribution of power is complete with the destruction of the reserves of the Bank of Japan and the presses needed to print new bills. The avengers of the underclass make their escape thanks to the rising of the oppressed masses that come out in support, dressed in ubiquitous gray.

Gray Men fits in with other dystopian texts that build up to the rising of the individual (or the masses) against the oppression of the totalitarian state. And yet, the novel's plot does not unfold against the backdrop of a futuristic nightmare metropolis but remains firmly rooted in the realities of early twenty-first-century Japan. Although the criminal events described are a work of fiction, they offer a reflection on the way the excesses of global neoliberal politics have reshaped the social structures of countries like Japan. According to World Bank statistics, Japan has the third largest economy in the world based on GDP, and while many sources claim that income inequality is almost non-existent, others speak of a rapid increase in 'hidden poverty' attributed to 'falling real wages, rising inequality and the rise of low-paid non-regular employment'.[34] In 2012, over 16 per cent of the Japanese population found itself living below the poverty line, a situation that mostly affects single-parent households.[35] These are the people the novel calls 'gray men' – both alien and invisible to the system that continues to disregard individuals for the benefit of the richest elites.

Studies indicate that apart from illness, most suicides in Japan are caused by financial or life-related problems (mostly debt and poverty), family issues (including conflict and divorce) and work-related problems (e.g. bullying or unemployment).[36] Many of these are intricately related and aggravated by economic recession and growing income disparity. Gray speaks of a civil war waged by Japan against her own people:

> People say Japan is a good country, that her people [are] among the world's fortunate. Tell me, then, why does the suicide rate never go down? We know that over thirty thousand people end their lives each year. If you add in those who go missing, it's two hundred thousand. That's how many meet their deaths. This country is at war. Why does no one look more closely?[37]

Social problems highlighted in the novel include dysfunctional families, ineffective educational institutions, underage prostitution, rising crime rates, widespread acceptance of corruption, a flawed legal system and general devaluation of human life. These represent the 'socially unspeakable' taboos of neoliberal capitalism that many contemporary Gothic texts credit with creating monsters. Suicides, for Gray, are neither altruistic sacrifices for the greater good nor individualistic choices, but are part of the mechanism of oppression allowing for the elimination of those who cannot be further exploited. Suicide prevention is thus a form of resistance.

Despite his 'salaryman' appearance and old-fashioned manners, Gray does not stand for 'traditional Japan' but rather belongs with comic-book heroes, his suit and smile replacing the mask. His goal is '*to grant the weak the possibility of resisting the powerful and to plant the seeds of fear in the strong*, thereby evening out the lopsided seesaw' (224, italics in original). Like Batman, he is a dark avenger haunted by his past, but unlike Batman, Gray is too damaged to rise above it. The final stage of his master plan involves eliminating three criminals who raped and murdered his wife and daughter several years before. The men were caught and prosecuted but were given a lenient sentence because of their youth. The photographic evidence of rape, torture and murder was leaked by the police and turned into sensational entertainment by the media. Gray kidnaps the criminals, subjects them to psychological torture and intends to end his plan with murder-suicide. Ironically, the man who saved countless young people from taking their own life has done it to license his own death.

Gray sees his suicide in terms of the accomplishment of his goals. His vengeance achieved, his life will be devoid of purpose, therefore removing himself is the logical act that follows. Yet this motivation, which seemed acceptable for a Zen philosopher like Sensei, is oddly jarring in the world described in the novel. Gray's suicide is thus interrupted by the reappearance of an old enemy, who takes his life – when Gray eventually steps off the cliff, he is already dying, shot through with several bullets, which makes this gesture merely a dignified reaction to something inevitable. It is his attempt to have the last word: 'All stories require an ending ... My disappearing ... Disappearance is the most fitting one for this tale' (239).

In contrast to other crimes that unfold through the action or negligence of specific perpetrators, the novel portrays suicide as the ultimate form of social injustice, an act of violence carried out by 'the system' that becomes the Gothic unnameable. Ironically, the actual suicides are a negative space in the text – Ryotaro's death is averted, and Gray is already dying. His fall into the pit is symbolic of sowing the seeds of revolution and results in multiplication:

The masses were staging 'rebellions' across the world. Tackling the full spectrum of sources of their suffering, the oppressed all over the globe were putting on gray garbs and making their voices heard. A new wave of Grays encircled the planet. (252)

Suicide inspires retaliation.

Repetition

The bizarre opening of Sion Sono's film *Suicide Circle* shows a mass suicide of fifty-four schoolgirls who join hands and, still chatting and giggling, jump under the Tokyo Express train, their bodies exploding violently all over the platform. In a different part of the city, a night nurse jumps out of a hospital window. Her friend returns with food, offers it to a night guard and follows her without a word of explanation. After the suicides, two bags containing 200 stitched pieces of human skin are found. The police are alerted to the existence of a mysterious 'Suicide Club' that is responsible. The film continues with a surreal kaleidoscopic montage of unrelated scenes: children jumping off the roof of the school, a girl hit by the falling body of her boyfriend, the family of the lead detective lost to murder-suicide. Subliminal messages are encoded in the songs of a teenage girlband, and a cryptic web board records suicides as red and white dots before they happen. 'Suicide Club' materialises in the guise of violent young men who kidnap, rape and murder women, but even when they are arrested, people keep dying. The message of the film is that to live, one must be 'connected to oneself'. When we die, our connections to other people remain, but if we are gone, are we still connected to ourselves?

In the film, the suicides are blamed on a Suicide Club said to encourage people to kill themselves. Suicide Club is a myth akin to a viral Internet curse that kills anyone who stumbles on the 'forbidden' website (a common Japanese urban legend). In reality there is no club, but there is a Suicide Circle, a reference to the cyclical nature of events portrayed in the film. This is even more visible in the manga version of the story. Here, the focus is on repetition. A young girl descends into depression following family problems, bullying and abuse. She begins to cut herself and sell her body and develops an eating disorder. Then she meets Mitsuko and becomes her obsessive follower. Mitsuko invites her to commit joint suicide with other girls. The girl survives. She adopts the name Mitsuko, and the story repeats itself.

While those left behind keep searching for a monster, we realise that there is no monster – every girl is Mitsuko, because every girl has the power to hurt herself and to hurt others.

Although never identified as Gothic, all the texts examined in this chapter employ a variety of Gothic conventions – from monstrous landscapes and Gothic heroes, victims and villains torn by internal conflict, to depictions of cruelty and violence, often sexualised, grotesque monstrous bodies and minds, disease, political upheaval, abuse of power, conflicts of memory, trauma and haunting. While the portrayal of suicide in modern Japanese texts can be contextualised as Gothic, these texts also demonstrate that concepts such as monstrosity, death or sin are culture-specific and significantly expand our interpretation. Attitudes to gender and sexuality; perception of time and space; relations between sin, guilt and punishment; conceptualisation; and fear of death have different implications in Japanese culture. Suicide thus can be an admission of guilt but also a nihilistic withdrawal and merging into nothingness, where fear of death is replaced by fear of life. It can be a form of inertia, passive resistance or quiet rebellion of an individual against the group. It can be a form of a recurring, contagious disease or karmic repetition. Finally, it can be a form of systemic violence, linked to the terror of neoliberal capitalism. Depictions of suicide in these texts reject Japanese cultural normalisation that accepts it as altruistic sacrifice for social ends. But they also expose the confines of a Eurocentric worldview that Gothic scholarship needs to liberate itself from if it wants to become transcultural.

Notes

1 Émile Durkheim, *Suicide: A Study in Sociology*, trans. J. A. Spaulding and G. Simpson (London and New York: Routledge, 2005), p. 180.
2 Tsunetomo Yamamoto, *Hagakure: The Book of the Samurai*, trans. W. S. Wilson (Tokyo: Kodansha International, 2002), p. 17.
3 Durkheim, *Suicide*, p. 178.
4 Masaru Fujimoto, 'Chushingura Chushingura', *Japan Times*, 15 December 2002, para 25. Retrieved from www.japantimes.co.jp/community/2002/12/15/general/chushingura-chushingura/#.WJXryH-Qp_k, accessed 17 January 2017.
5 Aleksandr Fedorovich Prasol, *Modern Japan: Origins of the Mind* (Singapore: World Scientific Publishing, 2010), p. 209.
6 Henry J. Hughes, 'Familiarity of the Strange: Japan's Gothic Tradition', *Criticism*, 42:1 (2000), 59–89, at 60.

7   Ibid., 74.
8   Daniel Wright, 'Spiritual Discernment in Soseki Natsume's *Kokoro*', *The International Fiction Review*, 17:1 (1990), 14–19, at 14.
9   Natsume Soseki, *Kokoro*, trans. M. McKinney (London: Penguin, 2010), p. 217.
10 Following one's lord in death.
11 Meredith McKinney, 'Introduction', in Soseki, *Kokoro*, pp. vii–xvi, at p. xi.
12 Ibid.
13 David Punter, *The Literature of Terror* (London: Longman, 1980), p. 6.
14 Eve Kosofsky-Sedgwick, *The Coherence of Gothic Conventions* (London: Methuen, 1986), p. 10.
15 Wendy Jones Nakanishi, 'The Dying Game: Suicide in Modern Japanese Literature', *Electronic Journal of Contemporary Japanese Studies*, 2005, para 19. Retrieved from www.japanesestudies.org.uk/discussionpapers/2005/Nakanishi.html, accessed 20 December 2016.
16 Ibid.
17 Wright, 'Spiritual Discernment', 17.
18 Ibid.
19 Ibid., 16.
20 Michael F. Marra, *Essays on Japan: Between Aesthetics and Literature* (Leiden: Brill, 2010), p. 203.
21 Yasuko Claremont, *The Novels of Oe Kenzaburo* (London: Routledge, 2009), pp. 69–70.
22 Kenzaburo Oe, *The Silent Cry*, trans. John Bester (London: Serpent's Tail, 2011), p. 4. Subsequent references are to this edition and are given in parentheses in the text.
23 See Claremont, *Novels of Oe Kenzaburo*, p. 67.
24 Justin D. Edwards and Rune Graulund, *Grotesque* (London: Routledge, 2013), pp. 39–40.
25 Akira Nishiyama, 'Exploring Suicide in Japan: In the Light of Mental Illness and Socioeconomic Factors', SFC Discussion Paper 2010-004 (2010), 1–38, at 7. Retrieved from gakkai.sfc.keio.ac.jp/dp_pdf/10-04.pdf, accessed 17 January 2017.
26 Sigmund Freud, *Beyond the Pleasure Principle*, trans. J. Strachey (New York: W. W. Norton, 1975), p. 32.
27 Julia Kristeva, *Black Sun: Depression and Melancholia* (New York: Columbia University Press, 1980), p. 12.
28 Ibid., pp. 12–13.
29 Haruki Murakami, *Norwegian Wood*, trans. Jay Rubin (New York: Vintage Books, 2010), p. 193. Subsequent references are to this edition and are given in parentheses in the text.
30 Kristeva, *Black Sun*, p. 4.
31 Ibid., p. 13.
32 Joe Chen, Yun Jeong Choi, Kohta Mori, Yasuyuki Sawada and Saki Sugano, 'Recession, Unemployment, and Suicide in Japan', *Japan Labor Review*, 9:2 (2012), 75–92, at 78.
33 In 2011, Japan's National Police Agency reported that 56 per cent of all suicides were committed by people over fifty years old (Ulrike Schaede, 'Sunshine

and Suicides in Japan: Revisiting the Relevance of Economic Determinants of Suicide', *Contemporary Japan*, 25:2 (2013), 105–26, at 112).

34 Noah Smith, 'Japan's Growing Poverty Defies Glib Explanations', *Bloomberg*, 26 April 2016, para 5. Retrieved from www.bloomberg.com/view/articles/2016-04-26/japan-s-growing-poverty-defies-glib-explanations, accessed 17 January 2017.

35 Tomohiro Osaki, 'Hidden Poverty Growing under Abe, Particularly among Young and Single Mothers', *Japan Times*, 26 April 2016, para 10, 18. Retrieved from www.japantimes.co.jp/news/2016/04/26/national/social-issues/hidden-poverty-growing-abe-particularly-among-young-single-mothers/#.Wgj-sYhx3IU, accessed 17 January 2017.

36 Chen *et al.*, 'Suicide in Japan', 78.

37 Tomotake Ishikawa, *Gray Men*, trans. J. Lloyd-Davies (New York: Vertical, 2013), pp. 213–14.

11

Dawn Stobbart

'I will abandon this body and take to the air': the suicide at the heart of *Dear Esther*

> *Dear Esther. I am on a stone jetty, the sun is setting and I am alone on this island. I cannot interact with anything: all I can do is walk, look and listen. As I walk, I hear a voice speak, reading fragments of letters to you. It becomes clear, as I listen to the fragments, that I am following the path that someone else has already trodden; the author of the letters has preceded me in my traversal of this island. I walk on, exploring this silent twilight, the fragments of letters becoming more confused, the mental state of the writer deteriorating as I move, until I have a vision of climbing an aerial tower, and plunging to the ground. I fly over the island, over all the locations I have visited, until once again I am at the stone jetty, and the screen fades to black, with the words 'come back' ringing in my ears. Then I am back – back at the stone jetty; the sun is setting and I am alone on this island.*[1]

As this brief (but concise) walkthrough shows, *Dear Esther* is part of a growing category of games known as the first-person walker, or walking simulator, a genre whose sole activity comprises of traversing a game space, often at a walking pace.[2] This non-ludic structure allows the player to become immersed in the world of the game through the use of her eyes and ears, rather than through quick reflexes or learned techniques, as is the case with many popular videogames.[3] This means that rather than engaging in combat or competition, the player of *Dear Esther* is required to interpret a landscape, in conjunction with the one-sided dialogue that an unnamed protagonist has with the Esther of the game's title. The 'story' of the game is told in an epistolary form, delivered through fragments of letters, and is augmented by the player's ability to observe the landscape, using both together to build a cohesive narrative of loss, grief, guilt and suicide.

Catherine Spooner reminds us that the Gothic has never been solely restricted to books.[4] Thus, 'given that a great majority of video games are based on the need to stay alive',[5] it is not surprising that the 'Gothic obsession with death' allows it to be a source of much inspiration for this branch of new media.[6] Gothic tropes and elements frequently appear in a variety of videogames, including *Doom*, as Fred Botting argues,[7] and more recently, the *Portal* franchise, which Ewan Kirkland considers to be 'distinctly Gothic in theme and tone'.[8] Gothicism can also be seen in the settings, aesthetics and narratives of many of the new videogames released every year, a space into which *Dear Esther* fits.

Whilst videogames ably represent the monstrous – and the need to kill the monster – recent years have seen an evolution in terms of content, with developers turning their attention from solely ludic enjoyment to 'serious' games that explicitly foreground a moral aspect, didactic content or a strong narrative. Games such as *Gone Home* deal with sexuality and acceptance, whilst *Depression Quest* tries to offer a way to understand depression, through a narrative that requires the player to make decisions and react to some of the situations that a depressed person might recognise, including suicidal feelings and the reaction to those feelings – something not frequently explored in most videogames.[9]

Gothic themes, tropes and narrative converge in the 2012 videogame *Dear Esther*. Set in the perpetual twilight of a deserted Hebridean island, this game involves the player exploring a typically Gothic landscape, which is 'more than just a mere backdrop to the main action', being central to the game and its story.[10] There are two major interpretations of *Dear Esther*, according to Pinchbeck's notes: a literal one, where 'the narrator has a nervous breakdown and strands himself on a deserted Hebridean island', or a version of the island that 'is not a real space at all … a visualisation of the destroyed interior landscape of the narrator's mind'.[11] Both of these interpretations can be supported by the ambiguous letter fragments; this chapter, however, is concerned with the second interpretation. In this reading, I contend that through a subversion of gaming expectations and tropes, *Dear Esther*'s simple control system and the lack of interactivity with the game's landscape, the player takes on the role of a ghost that haunts the island, occupying a liminal space between the player and the narrator in the game, and forcing the narrator to endlessly repeat his suicide and the events that lead to it.

Dear Esther was originally released in June 2008 for the popular game *Half-Life 2*. Using many of the structural elements of its 'parent' game, such as the graphics and sounds, players are able to adapt them to create new elements, or even a wholly original game that bears little resemblance to its parent, even though accessing it requires the original game. Following its initial release, *Dear Esther* was entirely remade and rereleased in February 2012 as a stand-alone title, with extra content and an amplified and richer landscape. It was again rereleased in late 2016, taking advantage of technological advances that allow even more photorealistic visuals and sound, and further enhancing the narrative experience of the game, creating a more 'real' space for the narrator to haunt. The result of the non-ludic strategy means that the player must concentrate solely on the narrative, the setting and the soundscape – these being commonly the forgotten or unnoticed elements of a videogame, though their importance in the representation of videogame narratives is as great as their comparable elements in other media such as film. The landscape is complemented by a Gothic musical score, resulting in feelings of solitude and an increasing sense of uneasiness as the game progresses and the disparate elements of the narrative begin to knit together. Through its narrative and through ludic disempowerment, *Dear Esther* offers the player a ghost story and provides an insight into the mind of the suicidal protagonist via a tale of death, imprisonment, madness and escape that is recognisable throughout the history of Gothic fiction. It does so by placing the player within the narrative itself, physically driving it onward, both through her actions and the replay necessary to come to a full understanding of that narrative, and asking her to interpret the information she finds to discover the game's suicidal and Gothic heart.

The control system for *Dear Esther* is simple; all that is required is basic movement: no running, jumping, ducking or shooting is required to play, something unfamiliar to most players. Yet, this momentum allows the player to uncover three distinct stories: that of a Scandinavian hermit named Jacobson and an eighteenth-century explorer named Donnelly, and (most importantly for this paper) the narrator's own story. The game reaches a climax with the suicide of the unnamed (male) narrator, where he hopes to be reunited with Esther. Instead, as the walkthrough at the beginning of this chapter shows, he (and the player) is transported back to the stone jetty to begin again. Reaching specific areas in the landscape triggers the recitation of these fragments of the letters (generally one of three or four available, which contain slightly different information). Canonical Gothic narratives such as *Dracula* and *Frankenstein* and more recent works such as Max Brooks' *World War Z* (2009) and Lionel Shriver's *We Need to Talk About Kevin* (2010) all make use of this structure, with the potential for unreliable narration being a key factor in these texts. It is into this tradition that *Dear Esther* fits: the unreliability of the narrator becomes a major factor in the interpretive nature of the narrative. The fragmentary nature of the letter delivery means that the player, to understand the narrative fully, must repeatedly force the narrator to relive his suicide, haunting this landscape with his continued presence each time the game is switched on and the journey begun anew. The narrator himself appears to have an awareness of his status as haunter, telling Esther 'I have lost track of how long I have been here, and how many visits I have made overall' as the game opens, something Pinchbeck also signals when he writes that 'the idea of a cycle is important here, that the player is given the sense this is all a repeat'.[12] Usually, videogames use death and reincarnation as a way to learn from past mistakes, and thereby to progress, the cycle being broken as the player becomes sufficiently skilled to continue. *Dear Esther* refutes this classic gaming trope; instead, the game forces the narrator to relive the same events over and over again, and enshrouds him in his own version of hell.

The physical setting of *Dear Esther* is a beautiful, deserted Hebridean island, but even this is called into question by the ambiguous and interpretative nature of the game. Playing the game, the landscape foregrounded and interactivity limited, the player begins to question its verisimilitude as she finds herself 'slipping into the delusional state of ascribing purpose, deliberate motive to everything', in a landscape that is wholly created, whether that is by a game designer or by the narrator's own mind. One of the opening narrative fragments has the narrator reveal 'I sometimes feel as if I've given birth to this island', while another fragment asks 'was this island formed during the moment of impact, when we were torn loose from our moorings and the seatbelts cut motorway lanes into our chests and shoulders? Did it first break surface then?' The island is created as a result of the narrator's own suicide, with his guilt functioning much as the infection in his body, preventing healing and causing him endless pain. This island, then, is kept alive by the narrator's own haunting of this space. This is made even more explicit when he relates having kidney stones removed in hospital, remarking 'now my stones have grown into an island and made their escape and you have been rendered opaque by the car of a drunk'. He, himself, understands the island's structure, yet is unable to escape its confines.

The landscape of *Dear Esther* is a clearly Gothic space: the barren yet beautiful environment is as sublime as that found in *Frankenstein* or *Wuthering Heights*, and it inspires awe as the player walks around the island. Equally, it embodies the capacity to chill the player with its bleak emptiness. This landscape, in other words, may be 'comparable to eighteenth-century aesthetic notions, in which a sense of the sublime occurs in an encounter with an immensity the mind cannot comprehend, a natural and divine power found in the sovereign shape of rugged, mountainous landscapes'.[13] The player passes, but is unable to interact with the evidence of, previous human habitation, ranging from a stone circle thousands of years old to an aerial that sends a red beacon into the perpetual twilight of the game, with old buildings being part of this landscape, their ruinous presence a reminder of the Gothic spaces of many other narratives. This creates a feeling of gloom and deterioration that pervades the entire landscape, which encompasses the extreme contrasts regarded as crucial by Linda Bayer-Berenbaum, when she writes 'the Gothic landscape plunges from extreme to extreme; from the height of an airy bell to the depth of a dungeon vault'.[14] Removal of all the ludic elements of the game forces the player to pay attention to these details, found in many videogames but which conventionally remain unnoticed, as she engages in battles, competition and point scoring.

Whilst the player walks, and the information the narrator delivers becomes increasingly disjointed (due to his blood poisoning), it becomes clear that the player is following the narrator's path as he contemplates and commits suicide, before being returned to the stone jetty, to begin his journey again. The letters contain details that appear out of joint with the landscape: for example, near the end of his journey, the narrator relates finding a cargo of paint that he will mix with 'ashes and tarmac and the glow from our infections' long after this has been seen by the player. The letters also allow the player to gain an understanding of the reasons for his suicide: as the narrator becomes increasingly confused, the letters become more frequent, and refer to himself, rather than another character, Paul, as being responsible for Esther's death. In these fragments, the narrator suggests that he has an alcohol problem and intimates that he was drunk-driving when the accident that claimed Esther occurred. He admits to being drunk as he arrived at the island and has painted the chemical symbol for alcohol (CH_3CH_2OH) over the island in his delirious state, using the paint he has found. The landscape itself aids in providing the information that the player needs to understand the narrative, alongside the spoken words.

The relationship the narrative has with the landscape can be summarised best by one of the fragments the narrator relates as he crosses the third beach of the island:

> To explore here is to become passive, to internalise the journey and not to attempt to break the confines ... It will take a number of expeditions to traverse this micro continent ... to arrive at the point of final departure.

This is joined by one of the opening fragments, where the narrator states, 'I return each time leaving fresh markers that I hope, in the full glare of my hopelessness, will have blossomed into fresh insight in the interim.' For the player, this will involve repeating the game, whilst for the narrator, it will mean reliving of the events leading up to his suicide, where he hopes he will be able to end the cycle of haunting and be reunited with Esther.

The visual construction of the island supports the supposition that landscape is created in the mind of the narrator. As the game progresses, the player sees that the landscape is littered with detritus from the car accident, and surgical equipment that would not be present if the narrator washed ashore, as he says. Interestingly, these objects are randomised, with each play inserting or omitting objects that may be important to the narrative. The final passage of the game, at the point of the narrator's suicide, is a last letter to Esther, in which he tells her that he has 'painted, carved, hewn, scored into this space all that [he] could draw from him' and that he 'will rise from the ocean like an island without a bottom, come together like a stone, become an aerial, a beacon'; it gives further credence to the island's internal construction in the mind of the narrator, and his reappearance at the beginning. This island is a place of memory and of guilt, of repeated attempts to come to terms with the loss of Esther and failing.

In keeping with many Gothic texts across media, doubling plays an important part in the construction and delivery of this game's narrative. There is a very evident doubling of the narrator and the player in *Dear Esther*, as well as with the other characters mentioned in the letters, primarily Donnelly and Paul. First, and most obviously, the player is continually retracing the footsteps of the narrator and reliving his final days on the island, haunting the island in a very literal sense, and forcing the narrator to relive these events every time the game is loaded. However, the doubling between the narrator and the other characters is subtler than this. Indeed, the narrative itself (and the notes Pinchbeck produced for his development of the game) suggests that the other characters (with the exception of the hermit) are manifestations of the narrator's own psyche and that this doubling is a further haunting, where the narrator is haunted by himself and his own previous actions. This concept is first indicated near the beginning of the game, when the player is walking up a cliff path, and a letter fragment discussing a book written by Donnelly relates that

> if the subject matter is obscure, the writer's literary style is even more so, it is not the text of a stable or trustworthy reporter. Perhaps it is fitting that my only companion in these last days should be a stolen book written by a dying man.

For the player, this is an ironic statement, especially if it is not the first time she has played the game. The letter fragments show the narrator to be increasingly unstable as the game progresses and he approaches his death, suggesting that in some way, the narrator is referencing himself. Several times, the narrator speaks of Donnelly in the present tense: he relates that Donnelly speaks to him and that he physically carries Donnelly's corpse on his back, which 'whispers of guilt … He tells me I was not drunk at all'. This aligns the narrator with Donnelly; the corpse the narrator carries is analogous to the popular phrase describing addiction as a 'monkey on your back', and the oft-repeated denial of the alcoholic that they are drunk.

Central to the narrative of the game – and the suicide of the narrator – is the car accident and its resulting question: was the narrator drunk, and thus responsible for the death of Esther, or is his guilt misplaced? The game does not reveal the answer to this question, but leaves the player to interpret the letter fragments as they become increasingly more confused. At the beginning of the game, the letter fragments are lucid, relating the events that brought him to the island, the theft of Donnelly's book from an Edinburgh library to guide him around the island, and visiting Paul, attempting unsuccessfully to come to terms with his loss. This coherent structure changes as the narrator's health breaks down and he approaches his death, producing a narrative technique in which the player becomes confused, mirroring the disorientation of the narrator. As the narrator's state of mind deteriorates, he begins to become muddled about facts and starts to contradict previous statements; this results in the player not being able to decide who is responsible for what actions in the narrative, just as the narrator himself seems unable to distinguish between different people and their actions. For example, the narrator, early in the game, suggests that Paul was the driver of another car and is responsible for Esther's death, saying 'He still maintains he wasn't drunk, but tired' at one point. When delirious, however, the narrator's ravings suggest that it was not Paul's fault, but his own actions that caused Esther's death: the guilt that Donnelly whispers of, which tells the narrator he was not drunk, along with 'I saw only bruises, cut into the cliffs by my lack of sobriety', offer an implicit admission of his own guilt. He also admits to 'being increasingly unable to find that point where the hermit ends and Paul and I begin'.

As well as being a character, Paul also alludes to what is an explicitly religious theme in the game. Within the letter fragments, and written on the landscape itself, there are repeated references to Damascus, which links to Paul and is a clearly religious allusion (as is Esther). According to Christian religion, Paul, whilst travelling to Damascus, underwent a dramatic conversion to Christianity, becoming a key figure in creating the doctrine that transformed Christianity from a small sect within Judaism into a worldwide faith. At various points in the game, Paul (the game character) is compared to the biblical apostle; the journey of the player and the narrator is compared to that of Paul and his journey to Damascus, and the literal road to Damascus is compared to the stretch of the M5 motorway where Esther was killed. The religious theme is seen in more than these references, however, for instance in the musical score; and the content of the letters to Esther, such as those describing the island, is considered in religious terms:

> Donnelly tells me that [the shepherds] had one Bible that was passed around in strict rotation. It was stolen by a visiting monk … did they assign chapter and verse to the stones and grasses, marking the geography with a superimposed significance; that they could actually walk the Bible and inhabit its contradictions?

There are several other references to religion in the letters, the first being at the opening of the game, when the narrator mentions an 'alpha point'. Pinchbeck explains that this is a reference to 'the religious idea of God being the alpha and the omega, the beginning and the end of all things'. There are also references in the letter fragments to the Sermon on the Mount, to Lot and his wife and to the lid of the Ark of the Covenant, all of which point to a religious undertone to the game.[15] All of these clues in the text which allude to the Christian religion support the concept of the island being a personal purgatory for the narrator, constructed of his own guilt and sin. Many religions historically believed that suicide was a major sin, and 'the Roman Catholic Church forbade the Christian burial of those who committed suicide', and 'the same norms were held by other Christian churches, or other religions and ethnic denominations'.[16] Therefore, the act of suicide that ends (and begins) the game denies the narrator forgiveness, and dooms him to repeat his actions.

It is impossible to discuss the cyclical and repetitious nature of *Dear Esther* without making reference to Freud. In *Beyond the Pleasure Principle*, Freud writes that there is a 'compulsion to repeat' things, even to the point where this repetition is harmful and counterproductive, as the 'compulsion to repeat also recalls from past experiences which include no possibility of pleasure' to the person who is engaged in the repetition.[17] Freud explains that the activity being repeated is 'intended to lead to satisfaction; but no lesson has been learned from the old experience of these activities having led instead only to unpleasure. In spite of that, they are repeated, under pressure of a compulsion'.[18] This informs the underlying structure of the game. The narrator, having committed suicide, is then driven by a compulsion to repeat his actions again and again; each time, the intention is to achieve the satisfaction of being reunited with Esther – but instead of the reward he seeks, he is once again returned to the opening of the game, where the repetition will begin again. I consider that the narrator's guilt brings about this repetition, functioning in the same way as Freud's 'punishment dreams', which 'merely replace the forbidden wish-fulfilment by the appropriate punishment for it', and that the island itself is a dreamlike space which the narrator has himself constructed from his suicide on the real island.[19]

The ideal way to play *Dear Esther*, as with many other videogames, is in a darkened room, with the sound playing through earphones to block out any external noise, thus allowing the player to focus solely on the game. This enables the sounds of the landscape and the musical score to become foregrounded alongside the narrative and to take their place as an integral part of the narrative experience. Music has a sonic space of its own making, as Jean-Luc Nancy, amongst others, argues.²⁰ Thus, music engenders a time and space of its own, which alongside the perpetual twilight of the island means that the player is invited to leave behind the here-and-now of reality and to allow herself to feel the immersive effect of the soundtrack to *Dear Esther*. The ambient sounds, the disembodied human noises and the musical score combine with the landscape to raise the player's awareness of sight and sound – to feel part of the diegesis. Isabella van Elferen, in *Gothic Music*, considers Gothic 'game music [to] defy the borders of the screen and envelope game and player alike in its own, sonic version of virtual reality' with the inclusion of Gothic sounds, ranging from 'hollow footsteps' to 'ghostly melodies'.²¹ *Dear Esther* is filled with the diegetic sounds of the landscape, which combine with the musical score to assist in this enveloping of the player in the game. The crash of the waves on the sea, the sound of the wind across the island and the plaintive cry of a single seagull as it is disturbed all feature in this soundscape, with the only diegetic manmade sounds being footsteps as the player walks the island, as the Gothic music is exchanged for the natural noises of the derelict landscape in places. Serving to highlight the link between the music and the sounds of the landscape, the source of the footsteps the player hears as she walks the island is enigmatic; are they the footsteps of the player, or are they the footsteps of the narrator, reminding the player of his prior claim on the narrative, and the setting, as well as his journey to death? Are they a supernatural echo that only the player can hear, though their source is not locatable, as there are no feet to create the steps evident in the game? Occasionally, the sound of a female voice whispering 'come back', reminiscent of Catherine Earnshaw's 'Let me in', can be heard if, for example, the player sinks into the sea – refusing to let her fade into nothingness, calling her back to the beach and the endless repetition of the journey over and through the island, and that final plunge from the beacon.²²

Throughout the game, music seems to play randomly as the player walks; a solo violin or the unaccompanied voice of a piano penetrate the diegetic sounds, dragging the player, as van Elferen says, 'along in the musical movement from the mundane to the divine or the occult' and enveloping her in the timeless nature of the narrative, a time parallel to, within and yet without the present outside the game.²³ Since music is a temporal art form it cannot possibly exist in an atemporal vacuum, and therefore its presence detracts from the timelessness that the visual representation of the landscape suggests, causing a dissonance in the listener and in her interpretation of the game. Usually, a listener would expect the mundane – a complete and unified melody; however, in Gothic music, the divine and/or occult can be represented in the fragmented and broken snatches of melody that are heard throughout *Dear Esther*. Musical theory uses expectation and deviation as part of its basis, and so the refusal of Gothic music to lead to a mundane outcome suggests that the composer is deliberately subverting the musical score to create an unsettling piece. A female voice can be discerned within the music, her voice a non-diegetic element of the game, seemingly indistinguishable from the diegetic noise of the landscape, and her litany a religious undertone to remind the player of the island's position as limbo – the place between life and death that the narrator inhabits. This example also functions as an instance of stylistic awareness; that is, the player will consider this as religious through expectations, even as the narrative subverts it. The musical score aids the interpretation of the narrative as being endless, as the repetition of the events and the lack of perfect cadences (the traditional way to 'end' a piece of music or to 'resolve' dissonance) means the music refuses to have a final ending, allowing the return to the game's beginning to be deliberate and part of the fragmented narrative that the score suggests.[24]

At the point where the narrator begins the climb up the radio mast, and commits suicide, control is completely removed, placing the player in a passive position: even the prospect of movement is denied her. Again, the links with religion are made manifest, the predetermined nature of the journey made explicit at this last moment – there is no choice in this act, and the narrator will once again take his own life. For the narrative, this is the culmination of the narrator's journey: he believes he is about to be reunited with his beloved Esther. The player soars across the island, the music reminiscent of a religious litany, the religious echoes becoming louder and more dominant in the piece as the player approaches the place where the game began. There is a discordant note, and the screen starts to get darker, fading slowly to black. There is a final 'come back' and the game begins anew; the narrator begins his journey once again. He is denied redemption and must repeat his journey endlessly, every time the player loads the game.

At first glance, *Dear Esther* seems to be a simple game, the lack of interaction being counterintuitive to many gamers' expectations. However, this game is a sophisticated and deeply thought out piece of software, with the focus on the narrative as gameplay, specifically in the interpretation of the narrative through the events, landscape and soundscape of the game. Each element of the game is a constituent portion of the narrative, and the player combines these to create a narrative based on her own elucidations of the letter fragments, the landscape and the musical score - one that allows the player to act as a quasi-author of the piece, bringing her own understanding and experience to a deliberately ambiguous work that allows multiple interpretations. The suicide of the narrator forms the basis of the game's cyclical structure and explains the need to replay the game several times to understand the narrative. The suicide also informs the narrator's mental state and explains the island as a manifestation of his own tortured psyche – literally a religious purgatory from which he can never be freed, brought about because of his sins: the death of Esther, his responsibility for her death and his suicide.

Notes

1 This walkthrough is based on my own primary playing experience.
2 Dan Pinchbeck, *Dear Esther* (Portsmouth: The Chinese Room, 2012). All in-game quotations are taken from this version of the game.
3 Mark J. P. Wolf, 'What is a Video Game?', in Mark J. P. Wolf (ed.), *The Video Game Explosion: A History from PONG to Playstation and Beyond* (Westport, CT: Greenwood Publishing Group, 2008), pp. 3–8, at p. 4.
4 Catherine Spooner, 'Gothic Media', in Catherine Spooner and Emma McEvoy (eds), *The Routledge Companion to Gothic* (Abingdon: Routledge, 2007), pp. 195–8, at p. 195.
5 Bernard Perron, 'Introduction', in Bernard Perron (ed.), *Horror Video Games: Essays on the Fusion and Fear of Play* (Jefferson, NC: McFarland, 2009), pp. 3–13, at p. 7.
6 Coral Ann Howells, 'The Gothic Way of Death in English Fiction 1790–1820', in Fred Botting and Dale Townshend (eds), *Gothic: Critical Concepts in Literary and Cultural Studies* (London: Routledge, 2004), pp. 223–32, at p. 223.
7 id Software, *Doom* (Mesquite, TX, 10 December 1993); Fred Botting, 'Aftergothic: Consumption, Machines, and Black Holes', in Jerrold E. Hogle (ed.), *The Cambridge Companion to Gothic Fiction* (Cambridge: Cambridge University Press, 2002), pp. 277–300.
8 Valve, *Portal* (Kirkland, WA, 2007–11); Ewan Kirkland, 'Gothic and Survival Horror Videogames', in Glennis Byron and Dale Townshend (eds), *The Gothic World* (London: Routledge, 2014), pp. 454–64, at p. 455.
9 Fullbright, *Gone Home* (Portland, OR, 15 August 2013); Zoe Quinn, *Depression Quest* (14 February 2013), www.depressionquest.com/, accessed 28 February 2018.

10 Sharon Rose Yang and Kathleen Healey, 'Introduction: Haunted Landscapes and Fearful Spaces – Expanding Views on the Geography of the Gothic', in Sharon Rose Yang and Kathleen Healey (eds), *Gothic Landscapes: Changing Eras, Changing Cultures, Changing Anxieties* (London: Palgrave Macmillan, 2016), pp. 1–18, at p. 1.
11 thechineseroom. *Some Old Dear Esther Archive Stuff* (6 September 2013), www.thechineseroom.co.uk/blog/blog/some-old-dear-esther-archive-stuff, accessed 24 February 2017.
12 *Ibid.*
13 Botting, 'Aftergothic: Consumption, Machines, and Black Holes', p. 278.
14 L. Bayer-Berenbaum, *The Gothic Imagination* (Madison, WI: Fairleigh Dickinson University Press, 1982), p. 22.
15 thechineseroom. *Some Old Dear Esther Archive Stuff*.
16 L. Ramon Martinez de Pison, *Death by Despair: Shame and Suicide* (New York: Peter Lang Publishing, 2006), p. 51.
17 Sigmund Freud, *Beyond the Pleasure Principle* (Mineola, NY: Dover Publications, 2015), pp. 13, 14.
18 *Ibid.*, p. 14.
19 *Ibid.*, p. 26.
20 Jean-Luc Nancy, *Listening* (New York: Fordham University Press, 2007), p. 13.
21 Isabella van Elferen, *Gothic Music: The Sounds of the Uncanny* (Cardiff: University of Wales Press, 2012), pp. 106, 1.
22 Emily Brontë, *Wuthering Heights* (London: Collins, 1968), p. 54.
23 Isabella van Elferen, 'The Gothic Bach', *Understanding Bach*, 7 (2012), 9–20, at 19.
24 Dr Vivien Leanne Saunders, in conversation with Dawn Stobbart (Lancaster University, 2016).

Index

Alfredson, Tomas
   Let the Right One In (film) 143
Alvarez, Al
   The Savage God 38, 39
antinatalism 128
antiquarianism 22–5, 26, 27
atonement 2, 8, 9, 55, 60, 62, 165

Brontë, Emily
   Wuthering Heights 14, 180, 185
Brooks, Max
   World War Z 179
Brown, Charles Brockden 12, 96, 103, 105, 106, 107
   Edgar Huntly 98–9, 100
   Wieland 98–9
Byron, George Gordon (Lord) 3–8, 38
   Don Juan 3–5
   Manfred 3, 7
Byronic hero 3, 103

Castlereagh, Robert Stewart (Viscount) 3–8
Chan-wook, Park
   Thirst 14, 139, 145–6, 148
Chatterton, Thomas 38
clergy 2, 8, 10, 11, 20, 37, 43, 55, 58–9, 60, 78, 162, 183
climate change 153
Cobain, Kurt 7, 17n.24

Crain, William
   Blacula 139, 157
crime fiction 116, 117, 123

Dacre, Charlotte
   Zofloya 10, 39–40, 46
Darwinism 66, 67, 70, 75, 76, 77, 79
degeneration 11, 66–9, 70, 77–8, 91, 143
depression 14, 57, 63, 112, 161, 166, 167–9, 172
diet 56, 57, 62, 63, 142
doctors 7, 54, 55, 56–7, 59, 61–3, 72, 73, 81, 89, 104, 162
doppelgänger 8, 10, 20, 69–70, 181–2
Durkheim, Émile 85, 92, 106, 160

ennui 14, 69, 74, 121, 140, 149–54, 157
environment 117, 153

Farrell, Sarah
   'Charlotte' 43–4
Freud, Sigmund
   'Beyond the Pleasure Principle' 115, 184
   'The Uncanny' 117

ghosts 14, 43, 99, 117, 119, 178
Goethe, Johann Wolfgang von 8, 37, 44, 45

Die Leiden des jungen Werthers 6, 10, 36, 37–9, 41, 43, 44–5, 46, 47, 48, 117
Gothic hero 1, 3, 36

hanging 11, 13, 32, 89, 164
Hardy, Thomas
  Jude the Obscure 81
hell 3, 60, 61, 150
Highsmith, Patricia 12–13, 110–12
  The Blunderer 111, 112
  The Boy Who Followed Ripley 112, 118, 120–2
  Carol 111
  Edith's Diary 110
  Ripley Under Ground 13, 112, 113, 118–20, 122–3
  The Talented Mr Ripley 118
  Those Who Walk Away 112
Hogg, James
  Confessions of a Justified Sinner 7
Holocaust, the 112–13
Hopkins, Pauline
  'The Mystery Within Us' 104–5
  Of One Blood 12, 96, 99–107
hypochondria 52

incest 1, 3, 39, 99, 100, 165, 166
insanity 4, 5, 6, 7, 8, 11, 85, 98, 104, 114, 125, 167
Ishikawa, Tomotake
  Gray Men 14, 161, 169–72

Japanese culture 160–1, 163, 169, 170–1
  Buddhism 162, 164
  Shinto 164
  urban legends 172
  Zen 171
Japanese Gothic 161, 173
Jarmusch, Jim
  Only Lovers Left Alive 152–4

Knighton, William
  'Suicidal Mania' 11, 81
Koestler, Arthur 13, 110

Lacan, Jacques 113–15
Lankester, Edwin Ray 11, 67, 68
law 5, 8, 10–11, 15n.4, 19, 69, 86, 118
Le Fanu, Joseph Sheridan 52, 63–4
  'The Familiar' 10, 11, 54, 55, 56, 57, 58–60, 61, 63
  'Green Tea' 10, 11, 54, 55, 56–8, 60–2
  'Mr Justice Harbottle' 10–11, 55, 57, 59, 60, 61, 63
Ligotti, Thomas 124, 128, 136n.2
  The Agonizing Resurrection of Victor Frankenstein 125
  Born to Fear 13
  The Conspiracy Against the Human Race 13, 124, 126, 129
  Grimscribe 13, 124
  'The Lost Art of Twilight' 125
  'The Medusa' 131
  'Metaphysica Morum' 134–5
  My Work Is Not Yet Done 125, 132–3, 134
  'The Night School' 130
  'Notes on the Writing of Horror' 129
  'Professor Nobody's Little Lectures on Supernatural Horror' 129
  Songs of a Dead Dreamer 13, 124
  The Spectral Link 13
  'The Strange Design of Master Rignolo' 133–4, 135
  'Suicide by Imagination' 131
  Teatro Grottesco 125
Lovecraft, H. P. 124–5, 130

Machen, Arthur
  The Great God Pan 11, 66, 72–4, 75, 77, 78
manga 161
Marsh, Richard 11–12, 82–3
  The Beetle 82, 87
  Crime and the Criminal 87, 88, 93
  A Master of Deception 88, 90–1, 92
  Mrs Musgrave – and her Husband 88–90, 92
  The Mystery of Phillip Bennion's Death 87–8, 91, 93
  A Spoiler of Men 87, 91–2

Index

'Suicide' 12, 83–7, 91, 92, 93
Marshall, Frederick
   'Suicide' 67, 68, 78–9, 83–7
medicine 5, 7, 53–4, 69
mental illness 7, 11, 14, 20, 52, 55,
   56, 57, 59, 61, 62, 63, 68,
   85, 89, 96, 99, 104, 106,
   124, 167, 176
mesmerism 100, 101, 102–3, 104, 105
Meyer, Stephenie
   Breaking Dawn 156
Murakami, Haruki
   Norwegian Wood 14, 161, 167–9

Nordau, Max 11
   Degeneration 67
Norrington, Stephen
   Blade 154–5

Oe, Kenzaburo
   The Silent Cry 14, 161, 164–7
'Ossian' (James Macpherson) 19, 21,
   28, 37

Peacock, Thomas Love
   Nightmare Abbey 48–9
Percy, Thomas
   The Reliques 9, 10, 18, 19–33
      'The Boy and the Mantle' 31
      'Edward, Edward' 29–30
      'Jemmy Dawson' 32–3
      'The Legend of King Arthur' 31
      'The Murder of the King of
         Scotland' 31–2
      'Sir Patrick Spence' 30, 32, 33
Poe, Edgar Allan 82, 125
   'William Wilson' 8
poison 8, 40, 84, 88, 93, 96, 97, 98,
   102, 105
pregnancy 155–6, 166
Protestantism 53

Radcliffe, Ann 12, 96, 103, 105, 106,
   107
   The Italian 8, 97–8
   The Mysteries of Udolpho 42

The Romance of the Forest 96–7
Rice, Anne 14, 139, 143, 150
   Interview with the Vampire 143–4,
      145, 147–8
   Memnoch the Devil 144–5
   Merrick 144, 145
   The Vampire Lestat 150
Romanticism 36, 38, 39, 48–9
ruins 22, 23, 46, 99
Rymer, James Malcolm
   Varney the Vampire 139, 141–2,
      144, 147

Scotland 9–10, 18–35 passim,
   177, 179
self-sacrifice 8, 71, 102, 154–6, 171
Shelley, Mary 46–7, 125
   Frankenstein 10, 14, 47–8, 75, 117,
      120, 179, 180
   Mathilda 48
Shriver, Lionel
   We Need to Talk About Kevin 179
Slade, David
   30 Days of Night 155
Smith, Charlotte
   Elegiac Sonnets 40–3, 44
Sono, Sion
   Suicide Circle 161, 172–3
Soseki, Natsume
   Kokoro 14, 161, 162–4, 171
Spierig, Michal and Peter
   Daybreakers (film) 143–4
stabbing and cutting 2, 4, 8, 60, 78, 98
Stevenson, Robert Louis
   Dr Jekyll and Mr Hyde 7, 8, 11,
      66–71, 72, 74, 76, 77,
      78, 117
   The Suicide Club 71, 72
Stoker, Bram 82, 125
   Dracula 139, 179
Strahan, S. A. K.
   Suicide and Insanity 67–8, 70, 71–2,
      81, 85
suicidal mania 11, 58, 81

True Blood (HBO) 150–2

Ukumaru, Furuya
  Suicide Circle (manga) 161, 172

vampires 4–5, 13–14, 16n.11, 117, 125, 139–58 passim
video games 14–15, 176–87 passim
  Dear Esther 176, 177–84
  Depression Quest 177
  Doom 177
  Gone Home 177
  Half-Life 2 178
  Portal 177

Walpole, Horace
  The Castle of Otranto 1–3, 6, 7, 8

Wells, H. G. 82
  The Time Machine 77
Wertherism 6, 10, 19, 36–7, 38, 40, 45, 47, 48–9
Whedon, Joss
  Angel 155–6
  Buffy the Vampire Slayer 155
Wilde, Oscar
  Dorian Gray 8–9, 11, 66, 74–8
Wollstonecraft, Mary 44
  The Wrongs of Women 10, 45–6

Zapffe, Peter Wessel 126–7
zombies 152–3, 154, 179
Žižek, Slavoj 113–14, 115

EU authorised representative for GPSR:
Easy Access System Europe, Mustamäe tee 50,
10621 Tallinn, Estonia
gpsr.requests@easproject.com